CB135558

Second Edition

Skillful Foundation

Reading & Writing Teacher's Book

Author: Stacey Holliday Hughes
Series Consultant: Dorothy E. Zemach

macmillan education

Macmillan Education
4 Crinan Street
London N1 9XW

A division of Macmillan Publishers Limited
Companies and representatives throughout the world

ISBN 978-1-380-01041-4

Written by Stacey Holliday Hughes
The author has asserted their right to be identified as the author of this work in accordance with the Copyright, Designs and Patents Act 1988.

This edition published 2018

First edition entitled "Skillful" published 2012 by Macmillan Publishers Limited

Designed by emc design ltd
Cover design by emc design ltd

The publishers would like to thank the following for their thoughtful insights and perceptive comments during the development of the material:

Dalal Al Hitty, University of Bahrain, Bahrain; Karin Heuert Galvão, i-Study Interactive Learning, São Paulo, Brazil; Ohanes Sakris, Australian College of Kuwait, Kuwait; Eoin Jordan, Xi'an Jiaotong-Liverpool University, Suzhou, China; Aaron Rotsinger, Xi'an Jiaotong-Liverpool University, Suzhou, China; Dr. Osman Z. Barnawi, Royal Commission Yanbu Colleges & Institutes, Yanbu, Saudi Arabia; Andrew Lasher, SUNY Korea, Incheon, South Korea; Fatoş Uğur Eskiçırak, Bahçeşehir University, Istanbul, Turkey; Dr. Asmaa Awad, University of Sharjah, Sharjah, United Arab Emirates; Amy Holtby, Khalifa University of Science and Technology, Abu Dhabi, United Arab Emirates; Dr. Christina Gitsaki, Zayed University, Dubai, United Arab Emirates.

Printed and bound in Dubai
2022 2021 2020 2019 2018
10 9 8 7 6 5 4 3 2 1

CONTENTS

SCOPE AND SEQUENCE

	Video	Reading	Vocabulary
1 SELF **PAGE 8** **Campus life** ➤ **Personal profiles:** Welcome new students **Campus life** ➤ **Article:** Students of the month	Happy countries	Prepare to read by finding and analyzing text parts	Use names for countries and languages Use names for subjects of study
2 FAMILY **PAGE 26** **Sociology** ➤ **Article:** It's 5:54—time for dinner! **Culture** ➤ **Message board:** Family fun	Family time in China	Preview a text by thinking about its topic and searching for key text parts	Use names for family members Use words and phrases to describe how often things happen
3 STUDY **PAGE 44** **Design** ➤ **Discussion forum:** Dorm spaces **Architecture** ➤ **Article:** What works for me	Box hotel	Learn and practice skimming to help you understand the main idea of texts	Use prepositions of place to describe where things are Use names for classroom and college objects
4 MONEY **PAGE 62** **Personal finance** ➤ **Article:** Money types **Economics** ➤ **Online seminar:** Daily spending	Money lessons	Use previewing and skimming to recognize the topic of the text and each paragraph	Learn and practice saying and writing numbers Learn words to give more information about numbers
5 TASTE **PAGE 80** **Business** ➤ **Article:** Food jobs **Tourism** ➤ **Reviews:** Time for something new?	Real food	Practice reading for gist to find general meaning in texts	Use collocations to talk about food Use adjectives to make writing more interesting

Grammar	Writing	Study skills	Unit outcomes
Practice and use the present tense of *be*	Practice and write simple sentences with correct punctuation and capitalization Plan and write simple sentences about your classmate	Introduction: learn about life at college	Prepare to read texts by finding and analyzing text parts Plan and write descriptive sentences about a classmate
Use subject pronouns and possessive adjectives	Practice writing sentences without repeating words Plan and write descriptive sentences about your family	Find out how you prefer to learn	Preview a text by thinking about its topic and searching for key text parts Plan and write a series of descriptive sentences about your family
Practice and use the verb *have* to talk about possessions	Learn to add information to your sentences by using *and*, *also*, *too* Write and share a description of a study space	Think about what you have (and what you need) to learn well	Learn and practice skimming to help you understand the main idea of texts Write and share a description of a study space
Practice and use verbs in the simple present tense	Learn to use numbers in your sentences Check information and describe how much a family spends each month	Learn to understand percentages in English	Use previewing and skimming to recognize the topic of the text and each paragraph Check information and describe how much a family spends each month
Learn and practice using articles and adjectives with nouns	Learn to write interesting sentences using adjectives Plan and write a description of a restaurant you know	Learn to read better by improving your understanding	Practice reading for gist to find general meaning in texts Plan and write a description of a restaurant you know

SCOPE AND SEQUENCE

	Video	Reading	Vocabulary
6 HEALTH **PAGE 98** **Sports science** ➤ **Survey:** How healthy are you? **Medicine** ➤ **Interviews:** Healthy habits	Robots and health	Look for information in texts quickly by scanning	Use verb / noun collocations to talk about health Use words and phrases to talk about comparing actions
7 PLACES **PAGE 116** **Urban studies** ➤ **Online comments:** Favorite neighborhoods **Architecture** ➤ **Article:** A greener Seoul	A special bench	Read to find specific information in texts	Use words and phrases to name places and buildings Use phrases to give information about the number of things
8 PLANS **PAGE 134** **Education** ➤ **Invitation:** TechQuest Conference **Business** ➤ **Email thread:** Will you speak at TechQuest?	Kenya tech plans	Learn to identify different text types to understand their aim	Use words for days, months, and time Use words and phrases to say how possible something is
9 JOBS **PAGE 152** **Productivity** ➤ **Résumé:** Looking for a job **Sociology** ➤ **Article:** Tell me about your job	An urban farm grows in Brooklyn	Practice highlighting and annotating texts to choose information to remember	Use names for popular jobs Use names for jobs and careers at colleges
10 SKILLS **PAGE 170** **Psychology** ➤ **Lecture notes:** Children and their skills **Social studies** ➤ **Article:** The people I know	Skills of a champion	Learn how to organize information into a chart when reading	Use collocations to talk about skills people have Use adjectives to describe people and their skills

Grammar	Writing	Study skills	Unit outcomes
Use adverbs of frequency to talk about how often things happen	Practice joining and comparing sentences with *and* and *but* Write a comparison of two people's health habits	Think about creative learning	Learn to scan texts to find key information Prepare and write a comparison of health habits
Modify adjectives in your sentences using *very*, *really*, *not … at all*	Learn to expand your notes into sentences Prepare and write a paragraph describing your neighborhood	Learn and decide: how helpful are your notes?	Read to find specific information in texts Prepare and write a paragraph describing your neighborhood
Use the simple present and *will* to talk about schedules and plans in the future	Learn about and practice writing emails Plan and write an email message with an invitation to a conference	Practice using a planner to organize your study	Learn to identify different text types to understand their aim Plan and write an email message
Practice using *like*, *would like*, and *be like*	Support your writing by giving reasons Write a paragraph describing a job you would like to have	Learn more about writing an English résumé	Practice highlighting and annotating texts Plan and write a paragraph describing a job
Describe ability and possibility using *can*	Learn more about writing paragraphs to make your sentences support your main idea Write a paragraph describing your classmate's skills and abilities	Think about checking and editing your paragraphs	Learn how to organize information into a chart when reading Write a paragraph describing your classmate's skills and abilities

To the teacher

Academic success requires so much more than memorizing facts. It takes skills. This means that a successful student can both learn and think critically. *Skillful* helps teachers prepare their students for academic work in English by teaching not only language—vocabulary and grammar—but the necessary skills to engage with topics, texts, and discourse with classmates.

Teachers using *Skillful* should:

- Encourage students to ask questions and interact. Many of the tasks and exercises involve pairwork, groupwork, and whole-class discussion. Working with others helps students solidify their understanding, and challenge and expand their ability to think critically.
- Personalize the material. Help students make connections between the texts in their book and their own world—home, community, and country. Bring in outside material from local sources when it's relevant, making sure it fits the unit topics and language.
- Provide a lot of practice. Review exercises and material from previous units. Use the *Skillful* digital components to develop the skills presented in the Student's Book.
- Provide many opportunities for review. Remind students of the skills, grammar, and vocabulary they learned in previous units. Have students study a little bit each day, not just before tests.
- Show students how to be independent learners. Point out opportunities to study and practice English outside of class, such as reading for pleasure and using the Internet in English. The *Study skills* section in every unit gives students valuable tips for successfully managing their own learning.

Learning skills, like learning a language, takes time and practice. Students must be patient with themselves as they put in the necessary time and effort. They should set and check goals. Periodic assessments the teacher can print, such as the unit tests, progress tests, mid and end tests in the digital components let students see their own progress and measure how much they've learned, so they can feel proud of their academic and linguistic development.

Opening page

Each unit starts with two opening pages. These pages get students ready to study the topic of the unit. There is a video to watch and activities to do before class.

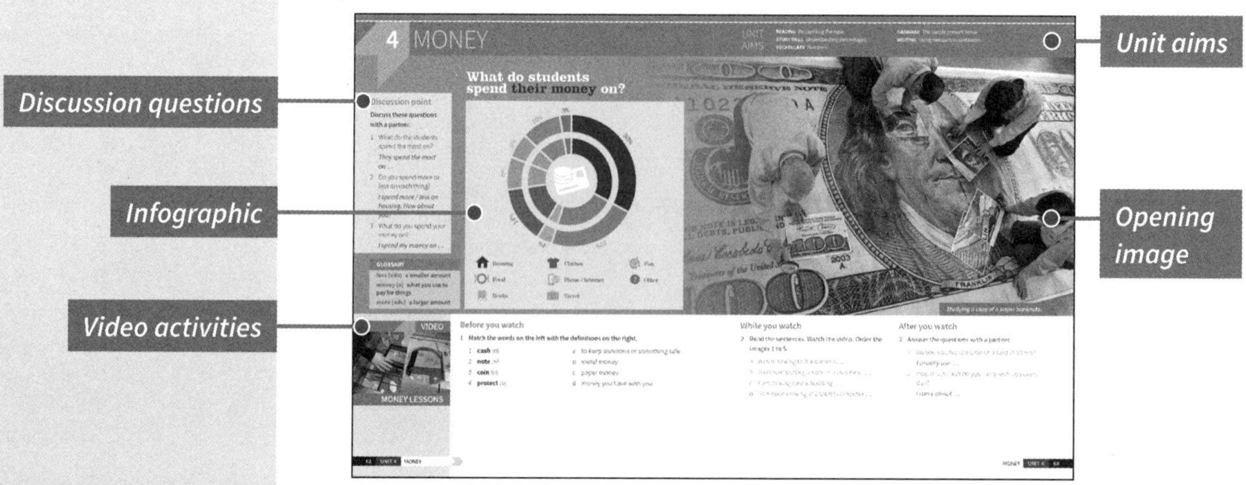

Reading lessons

In every unit, there are two reading lessons and they present two different aspects of the unit topic and help students with ideas and language for their *Writing task*.

Vocabulary to prepare students for the reading activities.

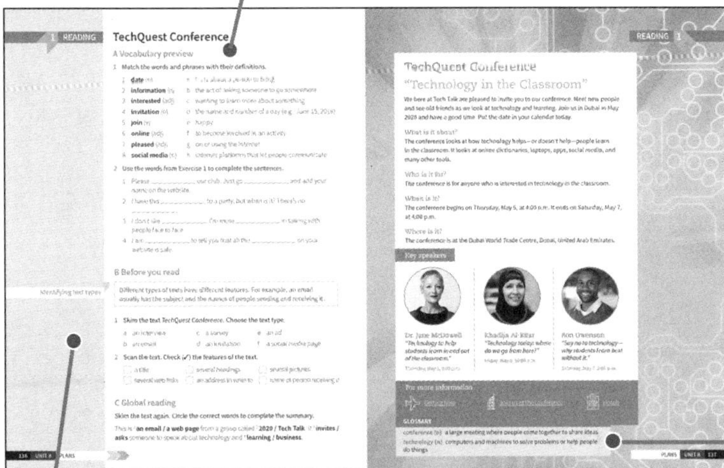

Every reading section helps students use a new reading skill.

Glossaries help students understand higher-level words from the reading text.

Develop your students' reading skills in each part of the reading lesson.

Writing lessons

After the reading lessons, there is a page for students to analyze a model answer to a writing task. This will help them organize their ideas and language and prepare for the final task at the end of the unit.

Students analyze the model answer.

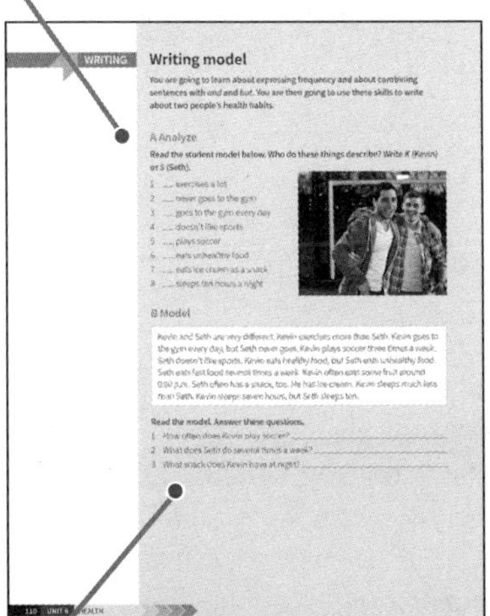

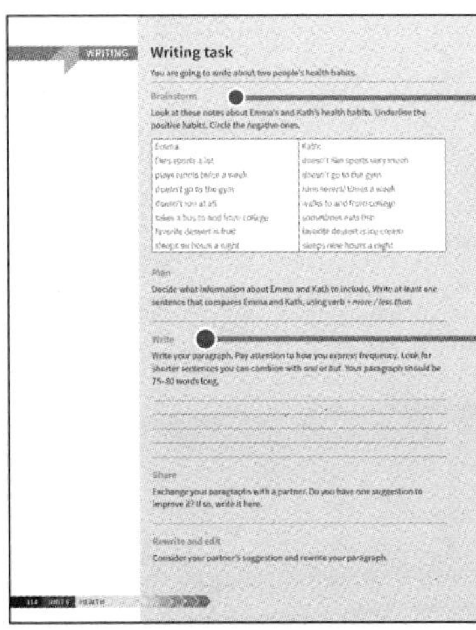

Brainstorm and plan the final writing task.

Finally, write a paragraph or essay.

Next, discuss ideas.

1 SELF

READING	Preparing to read
STUDY SKILL	Life at college
VOCABULARY	Countries and languages
GRAMMAR	Present tense of *be*
WRITING	Writing simple sentences

As this is the first lesson, it is worth spending some time making sure that students feel relaxed and comfortable since students learn better when they are engaged and not under stress, that is, when they have a lowered "affective filter." In order to build students' confidence and aid understanding, keep sentences short and simple. Where appropriate, use gestures. For example, students may not understand the concept of working in pairs, so you might have to use your hands to help explain, such as pointing to one student with one hand and another student with the other hand, and then bringing your hands closer together. Whichever gesture you use, make sure to use the same gesture each time, along with the spoken instruction, to avoid confusion and to build continuity. Be careful about using hand gestures that might be offensive. For instance, where pointing is considered impolite, point with your entire hand, fingers together with thumb on top.

Research has shown that students are more motivated when they feel like the teacher knows and cares about them. This unit provides a good opportunity for the teacher to get to know a little about each student, and for the students to learn more about each other. Getting to know one other is an important part of building the classroom community.

Warm-up

Start the lesson with an activity to engage the students and lay the groundwork for the unit. If it is allowed at your institution, ask students to take out their smartphone and take a photo of themselves. Ask them to show their photo to another person (or even send it with a message saying, *Me in English class!).* Then tell them to turn off their smartphone and put it away for the rest of the lesson. See if anyone knows what the picture is called and write *selfie* on the board. Ensure that students understand that a selfie is a picture that you take of yourself. Ask students to look at the title of the unit and the photo. Ask them what they think *self* means and how it relates to *selfie*. Students should understand that in this unit, they will learn to read and write about themselves.

If smartphone use is forbidden in your institution, you could bring in some selfies of yourself (in appropriate clothing and situations) to show the students and prompt discussion, e.g., *Where am I here? Is this a good selfie? When do you take selfies*? For homework, students could print out or upload some selfies into a class wiki or closed online group.

Discussion point

1 Ask students to look at the graph. Draw their attention to the title *Where are the students from?*, the numbers on the left, and the countries at the bottom. Review numbers zero to ten and make sure students understand that the words at the bottom are countries. If possible, bring in a large world map and ask students to find the countries listed in the graph on the map. Alternatively, if you have a projector hooked up to a computer, project a world map from the Internet. Ask students to look at the graph and complete Exercise 1. Check that they have the right answers.

ANSWERS
1 Japan **2** Four **3** China

2 If you have a class with students from different countries, give each student a slip of paper. Ask them: *Where are you from?* They should write their country on the slip of paper. (In a class where all students are from the same country, give students a slip of paper with a country name on it.) Ask them to stand up and ask other students *Where are you from?* The other students show what they have written. Ask students to write the names of their countries on the board before moving on to Exercise 2. Assess and discuss the demographic of where students in your class are from.

Extension activity

Students review the spelling of numbers zero to ten for homework. For the following lesson, start with a short competition. Put students into pairs. Call out a random number from zero to ten. Each pair writes both the number and the number word, concentrating on correct spelling. Do this for a total of five or six numbers. Then ask pairs to exchange papers for checking. Say the number and spell it aloud while writing the number and number word on the board so that students can hear the spoken letters and see the spelling. Congratulate students for their effort and encourage them to review any that they got wrong.

VIDEO

Before you watch

Introduce the topic of the video and ask students to read the exercise and identify any new words. Write these on the board and discuss the meanings as a class. Then, ask students to complete the *Before you watch* section. Monitor and provide feedback as a class.

ANSWERS
1 d **2** a **3** c **4** b

While you watch

Play the video once. Ask the students to watch the video and complete the exercise. Play the video again so that students can check their answers. Go through the answers with the class.

ANSWERS
1 two **2** four (including the narrator) **3** happy
4 weather

See page 108 for the video script.

After you watch

Put the students into pairs or groups and ask them to complete the exercise. Encourage them to use what they have learned in the video and the example answers to answer the questions. Go through the answers with class.

READING 1

Welcome new students

A Vocabulary preview

Use the photographs in *Welcome new students* as a way to introduce the vocabulary in bold. Ask students to look at the photographs. If possible, use the presentation tool to project the image. Ask *What's her name?* to elicit some possible names. Agree on a name for him (i.e., one of the boys) and write it on the board. Ask *What's his age? / How old is he? 19? 21? 30? 56?* Elicit the age students think he is. Agree on an age and write it on the board. Continue asking questions to elicit and agree on his city, country, email address, hobby, and language. Check that students understand the terms by checking several times during the process of building up the information about him, e.g., *Name? Age? City?* Students' responses will indicate if they have understood the terms.

1 Ask students to look at the list of words in bold in Exercise 1. Make sure they understand that they should circle the example that doesn't belong. For example, ask *Is March 5 age? No? Circle it.* Check students' answers before moving onto Exercise 2. Ask students to work individually. Then ask them to check in pairs, and then check as a class. Students can also complete the *Vocabulary preview* as homework before class.

ANSWERS
1 March 5 **2** 19 **3** Saudi Arabia **4** Cairo
5 555-7711 **6** family **7** France **8** 2018

2 This exercise will show whether or not students have understood the meaning of the vocabulary from Exercise 1. Ask students to use the words from Exercise 1 to complete the sentences. Ask volunteer students to read the completed sentences.

Pay particular attention to spelling. Tricky words to spell include *address*, *hobby*, and *language*. Write the first letter of each vocabulary word on the board with spaces for the rest of the letters (e.g., l _ _ _ _ _ _ _). With books closed, say the word and see if the class can spell it aloud. Write the letters the students say in the spaces. Students look in their books to see if they have made any mistakes. This activity will also show which letter names students need to review.

ANSWERS
1 language **2** birthday **3** hobby **4** name
5 email address **6** city **7** age **8** country

Extension activity

This is a good time to review the alphabet and months. Make sure students can pronounce key terms: *age* /eɪʤ/; *birthday* /ˈbɜrθˌdeɪ/. Ask students to concentrate on making the /θ/ sound by putting their finger to their lips when they say *birthday*. Their tongue should come out far enough to touch their finger. For the /r/ sound in *birthday*, the tip of the tongue comes down while the back of the tongue rises. There is a lot of movement to go from the /r/ to the /θ/ sound; draw students' attention to this massive movement to help them with the pronunciation.

For the /l/ in *language*, the tongue comes forward and the tip of the tongue presses against the roof of the mouth just behind the teeth.

Country is /ˈkʌntri/ not /ˈkaʊntri/.

Address can have the stress on the first or second syllable: /ˈædres/ or /əˈdres/.

Teach students how to say the symbols in an email address: @ is *at*; . is *dot*.

B Before you read

Preparing to read

We unconsciously take in a lot of information about a text before we read it. This gives us information about what we are going to read and aids comprehension. This section aims to teach students to use information about a text before reading it.

This exercise will work best if you can use the presentation tool to project the reading text. Use a pointer to draw students' attention to the title, captions, photos, and bold words. Ask, e.g., *Which gives the main idea? Which describes the photos? Which shows the important words?* to elicit the parts listed in the *Preparing to read* box.

Students read the *Preparing to read* box and complete the exercise. Check understanding by asking students to point to each part in the text.

ANSWERS
A title, pictures, captions

C Global reading

Reading for gist

This exercise encourages students to read quickly to get the main idea of the text without getting stuck on unknown words. Ask students to read the sentences. Then give them 30 seconds to read the text quickly and complete the sentences.

ANSWERS
1 new **2** four **3** different countries

D Close reading

1 In this section, students read the text more carefully and answer the questions. Students can use a paper or electronic dictionary if needed. Have students complete the exercise individually. Ask students to check in pairs, and then check as a class.

ANSWERS
1 F (Bianca is from Brazil.) **2** T **3** T
4 F (Nilay's birthday is on April 10.)
5 F (Bianca studies sports science.) **6** T

2 Point out that *age* and *years old* are the same thing. When we talk about age, we say *I am / he or she is ___ years old. How old are you?* Students work alone to find the first names in the text to complete the sentences. Compare in pairs before having the class give feedback.

ANSWERS
1 Kenichi **2** Nilay **3** Kenichi, Bianca **4** Ahmed, Nilay
5 Ahmed, Kenichi **6** Bianca, Kenichi

Extension activity

Put students into three groups. Ask Group 1 to make a list of all the countries they see from the unit so far. Group 2 should make a list of all the languages, and Group 3 should make a list of all the hobbies. Students should look at the infographic on page 8, the *Vocabulary preview* on page 10, and the reading text on page 11. Give them five minutes to complete the task. Ask fast finishers to make sure they have spelled their words correctly by checking in the book. Ask one person from each group to read one of their answers. Check and drill pronunciation as needed. Check that students understand the meaning of the hobby terms, but don't spend too much time connecting language to country because this comes up later in the unit. Ask another person from each group to read another answer and so on until each group has read their list, and you have practiced pronunciation and clarified meaning.

E Over to you

In this section, students use the same structure from the reading text to talk about themselves. This is an important step that consolidates and personalizes their learning.

1 Students work alone to complete the information about themselves. Give support where needed. Teach students the terms for _ (*underscore*) and – (*dash* or *hyphen*) if needed to say their email address.

2 Write the sentence stems from Exercise 2 on the board and show students how to use them to compare

information, e.g., *We are 19 years old. We are from Tokyo. We like movies. I like movies, but he likes tennis. I am 18, but he is 20.* Orally drill briefly so that students are comfortable saying the sentences. Put students into pairs to compare information. Ask each pair to find another pair. Ask each student to tell the others one thing that is the same or different about their partner. When they have done this, ask two or three students to tell the class one thing that was the same or different about their partner.

STUDY SKILLS

Life at college

Warm-up

Students close their books. On the board, write *Student life at college*. With the class, brainstorm ways that life at college is different from student life at high school or secondary school. Write their ideas on the board. You may need to prompt students with questions, e.g., *Is it exciting? Is there more work? Can you choose what you study? Do you have take-home activities? Can you ask for help?* (Possible answers: more freedom; more work; you choose what to study; lots of take-home activities; more independence; more responsibility; not many classes, etc.).

1 Students read the *Life at college* box. Then they check the statements that are true for them. Give students three minutes, and then ask volunteers to say which statements they checked. Ask students to work in pairs to think of one or two more ideas to add to the list. Ask a few volunteers to tell the rest of the class what they added.

2 Students work alone to complete Exercise 2, and then they read their answers to their partner. Ask students to write their answers on a piece of paper or send them to you in an email so you can find out more about your students and build your relationship with them.

Extension activity

This would be a good time to advise students on where and how they can do the things that they have written in Exercise 2. For example, students may want to join a study group, but may not know how to find one. Put students into groups of three or four to discuss ways to achieve their aims. Some ideas include, e.g., creating a regular face-to-face or online study group with classmates, reading a graded reader or listening to a podcast and keeping a log of new vocabulary, recording yourself speaking—starting with one minute a day and working up to five minutes, etc.

READING 2

Students of the month

A Vocabulary preview

Warm-up

Write *Students of the month* on the board. Ask students what they think this means (Possible answer: students who are chosen to be showcased or honored in some way, often because of an achievement or as a way to inspire other students). Ask students why someone might be chosen for student of the month. Find out if anyone has ever been chosen for a similar award. If there is a similar award at your institution, talk about why students are chosen.

1 Students work together to match the words with their definitions. If required, students can use a paper or online dictionary to complete the exercise. When checking answers, ask for the whole definition from volunteer students, e.g., T: *What is a class?* ST: *A group of students with a teacher.* Ask students to say the words in an oral drill two to three times to practice pronunciation.

Draw students' attention to the parts of speech in parentheses after each word. Find out if they know what (n) [noun] and (adj) [adjective] mean. At this point, you don't need to go into too much detail, but you could explain that a noun is a person, place, thing, or idea and an adjective is a word that describes a noun.

ANSWERS
1 c **2** d **3** a **4** b **5** h **6** g **7** f **8** e

2 Students complete the exercise alone, and then check in pairs. To practice saying the new words in sentences, ask Student A to read the odd-numbered sentences aloud to his or her partner. Student B reads the even-numbered sentences.

Pay particular attention to spelling. Tricky words include *easy*, *favorite*, *movie*, and *third*. Use the same class spelling activity from the TB page 11 to continue working on letter names.

ANSWERS
1 favorite **2** class **3** first **4** movie **5** club
6 easy **7** second, third

B Before you read

Give students 30 seconds to read the instructions and sentences and check that they understand what to do. Reading the instructions and sentences before reading a text helps students know what information they should be looking for and is a good exam skill to develop early on. Give them 30 more seconds to read the text quickly to find the answers. If appropriate, you could do this as a competition—the first student(s) to get the answers could be "students of the day." (More opportunities to be "student of the day" can be given later in the lesson.)

ANSWERS
1 three **2** students **3** student magazine

C Global reading

Ask students to read the instructions and questions. Give them two minutes to read the text and find the answer. Alternatively, challenge students to find the answer as quickly as they can with the "winner(s)" being added to the list of "students of the day" from *Before you read*.

Reading quickly to get the main idea of a text is an important skill and helps students see that they don't need to look up every word in order to get a global understanding of the text.

ANSWER
1 They speak English

D Close reading

1 Students read the text again to complete the chart. Draw the blank chart on the board. Ask fast finishers to complete the information for one of the students in the chart. Ask the rest of the class if they got the same answers as those on the board and correct any mistakes.

ANSWERS

	Leila Abboud	Diego Garcia	Ji-won Kim
Age	20	18	21
Year	second	first	third
City	Sharjah	Tijuana	Busan
Country	United Arab Emirates	Mexico	South Korea
Studies	biology	music	east Asian history
Languages	Arabic, English, French	Spanish, English	Korean, English, Japanese, Chinese

2 Students work alone to complete the sentences with words from the text and compare with a partner. Ask volunteers to read aloud their sentences for checking as a class.

ANSWERS
1 old **2** movie **3** soccer **4** music **5** Chinese
6 teachers

Extension activity

Put students into pairs. Give each pair a chart like the one in Exercise 1, but without the names and information included. Students interview each other and complete column 1. Then they change partners and complete columns 2 and 3. Each student then chooses one of the people in their chart and gives a mini-presentation about that person to the class. In a large class, students can work in small groups for their mini-presentations. Less-confident students can read what they've written, while more-confident ones can try to present the information without looking at their notes.

E Over to you

1 Put students into groups of three or four. Students circle the free-time activities they do. Explain that free-time activities are the same as hobbies (They will see both of these terms throughout this unit.). Encourage students to ask each other follow-up questions. Write some questions on the board to support them, e.g., *What do you draw? Where do you swim? What do you sing? Where do you travel? What do you read? What do you cook? What do you watch on TV? What kind of movies do you watch?*

2 Students complete the sentences. Ask them to find one or more other people who like to do the same things. Let them move around the room if possible and mingle with other students.

3 Put students into groups of three or four, and ask them to make a list of school clubs. Compile a list on the board and encourage students to join. If your institution doesn't have clubs, ask students what clubs they would like to have—maybe they can put together a proposal for some clubs to take to the governing body of the school.

Extension activity

Students create a profile for a class study group, blog, or discussion forum. Ask students to read each other's profiles and find one thing they have in common with someone else in the class.

VOCABULARY

Topic vocabulary

Countries and languages

Warm-up

Put students into teams of three. Tell them they have three minutes to look through pages 1–17 in their books to find the names of as many countries as they can. They must write the name of the country and be careful about spelling—including capitalization. When the three minutes are up, ask teams to exchange papers. The team gets a point for each country they have found and another point for spelling the name of the country correctly. As they call out the countries, write them on the board in a column so the students can see the correct spelling. The team with the most points wins.

At the top of the column on the board, write *country*. At the top of a new column, write *language*. See if students can tell you what language they speak in each of the countries on the board from the *Warm-up*. Complete the *language* column and ask students if they see any patterns. For example, they may see that some languages end in *-ese* (Chinese, Portuguese), some in *-ish* (English, Spanish, Turkish), and some in *-an* (Korean).

Students open their books and look at the table with countries and languages. Draw students' attention to the fact that both languages and country names are always capitalized. Go through the pronunciation of each. Ask students to underline the stressed syllable in each word.

China	Chinese
France	French
Germany	German
Italy	Italian
Portugal	Portuguese
Russia	Russian
South Korea	Korean
Spain	Spanish
Thailand	Thai
Turkey	Turkish

Point out that, although *Thailand* and *Thai* is spelled with a *th*, the sound is /t/ not /θ/. The *g* in *Portuguese* is a hard /g/ and the second *u* is silent: /ˌpɔrtʃə'giz/.

1 Students circle the word that does not belong. When going over the first few items, ask students to tell you why the word does not belong, e.g., *They are languages. It is a country.*

ANSWERS
1 France **2** Russia **3** Thai **4** Japanese **5** Thailand

2 Students work alone to complete the sentence. They then check in pairs. Encourage them to pay attention to spelling. Volunteer students read aloud the entire sentence. When checking answers as a whole class, check that students are using the correct pronunciation.

ANSWERS
1 France **2** Russia **3** Italy **4** China **5** Japan

3 Students work alone to complete the sentence. They then check in pairs. Pairs self-check spelling. As the class gives feedback, ask volunteer students to read aloud the entire sentence. Monitor and check pronunciation.

ANSWERS
1 Spanish **2** Korean **3** German **4** Portuguese
5 Thai

4 Put students into pairs to ask and answer the questions. If appropriate, ask them to record their conversation and play it back to listen for good pronunciation of countries and languages.

Extension activity

Put students into pairs. Student A has the book closed. Student B says the name of the country. Student A says the language. Change roles and repeat. Later in the unit, review again—give each pair a set of cards with languages and countries mixed up. They sort them into two columns and match them up.

VOCABULARY

Vocabulary builder

Subjects of study

Ask a few students what subject they want to study or are studying at school. Ask them if they know how many subjects it is possible to study at the institution they are currently in. If possible, bring in brochures from the school. Ask students to work in small groups to find three or four subjects that are interesting to them.

1 Students work alone to match the subjects with what they are the study of. Have them check in pairs and give feedback to the class. Go over the pronunciation

of each subject. Some students struggle with *science* /'saɪəns/, *history* /'hɪst(ə)ri/, and the stress pattern in *geography* /dʒi'ɑgrəfi/. Ensure that students know that school subjects are not always capitalized, although languages, e.g., Spanish, are capitalized.

ANSWERS
1 c **2** f **3** a **4** e **5** d **6** b **7** h **8** g

2 Students match the subjects with the pictures, and then write sentences. Fast finishers can think of two more subjects. Have the whole class give feedback. Ask the fast finishers to say what the subject is the study of and see if the others in the class can guess the subject. When checking answers, ask volunteers to read their sentences to the class. Check and drill pronunciation as needed.

ANSWERS
1 Marta studies business.
2 David studies music.
3 Kwame studies art.
4 Ana studies history.
5 Kurt studies sports science.
6 Yumiko studies geography
7 Lucy studies film studies.
8 Salim studies science.

Extension activity

To review subjects, give each student a slip of paper. Ask them to write the subject that they study or want to study on the slip and put it into a hat or box. When everyone has finished, mix up the slips. Read the school subject and see if students can guess who wrote it. They have to use a complete sentence, e.g., if the slip reads *Languages*, the students might say, *Busan studies languages.* How many they get right shows how well they know each other.

WRITING

Writing model

Ask students to read the paragraph at the top of the page so that they know the aim of the *Writing* section. By having an awareness of the aim, students will better understand why the activities they are doing are important. The following exercises build the skills and language students will need in order to complete the *Writing task* at the end of the unit.

A Analyze

Students work alone to match the questions and answers, and then give feedback to the rest of the class. Teach students that the intonation of Wh- questions falls at the end of the question. Compare *Where are you from?* (falling intonation) with *Are you from China?* (a yes / no question with rising intonation). Once you have practiced pronunciation of the questions with students, put them into pairs. Student A reads questions 1 to 5 and Student B answers them. For questions 6 to 10, students exhange roles.

ANSWERS
1 c **2** e **3** a **4** b **5** d **6** h **7** i **8** j
9 g **10** f

B Model

1 Students read the text alone and then describe it to another student.

2 Ask students to match the sentences to what they describe. Have students compare answers in pairs, and then give feedback to the rest of the class. You may wish to explain that this is an example of the writing they will be doing at the end of the unit.

ANSWERS
1 e **2** a **3** f **4** b **5** c **6** g **7** h **8** d

GRAMMAR

Present tense of *be*

Ask students to read the *Present tense of be* information box as a take-home activity before the lesson so that they are better prepared to understand your presentation.

Ask students to close their books. Write the first three example sentences from the grammar box on the board. Underline *am*, *is*, and *are*. Ask students if they know which verb this is to elicit *be*. Ask students which form they should use with *he* (is), with *they* (are), with *you* (are), and with *it* (is). Conduct a short oral substitution drill:

T: *I am an English student. He.*

STS: *He is an English student.*

T: *She*

STS: *She is an English student.*

T: *They*

STS: *They are English students.*

Show the students how to make a yes / no question from the sentences on the board by swapping the subject and the verb: *I am --> am I?; Bianca is --> Is Bianca?; Mark and I are --> Are Mark and I?* Conduct a short oral substitution drill:

T: *I am an English student.*

STS: *Am I an English student?*

T: *Abdullah is from Jeddah.*

STS: *Is Abudullah from Jeddah?*

Encourage students to answer the yes / no questions, e.g., *Am I in this class? Yes, you are. / No, you aren't; Is Abdullah from Jeddah? Yes, he is. / No, he isn't.*, etc.

Move on to Wh- questions. Write the questions from the grammar box on the board. Draw students' attention to the word order by underlining the verb and circling the noun or pronoun:

Where is Sharjah? How old are you? What is your hobby?

Ask students: Can I say *Where Sharjah is?* (no)

Conduct a final short substitution drill:

T: *Sharjah is in the United Arab Emirates.*

STS: *Where is Sharjah?*

T: *I'm 21 years old.*

STS: *How old are you?*

The grammar section has a variety of exercises to practice using the verb *be*. If class time is short, you could assign some of the exercises for homework.

1 Students complete Exercise 1 alone, using the grammar box for support if needed. Ask students to check in pairs, and then check as a class. Ask volunteer students to read the entire sentence.

ANSWERS

1 is **2** am **3** am **4** is **5** is **6** are **7** is

2 This email is an example of a grammar-in-context exercise. Students must understand the context in order to complete the sentences. Some students may not have seen this type of exercise before and might need help from a stronger student to help them complete it. If possible, pair up a stronger and weaker student. Ideally, use the presentation tool to project this exercise when checking answers. Draw attention to the words that give the clues to what form of the verb to use, e.g., *How [1]_____ college life in California?*

ANSWERS

1 is **2** is **3** am **4** is **5** is **6** is **7** is **8** is **9** is **10** are **11** is

3 Ask the students to unscramble the words and do the first sentence together as a class so that students understand the task. Point out that they also need a capital letter at the beginning of the sentence and a period at the end. After checking that they are correct, ask fast finishers to write their answers on the board while the others are still working.

ANSWERS

1. Cassie is 23 years old.
2. Max is not in a club this year.
3. I am not a second-year student.
4. Tomas is a film student from Panama.
5. The teachers at this college are great. / The teachers are great at this college.
6. Korean and Chinese are not easy. / Chinese and Korean are not easy.

4 In this exercise, students write sentences with the correct form of the verb *be*. Do the first one together so that students understand what to do. Encourage students to write the entire sentence and not just the verb—this is so that they will internalize the structure better. Then tell the students to ask the questions to a partner.

ANSWERS

1. Are you 20 years old? Yes, I am.
2. What is your last name?
3. Where are you from?
4. Is your area of study English?
5. Are you a new student here?
6. How are your classes?

5 & 6 To add some variety, ask students to work in groups of three for this exercise and write two true sentences and one false sentence about people in the class. Ask each student to read aloud a sentence. The rest of the class has to say which sentences are true and which are false. If the sentence is false, the person it is about corrects it as in the example in Exercise 6. These exercises could also be done individually for homework with students bringing in their sentences to the following class.

WRITING

Writing skill

Writing simple sentences

Many students dislike writing because they consider it to be difficult. The *Skillful* series aims to build students' writing skills so that they feel more confident about writing and begin to see writing as an important means of communication. In this unit, students focus on simple sentence structure and punctuation as the groundwork for writing a short profile about another person.

Unlike many other languages, sentence structure in English is fixed with a finite number of patterns. Simple declarative sentences follow the pattern of SUBJECT + VERB (+ OBJECT). This is an important rule to point out to students, especially where their language has a different or more flexible word order pattern.

Ask students to read the *Writing simple sentences* box for homework before the lesson so that they are better prepared to understand your presentation. Write the sentences from the skill box on the board. Ask students what the verb, subject, and object are in each of the sentences. Double underline the verb, underline the subject, and circle the object:

I know. (no object)

Leila studies biology.

Ahmed and Nilay study business.

Ji-won speaks and understands Chinese.

Diego speaks Spanish and English.

Concept check: Ask *Can I say "Spanish and English Diego speaks"*? (no); *Can I say "Study Ahmed and Nilay business"*? (no), etc.

Ask students to say which words are capitalized in the sentences on the board. Check that students understand the concept by asking, e.g., *Do we capitalize verbs?* (no) *Do we capitalize names?* (yes) *What else do we capitalize?* (languages, cities, and countries), etc.

1 Students complete the exercise alone, and then compare answers in pairs. Ask fast finishers to write their sentences on the board to make it easier for students to check their answers. Sometimes students don't see the importance of capitals, commas, and periods, especially as they are not used in text speak. Explain that correct punctuation is an important part of academic writing.

ANSWERS
1 Derek speaks Greek and Italian.
2 Karachi is a large city in Pakistan.
3 My friend Roberto is from Bogotá, Colombia.
4 Berlin, Munich, and Cologne are cities in Germany.
5 People speak French and English in Canada.
6 Our teacher is from Los Angeles, California.

2 To help students struggling with this exercise, ask them to identify the words in the two sentences that are different and those that are the same. The different words are the ones that will form the compound subject, verb, or object.

ANSWERS
1 Isobel and Paul are first-year students.
2 Justine speaks English and Spanish.
3 Achara reads and writes Chinese.
4 Mark and Hassan are business students.

3 Students use compound subjects, verbs, or objects for this exercise. You could assign this exercise for homework. In class, ask students to read their sentences to each other, and then exchange them and check them for capitalization and periods. Although students may think they can't assess each other's work, peer review is an important skill. To support this, write the criteria on the board: *Does the sentence start with a capital letter? Does the sentence end with a period? Are languages, names of people, and countries capitalized?* Encourage students to ask you if they have any doubts or disagreements about the sentences.

WRITING

Writing task

Although it's tempting to assign writing as a take-home activity, there are good reasons for writing in class. First, students need to learn the steps in writing—brainstorming, planning, writing, peer reviewing, and rewriting and editing. The exercises in this section take students through those steps. Second, writing can be much easier if students are allowed to work together on some of the stages—brainstorming and planning, for example, can be done collaboratively. Finally, observing what the students do when they write can tell the teacher a lot about the students: Do they use their plan to help them write? Do they look back through the exercises in the book for support? Do they spend a long time looking up words? Do they struggle or do they find it easy? Do they stop and count the words in each sentence or wait until they have finished what they want to say before counting? How long does it take them to write 50 words? This information will help you plan future lessons and support for students.

In this task, students write about each other. To make this exercise extra engaging, tell students that they are going to publish their finished work. Ideas for publication include posting their work on a class blog, creating a "who's who" bulletin board, or making a "students-of-the-month" poster. Knowing that others besides the teacher will read their work is a good motivator.

Brainstorm

Put students into pairs to interview each other. Student A interviews Student B first. To ensure that Student A actually asks the questions verbally, Student B should have his or her book closed. Then ask students to change roles.

Plan

Students work alone to write about their partner. Ask students to think about how they will organize the information. Refer them back to the model on page 20 and the reading texts on pages 15–16 if they need some ideas. Ask them if there is any information they can put together using compound subjects, verbs, or objects. They should make notes at this stage.

Write

Give students about 20–25 minutes of class time to write their paragraphs.

Ask students to write 50 words about their partner and to remember to use the key points, e.g., to use capital letters, periods, and the verb *be*. Students then complete the *Writing task* in class.

Share

Students may not think they are qualified to comment on another student's work, so the rationale behind peer review may require explanation. When evaluating another person's work, students are improving their own skills as a writer because they are raising their awareness of what makes good writing. This also helps them become more independent of the teacher—an important skill as they progress into higher education. Finally, peer review is an important part of publishing in academia. Point out that in peer review, the reviewer provides an extra "set of eyes" to help support the writer.

Students exchange paragraphs with their partner. To help with the peer review, write guidelines on the board:

Is the information correct?

Are words capitalized correctly?

Is there a period after each sentence?

Can any sentences be combined?

Are the words spelled correctly?

Students should discuss each other's work with the guidelines in mind.

Tell students to look at the checklist on page 189. They use the checklist to compare their writing in pairs and offer suggestions for improvement.

Rewrite and edit

Students read and consider their partner's comments and rewrite and revise their paragraph on a clean sheet of paper, checking for errors before turning it in. This could be done for homework. Optionally, students could write their final paragraph directly into a class blog, or they could use a word processor and print out their work. Include a picture of the person the paragraph is about if appropriate.

REVIEW

Wordlist

Students work in pairs or small groups to work through the *Wordlist*, checking that they all remember what each word or phrase means, how to pronounce it, and how it was used in the unit. Go through the list carefully with the class.

Vocabulary builder review

Students work through the sentences, check in pairs, and report back to the class.

ANSWERS
1 art **2** geography **3** history **4** film studies

Unit review

Students work through the list alone to decide what they can and can't do. They discuss their answers in pairs, including what they remember from the unit about each point. Finally, open up the discussion to include the whole class. Pay particular attention to any boxes that the students didn't check. Explore with them ways of overcoming any remaining problems.

Extra research task

As a take-home activity, tell students to search online for information about a famous person whom they respect or admire. They should find out the person's age, country, job, and two other pieces of information about that person. In the lesson, ask students to share the information with each other in small groups. Alternatively, students can write about the person on the class blog.

2 FAMILY

READING	Previewing
STUDY SKILL	How I prefer to learn
VOCABULARY	Family members
GRAMMAR	Subject pronouns and possessive adjectives
WRITING	Not repeating words

The idea of "family" is a cultural construct. In some cultures, people's idea of family extends to cousins, aunts, and uncles, but in others, it generally means parents and children, or nuclear family. Cousins, aunts, uncles, and grandparents would be considered extended family. It may be necessary to treat the topic of family with some sensitivity as some students may have lost members of their family.

Warm-up

To begin the topic of family, show students pictures of your family. If possible, hook up your smartphone to the projector so that everyone can see the pictures. Talk about who is in the picture and where it was taken. If permitted, allow students to show each other pictures of their family from their smartphones. If technology is not available or permitted, use the photo at the beginning of the unit to introduce the topic. Find pictures online of different types of family, print them out, and put them around the room. Ask students to look at the pictures and discuss which is most like their family and why. Bring the discussion around to meal times with family to lead into the *Discussion point*.

Discussion point

Ask students to look at the two pie charts in their books. Make sure students understand that a pie chart shows the percentage out of 100, and that the symbol for per cent is %. Review numbers and show how to talk about per cent—point to the figures and ask *What is this number?* (5%, etc.). Review how to say the time—*six o'clock*, or simply *six*, etc. Check that students understand the concept, e.g., *What does the first pie chart show?* (the time students in the class have breakfast); *What does the second pie chart show?* (who the students eat lunch with); *What is a co-worker?* (someone you work with).

1 Ask students to read through the three sentences in pairs and circle the correct answers. Check as a class with volunteer students reading the complete answers.

ANSWERS
1 5% **2** 8:00 and 9:00 **3** a friend

2 Put students into pairs to discuss the questions. Ask three or four volunteers to report back their answers to the class in complete sentences, using the sentence stems in the exercise.

VIDEO

Before you watch

Introduce the topic of the video and ask students to read the exercise and identify any new words. Write these on the board and discuss the meanings as a class. Then, ask students to complete the *Before you watch* section. Monitor and go through the answers with the class.

ANSWERS
1 d **2** a **3** c **4** b **5** e

While you watch

Play the video once. Ask the students to watch the video and complete the exercise. Play the video again so that students can check their answers. Go through the answers with the class.

ANSWERS
1 China **2** visit **3** buy **4** cook

See page 108 for the video script.

After you watch

Put the students into pairs or groups and ask them to complete the exercise. Encourage them to use what they have learned in the video and the example answers to answer the questions. Go through the answers with the class.

READING 1

It's 5:54—time for dinner!

A Vocabulary preview

Warm-up

Note that there are two new parts of speech listed: verb (v) and pronoun. Tell students they will be learning more about pronouns later in the unit. Drill the pronunciation of the vocabulary orally with the whole class and individually, if necessary. Pay particular attention to the /θ/ in *both*, the /l/ in *clean*, and the /p/ in *pet* and *spend*. If students are pronouncing *both* like *boss*, then they aren't bringing the tip of their tongue forward enough to create the correct pronunciation. Emphasize the technique of bringing the tongue out between their teeth and demonstrate this to the class yourself. Remind students that the back of the tongue is pulled back and the tip sits on the ridge behind the teeth for the /l/ sound. If you have students for whom /**p**/ and /**b**/ are problematic, show them the difference between these two sounds. Ask students to put their fingers on their throat as they say /**p**/ (make sure it's /**p**/ and not /**p**ə/). Then as they say /**b**/, they should feel the vibration of the /**b**/ in their throat, but there should not be a vibration when they say /**p**/. Over emphasize the /**p**/ sound to practice it, releasing a lot of air.

1 Students work in pairs to match the words with the definitions.

ANSWERS

1 d **2** c **3** a **4** b **5** h **6** f **7** e **8** g

2 Ask students to work alone to complete the sentences with words from Exercise 1 before comparing answers in pairs. Students can use a paper or electronic dictionary if needed. Ask fast finishers to make vocabulary cards for the vocabulary box. Volunteers read their sentences to check answers as a class.

Pay particular attention to spelling. Tricky words include *clean* and *exercise*. With books closed, write the words on the board, but without vowels, e.g., *prtmnt*. Students work in pairs for five minutes to write the words in full on a piece of paper. Students exchange papers and check another pair's work with the words in the book.

ANSWERS

1 spend **2** clean **3** apartment **4** Both **5** pet
6 normal **7** exercise **8** cash

Extension activity

Find out if students have a vocabulary notebook, and if not, encourage them to keep track of vocabulary. There are many ways to do this: by unit, by topic, alphabetically, by word form, by spelling pattern, etc. Discourage simple translation alone since words can have many meanings, and encourage students to include example sentences and collocations in English.

In class, start a vocabulary box. Students write the vocabulary word on one side of a 3 x 5 card and on the other side they write the definition, example, or example sentence with a blank. When you have a spare five minutes, bring out the box, take out a card, read the definition, example, or sentence with a blank, and see who can give you the correct word. This encourages students to keep a vocabulary record not based on simple translation. If possible, use an online flash card maker with a game element.

B Before you read

Previewing

Ask students if they remember what they should do and why before they read a text (from Unit 1). Students open their books and read the *Previewing* box to see if what they said matches the advice given.

1 Students read the instructions. With books closed, agree on a time limit for completing this exercise, e.g., *Is ten seconds enough time? No? Fifteen seconds?* Ask students to open their books and start the timer. Repeat if needed for Exercise 2. Don't go over the answers yet.

ANSWER

b families in the U.K.

2 Put students into pairs. Ask them to write one thing they know about dinnertime and one thing they want to know from the text. Give some feedback about ideas to the rest of the class. Then, with books still closed, ask them to predict which four things are likely to be mentioned in the text. Don't review the answers yet, as with Exercise 1.

C Global reading

Students read the text alone quickly to see if their predictions from Exercises 1 and 2 were right. Set a timer so that students read the text quickly. Ask students if they found out what they wanted to know from the text. Have the class give feedback.

ANSWERS

children, food, money, exercise

D Close reading

1 Ask students to read the sentences before reading the text again to find the answers. Set a time limit—about three minutes—to read the text quickly and find the answers. Discourage dictionary use at this stage—students can spend more time at home looking up words from the text and reading it again. When going over the answers, point out that the picture shows the family eating take-out fish and chips. Note that in the U.S., *chips* are called *fries* or sometimes *French fries*, and *chips* are thin, fried, salted potatoes that come in bags. As British pounds sterling are mentioned in Exercise 2, find out if students know what the exchange rate is from British pounds sterling to the local currency—if permitted, students could use their smartphones to look up the exchange rate. Ask students to turn off their phones and put them away once the search is over.

ANSWERS
1 b **2** b **3** a **4** a **5** b **6** a

Exam skills

Students need to understand the importance of reading a text quickly to answer the questions. On exams, they have to find information quickly in a text without the use of a dictionary. Students who cannot read quickly will not be able to complete all the questions in the time allotted. Scanning (searching quickly through a text for specific information) might feel uncomfortable to those students who read slowly and carefully and try to understand every word. Point out that they can read again at home, but in class, you are teaching them the skill of quick reading. In scanning, it is important to read the questions first in order to know what information to look for.

2 Ask students to complete the exercise with words from the text. Allow students a little more time to find the words needed.

ANSWERS
1 outside **2** cash **3** exercises **4** normal

E Over to you

1 Ask students to check the sentences that are true for them.

2 Now ask students to compare their lists with a partner, using the sentence stem, *Both of our families ...*. As the class gives feedback, ask three to four volunteers to say how their families are the same, using complete sentences starting with the sentence stem. As a follow-up at home, if appropriate, ask students to take a selfie with their family eating dinner or just a picture of their dinner. Ask students to post the picture onto the class blog with a short caption. Alternatively, in the following class, students can share and talk about their pictures in pairs before putting their smartphones away for the rest of the lesson.

Extension activity

Create a "Find someone who ..." mingling activity on the topic of families to practice asking questions and to extend and practice vocabulary. Use the sentences in Exercise 1 as a starting point. Students turn the sentences into questions—*My family lives in an apartment. Does your family live in an apartment?* Students then write two more yes / no questions on the topic. Students stand up and walk around the room asking their questions. When they find someone who answers "yes" to the question, they write that person's name down. They must find different people who can answer "yes." Set a time limit of about ten minutes for this activity. Give feedback on some of the answers—maybe some of the surprising answers to the whole class. In a mixed-nationality class, there may be some differences in habits or traditions that could make for an interesting class discussion.

STUDY SKILLS

How I prefer to learn

Students often don't consider the learning preferences of other students in a class. For example, some students really enjoy working in pairs while others prefer to work alone. Teachers have to find the right balance between what they know is good methodology and the needs, preferences, and cultural expectations of each student in the class. This *Study skills* section is a good opportunity to examine the range of study preferences in the classroom and to highlight some effective study practices— both in and outside of class.

Ask students to raise their hand if they think they are a good learner. Ask volunteers to say what they do that makes them a good learner. Ask students if they think all students like to learn in the same way. Is how we like to learn always the best way to learn? Tell the students they are going to think about ways to learn in the *Study skills* section.

Ask students to read the *How I prefer to learn* box. Ask them, by show of hands, if they are more similar to Etienne, Claire, or Nita. Put students into groups of three. Ask them to identify some good ideas and not-so-good ideas in the three student comments. (Possible answers: Etienne—Good: to look for information on the Internet and put it together; Not so good: doing it late at night; Claire—Good: starting work early, taking notes; Not so good: writing and rewriting a paper [A lot of students write a messy copy, and then write a neat copy, but It is better to write a plan, and then write the final version. Rewriting a paper takes twice as long and can hinder students under exam conditions where there is time pressure]; Nita—Good: working alone and understanding that group work is sometimes important.) Ask students what a better idea is for the not-so-good ideas. (Possible answers: Etienne—look for the information earlier and take notes rather than waiting; Claire—make a plan that outlines what you want to say and then write the paper just once OR review and edit your work before writing it out again. Nita—use group-work time as an opportunity to practice speaking in English.

1 Students work alone to complete the chart, and then compare answers in pairs. As the class gives feedback, ask students if they think they should be doing these things more or less.

2 Ask students to work alone to circle what is true for them.

3 Students work in small groups to compare ideas. Encourage them to ask each other questions instead of just showing each other their answers. They take turns changing the statement into a question—*Do you like to ... / Do you prefer to ...*—or read their answer and ask *and you?* The group should write at least two sentences like the example sentences when they have found similarities. A volunteer from each group can read aloud one of these when class gives feedback. Ask students if their preferences are the best ways to do things. For example, if someone prefers to let others ask questions in class, what do they do if the question they have isn't asked?

Extension activity

The issue of whether listening to music while studying has been the subject of much debate. Ask students to do some online research to find some of the arguments for and against, and whether some types of music are any better than others. They can share their ideas on an online discussion forum or class blog or can discuss what they found in the following class.

READING 2

Family fun

A Vocabulary preview

Warm-up

It can sometimes be useful, especially if class time is short, for students to do the *Vocabulary preview* exercises at home and go over the answers in class. Once you are sure everyone has the right answers, conduct a group competition to help students remember the vocabulary. Write the words on the board and put students into groups of three. Each group should have one piece of paper numbered 1 to 8. Give the definition, e.g., *Which word means "one time"?)* and let the group decide together which word is the correct one. Move swiftly from one question to the next to keep the energy high. Exchange papers for checking. Alternatively, use the game element in an online learning tool of your choice.

In this exercise, *busy* / 'bɪzi/and *once* /wʌns/ are tricky since they are pronounced very differently from how they are spelled, so be sure to spend some time practicing their pronunciation.

1 Ask students to match the words with their definitions. Fast finishers can start to review in pairs. With books closed for Student A, Student B reads aloud the definition and Student A says the word. Change roles and repeat.

ANSWERS
1 c **2** a **3** d **4** b **5** h **6** f **7** e **8** g

2 Ask students to complete the sentences with the words from Exercise 1. Make sure students pronounce the vocabulary words correctly when going over the answers. Pay particular attention to the pronunciation of *special* /'speʃ(ə)l/, *busy* / 'bɪzi/, *once* /wʌns/, and *twice* /twaɪs/.

Add an element of personalization by asking, e.g., *Is this true for you? How many of you drink coffee at breakfast?,* etc. If necessary, repeat the spelling activity suggested on Teacher's Book page 21.

ANSWERS
1 once **2** keep **3** meal **4** busy **5** twice
6 Everyone **7** special **8** game

B Before you read

Family fun provides a nice contrast to *It's 5:54—time for dinner!* that presented what is typical in U.K. culture. Family traditions are not necessarily culture-specific, but rather they differ from family to family. In thinking about family traditions, students can begin to think about diversity within cultures.

Warm-up

Brainstorm free-time activities with the class and write students' ideas on the board (this also reviews vocabulary from Unit 1). Ask three or four students (choose students who haven't spoken much in class) to say which of these they do with their friends and which they do with their family.

1 Ask students to complete the chart alone and then share the information with their partner, using the sentence stems to make compete sentences.

Previewing

2 After students have read the question, give them ten seconds to read the text quickly and answer the question.

ANSWER
Six students

C Global reading

Ask students to read the instructions. Tell them they then have 20 seconds to read the text quickly to identify the person in each picture.

ANSWERS
Photo 1: Jared
Photo 2: Suzie

Extension activity

To raise awareness of this type of genre, ask students where they think they would read this text, e.g., in a magazine? newspaper? online? Find out if students contribute to any online discussion forums or if they ever post comments online. What topics do people post about in online forums?

D Close reading

1 Students work alone to complete the exercise, and then compare answers in pairs before giving feedback to the class. As the class gives feedback, ask students to say the number and the letter this time as a way of reviewing letters, names, and numbers. (The letters *a* and *e* are particularly tricky to pronounce).

ANSWERS
1 c **2** f **3** d **4** e **5** b **6** a

2 Ask students to complete the sentences with words in the box. When going over answers, have volunteer students read the whole sentence. You may need to work on the pronunciation of *restaurant* (/ˈrest(ə)rənt/—two syllables usually), *month* (/mʌnθ/ not /maʊnθ/), *photo* (/ˈfoʊtoʊ/), and *breakfast* (/ˈbrekfəst/ not /ˈbreɪkfæst/).

ANSWERS
1 old **2** fish **3** twice **4** first **5** once **6** has
7 pizza

Extension activity

Work on collocations with the verbs in the exercises to help students build their vocabulary. Down the left-hand side of a page in their notebook, students write the verbs *cook*, *play*, *watch*, *go*, *take*, and *eat*. They should leave two or three lines between each word. For homework, students think of three words or phrases to go with each verb. Possible answers include, e.g., *cook*—dinner, a meal, pizza; *play*—a game, soccer, tennis; *watch*—TV, a movie, a game; *go*—to a restaurant, to a movie, on vacation; *take*—a photo, a picture, a selfie; *eat*—in a restaurant, at home, a favorite meal. In the following lesson, students share their ideas with other students, and then volunteers share some with the rest of the class. Correct preposition errors as needed without going into too much detail.

E Over to you

1 Students write their sentences as a take-home activity.

2 In class, students read their sentences in pairs. Ask students to pair up two more times so that each student gets the opportunity to read their sentences a total of three times to three different people. As you walk around, listen and note down any errors you hear (but without interrupting the students). When they are finished, comment first on some of the interesting family activities. Then say that you heard a few things that were not right. Write down the incorrect sentence without saying who said it, and ask the class if they can correct it. For example, T: *I heard this: My family and I eats pizza on Friday. There is something wrong with* eats. *What should it be?* (eat) *Why?* (My family and I = we. We eat). This type of correction technique lets students know that you are monitoring them when they are speaking together. This can motivate them to speak in English rather than their L1 when doing pair-work activities. It is a non-threatening way of correcting errors, and it allows the entire class to think about how to correct them.

VOCABULARY

Topic vocabulary

Family members

Warm-up

Tell students you are going to tell them a riddle. Ask them if they understand the word and what it means (Answer: a question that seems impossible or silly, but has a clever or funny answer). Then tell them this riddle: A man is looking at a photograph. His friend asks, "Who is this?" The man says, "I don't have brothers or sisters. This man's father is my father's son." Who is in the picture? Give students a few minutes to work together to see if they can figure out the riddle. Some may get it quickly, so tell them not to shout out the answer so that others can have time to work it out. You may need to explain the possessive form *man's father* means *the father of the man,* or *his father.* The answer to the riddle is: He is looking at a picture of his son.

1 Students work in pairs to complete the exercise, using a dictionary if needed. Ask fast finishers to draw the chart on the board and write in the answers. Use this chart for drilling the words. Point to a word, say it, and have the students repeat it. Do this a few times, and then point to the word without saying it to see if students can remember the pronunciation. Tricky words include *aunt* (/ænt/), *daughter* (/ˈdɔtər/), *niece* (/nis/), *nephew* (/ˈnefju/), and *uncle* (/ˈʌŋk(ə)l/).

For homework, ask students to review the pronunciation using an online dictionary such as the Macmillan Dictionary, making sure to click on the American pronunciation of the words. Ask them to learn the spelling. In the next lesson, hold a team spelling competition completion as a review.

ANSWERS
Male: brother, father, husband, grandfather, nephew, son, uncle
Female: aunt, daughter, grandmother, mother, niece, sister, wife

2 Ensure that students understand that *mother's mother* means *the mother of your mother*. Write *'s* on the board and explain that using an apostrophe and "s," e.g., *'s*, is how we show possessive in English. Check that students understand the concept. T: *The mother of your mother?* STS: *mother's mother*; T: *the daughter of your son?* STS: *son's daughter*, etc.

ANSWERS
1 grandmother **2** niece **3** aunt **4** nephew
5 grandfather **6** uncle **7** brother **8** father

3 Students complete the sentences and then share with a partner. If appropriate, see who has the biggest family.

Extension activity

If appropriate, ask students to draw a family tree for homework. They can do this on a large sheet of paper or they could use a family tree making app. (Search for family tree maker; there are several free apps online.) In class, students describe their family tree as a way of consolidating and reviewing the vocabulary.

VOCABULARY

Vocabulary builder

How often do things happen?

Focus students' attention on the *How often do things happen?* box. Explain the concept of *How often …?* by telling the students something you do every day or every weekend, e.g., T: *Every Saturday, I go to a restaurant with my family. You can ask me: "How often do you go to a restaurant with your family?" And I would say, I go to a restaurant with my family every Saturday.* Point out that the *t* in *often* is silent: / ˈɔf(ə)n/.

Introduce the new vocabulary. Draw a calendar on the board.

Monday	Tuesday	Wednesday	Thursday	Friday	Saturday	Sunday
					go to a restaurant	

Ask students *How many times a week do I go to a restaurant?* Elicit *one time* is ***once*** *a week.* Continue in this way to introduce *twice*, *three times*, and *every*. Point out that the expression is "once a week" and not "once every week." Clap and drill the rhythm: ONCE a WEEK; TWICE a WEEK, etc.

Introduce *morning*, *afternoon*, *day*, and *night* with times on the board. *Morning*—5:00 AM–11:59 AM; *afternoon*—12:00 PM–5:59 PM, etc. Note that different cultures have different views on when morning ends and afternoon begins, or when night begins and ends. Another word for 12:00 is *noon*, and this is where we get the term *afternoon*—literally after 12:00.

1 Students read the *How often do things happen?* box and reorder the sentences. When checking in pairs, remind students to use a capital letter and a period. When reading aloud the sentences during a class feedback session, ask the students *Is this true for you?* to add an element of personalization.

It is possible to put these time expressions at the beginning of the sentence, e.g., *Once a week, my mother cooks pizza*, but they cannot go in the middle of the sentence, e.g., *My mother once a week cooks pizza*.

ANSWERS

1 My mother cooks pizza once a week. / Once a week my mother cooks pizza.
2 I chat with my brother every night. / Every night I chat with my brother.
3 I talk with my parents twice a month. / Twice a month I talk with my parents.
4 I cook for my family every week. / Every week I cook for my family.
5 My aunt and uncle visit us twice a year. / Twice a year my aunt and uncle visit us.
6 My family goes to a restaurant three times a month. / Three times a month my family goes to a restaurant.

2 Ask students to find and correct the mistakes in each sentence. This is excellent practice for editing students' own work. Ask students to work alone and compare answers in pairs. To ensure that students have the right answers, write them on the board so they can see the correct sentence.

ANSWERS

1 I text my sister **every day**.
2 My family calls **once a** week.
3 My grandparents visit me **three times a year**.
4 My mother has breakfast with my father **every day**.
5 I watch an old movie with my mother **twice a month**.
6 My father takes my picture **once a year**.

3 Students complete the sentences with their own ideas. This can be done as a take-home activity if class time is short. You could ask students to write two true sentences and two false ones. They read their sentences to a partner, who must say which are true and which are false.

Extension activity

Play a vocabulary tic-tac-toe game. Hand out five slips of paper to each student. Ask them to look through their vocabulary notebook and write one word or phrase on each slip of paper. Collect the slips and put them into a hat or jar. Make a 5 × 5 chart on the board. Divide the class into two teams—X and O. Pick one word out of the hat or box and explain or define it, e.g., *This is the boy child of your mother and father. Your father is the ___ of your grandfather.* Each team will get a chance to guess the vocabulary word based on your definition. If they guess correctly, they get to put an X (or O) in the square. The aim is to get five down, five across, or five diagonally. Teams may try to block the other team.

WRITING

Writing model

Read through the introduction paragraph with the students so that they know the aim of the *Writing* section. At this stage, they probably won't understand what subject pronouns or possessive adjectives are, so explain that they are going to learn their meanings. Revisit this paragraph later so that students can assess what that they have learned. Remind students that each section of the next part of the unit builds towards the final *Writing task*.

A Analyze

1 Students may not have seen this type of graphic before, so explain that this is a mind map, and it is a very good way to get ideas down on paper quickly. Students work alone to read the mind map.

2 Students now read the text based on the mind map about Talia and check what it includes. Note that the paragraph does not include all the information from the mind map.

ANSWERS

[✓] her parents' names [✓] her brothers' ages
[✓] what her mother always does
[✓] how often they go to school
[ ] what her father sometimes does
[ ] how often Talia goes to school
[✓] her brothers' names [✓] how often Talia studies

B Model

Ask the students who they think wrote the text about Talia (a student). How did that person get the information about her? (They probably interviewed her/ asked her questions.) Below the text is a list of questions that the writer asked Talia along with her responses. Students match the questions and answers, and then check in pairs. As the class gives feedback, have one student read the question using falling intonation for Wh- questions and rising intonation for yes / no questions, and have another student read the answer.

ANSWERS

1 e **2** h **3** a **4** d **5** g **6** b **7** f **8** c

Extension activity

Practice asking questions. Put students into teams of three or four. Ideally, group students so that there is at least one strong student and one weaker student in each group. Ask them to come up with a name for their team. Read the answer to a question (You could use the answers in the exercise or make up your own.). Teams must write the question. One person from each team reads their question. For a correct question with no mistakes, the team gets two points. If the question is mostly right, the team gets one point. Keep score on the board. The team with the most points wins.

GRAMMAR

Subject pronouns and possessive adjectives

Ask students to read the *Subject pronouns and possessive adjectives* box for homework before the lesson so that they are better prepared to understand your presentation. Copy the table on the board, but do not put in the pronouns and adjectives yet. Make sure students understand the terms *singular* and *plural*. With books closed, ask students to tell you what the subject pronouns are. Write them in the appropriate column. Ask students to give you some examples of *he* (Harold, Mr. Thomson, the man, grandfather, etc.), *she* (Maria, Mrs. Lee, the woman, nephew, etc.), and *it* (the pet, Tizzy the cat, the house, etc. [NOTE: Some people refer to their pets as *he* or *she*, too.].) Ask students which pronoun they would use for *Martin and I* (we) or *Martin and Toby* (they). If you are talking to one person, you can use (you) as well as more than one person (you). If needed, explain that unlike some other languages, there is no formal form of *you*.

Ask students what the possessive adjective is for *I*, *you*, *he*, etc., and write these in the appropriate column. In some languages, it is confusing to students to say *his niece*—the possessive adjective sometimes matches the gender of the noun it modifies. If this is true for the language of your students, you may need to clarify.

Its vs. *it's*—if students ask, point out that *its* is the possessive adjective while *it's* is the short form of *it is*.

Drill pronunciation before asking students to open their books. Ask students to look at the subject pronouns and underline the subject in each example sentence. What do they notice? (The subject is always the pronoun.) They do the same for the examples in the possessive adjective column. What do they notice? (The subject is the adjective + the noun: *My mother*, *Your house*, etc.) Noticing this may help some students who are confused about which to use when.

1 Ask students to choose the correct subject pronoun or possessive adjective. Compare answers in pairs before having the class give feedback. Volunteers should read the entire line. Check their pronunciation. You also may need to review titles: *Mr.* refers to a man; *Miss* refers to a single woman; *Mrs.* refers to a married woman; *Ms.* is the female equivalent to *Mr.* and can refer to a married or unmarried woman.

ANSWERS

1 They **2** She **3** his **4** We **5** your **6** My **7** His **8** My, Its

2 This exercise illustrates how possessive adjectives can help avoid unnecessary repetition. Do the first sentence with the students as an example. Read the sentence, repeating *my mother's* so the students can hear the repetition. By substituting *her*, the sentence sounds better and is shorter, too. Ask students to pay particular attention to question 2. Point out that it is talking about more than one teacher, so it is plural. When students have finished the exercise, have the class give feedback and discuss anything students feel needs extra clarification.

ANSWERS

1 her **2** Their **3** Its **4** Their **5** His **6** Her **7** Their **8** Our

3 Ask students to work alone to complete the sentences with the correct subject pronoun or possessive adjective. Check answers as a whole class. When checking answers, remind students about capitalization.

ANSWERS

1 They **2** We **3** Our **4** His **5** You **6** It **7** My **8** She **9** We **10** Their

4 If time is short, assign this exercise as a take-home activity. When checking answers, ask students to work together and have them ask for your help if they disagree on the correction.

ANSWERS

1 My uncle has a new car. **It is** / **It's** very nice.
2 I don't live with **my** family. I live alone.
3 Do you and **your** brother live with your family?
4 Our parents live in Los Angeles. **They** visit me once a month.
5 My sister lives in Germany, but **her** daughter lives in France.
6 My father likes sports. **His** favorites are baseball and soccer.
7 I want to write to your niece. Do you have **her** email address?
8 Mr. Hariri and his new wife live in Oman. **Their** children live there, too.
9 I really like your new home. **It is** / **It's** a special place for your family.
10 My nephew and I like to play games. **They** are fun on a Sunday afternoon.

Extension activity

In pairs, students write three to five sentences on a sheet of paper, some that use subject pronouns or possessive adjectives correctly, and at least one sentence in which there is a mistake. Pairs exchange papers with another pair who must find the sentence with a mistake. Students can use sentences from the exercises (lower level) or write their own sentences (higher level).

WRITING

Writing skill

Not repeating words

Explain that the work students completed in the *Grammar* section supports the *Writing skill*. At this point, you could return to the introduction paragraph in the *Writing model* and ask students to assess what they have learned. Explain that using pronouns and possessive adjectives instead of repeating words will make their writing sound much more sophisticated.

Write the sentences from the *Not repeating words* box on the board without the pronouns or possessive adjectives. Students tell you where they can put them to make the second sentence sound more natural. Ask the students which word the pronouns refer to. Draw a circle around the word and a line to the word it refers to, e.g.,

Dr. Jones is in the library. He is helping Susan with her homework.

Students work alone to rewrite the description in the space provided below the text, replacing the underlined words with subject pronouns or possessive adjectives. Students compare answers with a partner before checking as a class.

ANSWERS

My family is very special to me. I live with my parents and my grandmother. We live in an apartment in Shanghai. My father is a taxi driver. He works all day. My mother works in a restaurant. Her restaurant is open all day. They both work very hard.
I go to college. It is very good, and I get good grades. I like my teachers. They help me a lot. I study business. It is not easy.
I have a sister. Her husband is a college professor. They live in Wuhan. They have a new baby boy. His name is Jinhai.

WRITING

Writing task

Brainstorm

Put students into pairs to interview each other. To ensure they ask and answer the questions orally, the student being interviewed should have his or her book closed. Students check the information that is correct about them once the interview is completed—spelling of siblings' names and school, for example, might be difficult for the students to spell. Ask students to correct spelling mistakes in each other's work.

Plan

Students work alone to consider the information from the interview and which they will use. Refer them back to the model if they need some ideas. Ask students to discuss their ideas with a partner, comparing notes, and give them time to add to or adjust their notes as required.

Write

Give students about 20–25 minutes of class time to write their paragraphs. Ask students to write 60 words about their partner and to remember to use the key points, e.g., to use pronouns and possessive adjectives in order to not repeat words. Observe students while they write to see who finds writing easy or difficult, who stops to count words after each sentence, and who refers to their plan.

Share

Students exchange paragraphs with their partner and write one sentence about themselves for their partner to include. To help with the peer review, and to help support the sharing stage, write guidelines on the board:

Is the information about you correct?

Does the writer use pronouns and possessive adjectives correctly?

Are the right words capitalized? (first word in the sentence, names, etc.)

Tell students to look at the checklist on page 189. They use the checklist to compare their writing in pairs and offer suggestions for improvement.

Rewrite and edit

Students read and consider their partner's comments and rewrite and revise their paragraph on a clean sheet of paper, checking for errors, before turning it in. This could be done for homework. Optionally, students could write their final paragraph directly into a class blog, or they could use a word processor and print out their work. Include a picture of the person the paragraph is about if appropriate.

REVIEW

Wordlist

Students work in pairs or small groups to work through the *Wordlist*, checking that they all remember what each word or phrase means, how to pronounce it, and how it was used in the unit. Go through the list carefully with the class.

Vocabulary builder review

Students work through the sentences, check in pairs, and report back to the class.

ANSWERS
1 business **2** once a year **3** music **4** every week

Unit review

Students work through the list alone to decide what they can and can't do. They discuss their answers in pairs, including what they remember from the unit about each point. Finally, open up the discussion to include the whole class. Pay particular attention to any boxes that the students didn't check. Explore with them ways of overcoming any remaining problems.

Extra research task

In many countries it's normal to live at home with parents until after school, after marriage, or indefinitely. In Europe and in the U.S., more and more young people are living at home longer. Ask students to find out more about (1) why more people are living at home longer, (2) in which countries this is a growing trend, and (3) what are some of the problems parents and young adults face with living at home longer. Ideas for searches include, e.g., *average age of leaving home by country, what is the average age to move out of parents' house, living at home with parents in the U.S.* In class, students share their information and discuss how they feel about this trend. Ask them to make a list of the advantages and disadvantages of living at home as a young adult. Share ideas in a whole-class discussion. Alternatively, start a classroom discussion forum where students can practice writing and reading while sharing their ideas. Avoid correcting grammar because the focus should be on idea sharing and not accuracy. The best way to incentivize students is by making them feel engaged by the task and to feel that it is helping them in some way, so do emphasize how extensive practice such as this will improve their overall English.

3 STUDY

READING	Skimming
STUDY SKILL	What do I have? What do I need?
VOCABULARY	Prepositions of place
GRAMMAR	The verb *have*
WRITING	Writing sentences: adding information

Warm-up

The word *study* can have many meanings. Show students how to find the right meaning in a monolingual dictionary. If possible, project the Macmillan Dictionary entry for *study*. Show students that there aredifferent possible meanings. Ask them to look at the unit-opening picture and the infographic. Which meaning do they think is closest to the meaning of the unit title? Explore the categories. This activity shows students how a monolingual dictionary can be more helpful than a bilingual one that just offers a translation of a word. Students should gradually wean themselves off a bilingual dictionary as their English improves.

Discussion point

On the board, write *a good study space*. With books closed, students work in small groups to come up with some criteria for a good study space. Students then open their books and read the eight tips for a better study space. In pairs or small groups, students discuss the questions. Ask for feedback for each question from two or three volunteers. Ask them to give you reasons for why they disagree with any of the tips.

Extension activity

Ask students to draw and label their perfect study space using a dictionary to support any new language they want to use. Alternatively, they can find a picture of the perfect study space online. Students compare their ideal study space, using the labels to help describe why it's perfect.

VIDEO

Before you watch

Introduce the topic of the video and ask students to read the exercise and identify any new words. Write these on the board and discuss the meanings as a class. Then, ask students to complete the *Before you watch* section. Monitor and go through the answers with the class.

ANSWERS

1 b **2** a **3** d **4** c

While you watch

Play the video once. Ask the students to watch the video and complete the exercise. Play the video again so that students can check their answers. Go through the answers with the class.

ANSWERS

1 T **2** F (The weather is cold and it snows.)
3 F (The hotel is in big metal boxes.) **4** T

See page 108 for the video script.

After you watch

Put the students into pairs or groups and ask them to complete the exercise. Encourage them to use what they have learned in the video and the example answers to answer the questions. Go through the answers with the class.

READING 1

Dorm spaces

A Vocabulary preview

Warm-up

If your institution has student accommodations, lead in with a show of hands of who lives on campus and who lives off campus. Find out how many live in student accommodations (as opposed to an apartment). Explain that a *dorm* is student accommodation, usually provided by the school. Ask students who live in a dorm to briefly say what it's like. Do they share a room? Are there lots of other students? Can they cook in the dorm? *Dorm* is short for *dormitory* and comes from the Latin meaning *a place to sleep*.

1 Ask students to match the words with their definitions. If permitted, let students find pictures online (or use your computer and projector) of a closet and dresser because these are easier to conceptualize from a photograph. Point out that a dresser (also known as a chest of drawers) has drawers in it, and a closet is built into the room (i.e., it's not a piece of furniture). Some people have a walk-in closet.

Note that all the words are nouns. Ask students which subject pronoun they would use to replace these nouns (it). Drill pronunciation. Ask students which words have one syllable (bed, dorm, shelves /ʃelvz/) and which have two syllables (closet /'klɑzət/, dresser, poster, roommate, sofa), and which syllable is stressed (for these words, it's the first syllable).

ANSWERS
1 a **2** c **3** d **4** b **5** g **6** e **7** h **8** f

Focus students' attention on the spelling of the words in Exercise 1. With books closed, write the words on the board twice—one version is spelled correctly and the other is not. Put the students into pairs to work together and decide which is the correct spelling and write it down. Students then self-check by comparing the words to the ones in the book. Find out which words gave them the most trouble. Review spelling often with quick activities to provide a change of procedure, which can enliven the routine.

2 Students work alone to complete the exercise, and then compare answers in pairs. Fast finishers can test each other. Student A reads the sentence without saying the vocabulary word and Student B supplies the word (without looking at the book). Ask students to add these new words to the class vocabulary word bank or flash card set as suggested in earlier units.

ANSWERS
1 shelves **2** bed **3** closet **4** dresser **5** roommate, sofa **6** poster, dorm

Extension activity

Ask students to remember their room or dorm room and make a mind map from memory of all the different items of furniture in it. Compare with a partner and add any new furniture words. Put the mind map into their vocabulary notebook.

B Before you read

Write the letters *b*, *c*, *d*, *f*, *p*, and *s* on the board in a vertical column. Put students into pairs. Give students one minute to think of things you find in a dorm room beginning with the letters on the board. Tell the students they are not to look in their books or notebooks. They can use each letter more than once. The pair with the most words "wins."

1 Students work alone to rank the items, and then compare with a partner. Encourage them to give reasons for their choices. Ask students if there are any items that are not on the list that they think are very important or important, e.g., computer or laptop, Wi-Fi router, etc.

2 Focus students' attention on the pictures in *Dorm spaces*. Divide students into three groups. Group 1 will look at picture 1, Group 2 at picture 2, etc. Students find the page, and then close the book marking the page with their thumb. When you say *open*, students open their books and study the picture for 20 seconds. They close the book when you say *close*. With a partner, they then write down all the things from Exercise 1 they saw in their picture.

ANSWERS
Picture 1: window, bed(s), desk(s), chair(s), lamp(s), TV, dresser(s), shelf / shelves
Picture 2: window, bed(s), desk(s), chair(s), lamp(s), TV, dresser(s), closet(s), poster(s)
Picture 3: window(s), bed, desk, chair, lamp, sofa, dresser, shelves, closet

C Global reading

Ask students to read the *Skimming* box. Ensure that students understand the concept, e.g., skimming is when your eyes pass over the text quickly, without reading every word, in order to understand the general idea. To reinforce this, ask them *Do you read every word when you skim a text?* (no) *When you skim do you read quickly or carefully?* (quickly) *Why is it important to skim?* (Sometimes you need to just get the general idea of the text. Skimming happens first, and then reading more carefully comes later.)

Students read the instructions. Make sure they know they are just looking for the name of the person next to each picture. Give them 20 seconds to skim-read the text for the name of each person.

ANSWERS
Picture 1: Megan
Picture 2: Kyle
Picture 3: Rachel

D Close reading

Ask students where they might find this kind of text. It is an online discussion forum. Ask students if they have ever posted to an online discussion forum and if so, what kinds of forums they participate in. This would be a good opportunity to set up an online forum with students if you haven't done so before. Students are often more likely to communicate in a foreign language in an online forum than face-to-face, so discussion forums are a great way to get students to communicate in English. There are many blogs suggesting ways to set up forums online; search *online forums for students*.

1 Students complete the chart alone, and then compare with a partner before checking as a class.

ANSWERS
1 Megan, Kyle **2** Kyle, Rachel **3** Megan, Kyle
4 Megan, Kyle **5** Megan, Kyle **6** Megan, Kyle **7** Kyle
8 Rachel

2 Students work alone, and then compare in pairs. Ask fast finishers to make the false sentences true. As the class gives feedback, ask those students to tell you the true sentence that they've written.

ANSWERS
1 T **2** F (Megan doesn't have a picture of her closet.)
3 T **4** F (He keeps his books on the floor.) **5** T
6 F (Her room has a desk lamp.) **7** T
8 F (She lives alone.)

E Over to you

Students discuss the questions in small groups. If you have been noticing that some students don't participate or don't speak well in a group, or if some students dominate the conversation, one way to help is by giving each student three sticks or tokens of some kind. These are speaking tokens. When the student in the group answers the question, he or she can discard the token. The rule is that they must use a complete sentence. They may use the sentence frames provided or their own sentence. Encourage higher-level students to give reasons for their answers. The groups should use up all their tokens thereby ensuring that the students who are shy or nervous speaking have a chance to voice their opinions.

Extension activity

Students write two true sentences and two false ones about their room. They can use the sentences in Exercise 2 on page 48 for ideas. Other students guess which is the false sentence.

STUDY SKILLS

What do I have? What do I need?

Although many students have a study space or a system that works well for them, many students do not. These students may be poorly organized and consistently falling behind on assignment deadlines. It is worth spending time raising student awareness of the types of study tools that will help them cope with the demands of being an independent learner.

Some students won't have their own separate study space, especially if they have to share a room with brothers and sisters. This doesn't mean that they don't have a system in place. Find out how students cope in different situations to see if they have good ideas to share.

Warm-up

As a class, brainstorm things that help you study. Write student ideas on the board. Encourage them to think of people and places, as well as things. If there are any ideas that sound unusual for study (e.g., video games), ask the student why that will help him or her study. Put students into pairs or groups of three. Ask them to make a list of the things they have now that help them study and a list of things they need to help them study. Have the class give feedback. For the list of what students need, see if anyone can suggest ways to get the things. Where possible, direct them to the appropriate service at the college.

1 Students add the words to the correct places in the word map.

ANSWERS
1 parents **2** kitchen **3** printer **4** teachers
5 library **6** photocopier

2 Ask students to add other ideas to the word map. Ask them if they know of any online tools that can help them study—a podcast in English, dictionary apps, etc.

3 Students work alone, and then compare in pairs. Conduct a substitution drill (books closed) with individual students around the classroom:

T: *I have a desk at home. Computer.*

ST: *I have a computer at home.*

T: *I have a reading lamp on my desk. Dictionary.*

ST: *I have a dictionary on my desk.*

T: *I have a desk at school. We.*

ST: *We have a desk at school.*

Extension activity

Ask students what their study routine is, e.g., *Do they do assignments when they are assigned or wait until the day before they are due? Do they have a specific time they study or does it vary? Are they happy with the way they study or do they wish they had a better system? Do they study a lot but don't feel like they are improving?* Share ideas to raise awareness of the need for a study system—whatever that system may be.

READING 2

What works for me

A Vocabulary preview

Warm-up

Ask students what they think *It works for me* means. (It's fine with me; It's good for me.) Give them some examples of the expression in use, e.g., *Raul: Can we study in the library tonight? Paolo: It works for me.* You can also use the expression as a question, e.g., *Paolo: I'd like to play some music while I study. Does that work for you?* Put students into pairs to create a mini-dialogue with the expression.

1 Ask students to work alone to match the words with the definitions, using a dictionary if needed. Ask students to check in pairs, and then check as a class. Note that *light* and *plant* have several meanings, and *open* can be an adjective or a verb. Ask students if their study room is messy or neat.

ANSWERS
1 c **2** d **3** b **4** a **5** f **6** h **7** e **8** g

2 Ask students to work alone to complete the sentences with the correct words from Exercise 1. Then put them into pairs to compare their answers. Tell Student A to read aloud the odd sentences and Student B to read aloud the even sentences. For homework, ask students to write their own sentences with the vocabulary words. Collect sentences and use them for a quick vocabulary review in the next lesson. Read the sentence without the word; students supply the missing word.

Pay particular attention to spelling. Repeat the activity suggested on Teacher's Book page 21.

ANSWERS
1 plant **2** electricity **3** light **4** neat **5** office
6 best **7** messy **8** open

Extension activity

In their vocabulary notebooks, students make a 5 x 4 grid. In the left hand vertical column, they write *Noun*, *Verb*, and *Adjective*. Across the top, they write a letter from the alphabet. Give them one minute to complete the table with vocabulary words beginning with the letter in the correct part of speech (see example below). After one minute, they compare and help their partner think of more words to complete the chart. Have students give feedback about some of the words to the rest of the class. Note that they may not be able to fill in all the spaces. This is a good activity to repeat often and can be done as a group competition. Soon students will learn which letters of the alphabet are used more at the beginning of words.

	B	O	M	P
Noun	bedroom	office		plant
Verb			make	
Adjective	best	open	messy	pretty

B Before you read

If you introduced the expression *It works for me*, then ask students what they think the title *What works for me* means. Ask them to read the subtitle for clues. You could re-state the title as *These are the things that are good for me.*

Students look at the pictures and decide what they show.

ANSWER
b where people work

C Global reading

Skimming

This is an exam-type activity. Students must quickly skim the text to decide where the headings belong. Headings in texts provide short summaries of the paragraph that follows. Often in exams, there is one extra heading that doesn't fit. This type of question tests whether or not students can quickly skim for main ideas.

Draw students' attention to the heading in the first paragraph. Ask them to circle the words in the paragraph that relate to the heading (*neat, clean, open*).

Students read the headings, and then quickly skim the text to put them into the right place. Give them no more than 60 seconds to match them. As the class gives feedback, ask students which words in the paragraphs gave them clues. Ask students what they think the expression *keeping it green* means (to do things that help the environment). Ask students what Richard does to help the environment. Ask students what they do to *keep it green*.

ANSWERS
Messy is best 4
Keeping it green 3
Family and friends 1
Lots of light 2

D Close reading

1 Ask students to read the text and choose the correct answers. If class time is short, you can ask students to do this exercise for homework.

ANSWERS
1 b **2** c **3** c **4** c **5** a

2 Students use the words from the box to complete the sentences.

ANSWERS
1 work **2** neat **3** open **4** spaces **5** pictures
6 make

E Over to you

For question 1, put students into pairs to say whose work space they like and why. Change partners and repeat for more practice and so students can continue to get to know each other. Then ask pairs to agree on one or two adjectives to complete the sentence stem in question 2.

Extension activity

Neat and *messy* are opposites. Ask students to find the opposites of the other adjectives, e.g., *clean—dirty*; *large—small*; *open—closed*; *comfortable—uncomfortable*; *sunny—dark*.

VOCABULARY

Topic vocabulary

Prepositions of place

Warm-up

You can introduce prepositions of place with a box and a ball. Put the ball in the box and say, *The ball is in the box.* Do the same for *on, under, by, in front of,* and *behind*. Check often by placing the ball and asking students to say the preposition. Ask a student to come up and place the ball while the other students say the preposition. Ask another student to come up and place the ball where the other students tell him or her to. Put the ball in the box and elicit a complete sentence from the class, e.g., *The ball is in the box.* Continue to elicit complete sentences for the other prepositions. Note that *by* is the same as *next to*.

1 Ask students to look at the *Prepositions of place* box and complete the exercise alone. They can use a dictionary if they don't know a word. When the answers have been checked, students work in pairs to drill each other. Student A says, *Where's the …?* (choosing an item from Exercise 2). Student B says where it is using a complete sentence. For example, Student A: *Where's the box?* Student B: *The box is under the chair.* They then change roles.

ANSWERS
1 The book is on the table.
2 The phone is under the bed.
3 The lamp is in the closet.
4 The man is by the shelves.
5 The book is in front of the TV.
6 The plant is behind the sofa.
7 The TV is on the dresser.
8 The poster is on the wall.
9 The box is under the chair.

2 Students work in pairs to write the four sentences using prepositions of place. They form groups of four to compare sentences. As an alternative, ask students to write three true sentences and one false sentence. The other students have to say which one is not true.

Extension activity

In pairs, students write a short description of one of the workspaces from *What works for me*. Do one as an example, e.g., *There's a computer on her desk, and a phone by the computer. Whose desk is it?* (Lily's). Pairs read their description for another pair to guess.

VOCABULARY

Vocabulary builder

Classroom objects

If possible, bring in some of the items from Exercise 1 in a large bag. Begin to bring out the items to introduce the vocabulary. Point to the printer and map if you have them already in your classroom and ask students what they are. Revisit each item frequently. Hold it up and say, *What's this?* Ensure that students pronounce the words correctly. Note the stress pattern of *notebook* and *flash drive*. Both have stress on both syllables. Make sure students are saying /**p**/ and not /**b**/ in *map, printer*, and *pen. Highlighter* is a tricky word because of its spelling (/ˈ**haɪˌlaɪtər**/).

1 Students write the words under the correct pictures. In pairs, Student A covers the words 1–4, points to the pictures, and asks *What's this?* Student B tries to remember the vocabulary word. Change parts with Student B covering the words for 5–8.

ANSWERS
1 map **2** folder **3** tablet **4** notebook
5 highlighter pen **6** calendar **7** printer **8** flash drive

2 Students work alone to complete the sentences before checking in pairs. As the class provides feedback, ask volunteers to read the complete sentence to the class.

ANSWERS
1 map **2** tablet **3** notebook **4** highlighter pen
5 calendar **6** printer **7** flash drive **8** folder

3 After students discuss in pairs, find out who uses these things and how. For example, students may use the map and calendar on their smartphone. Some students may prefer the cloud to a flash drive, or a note-taking app instead of a notebook, for instance.

WRITING

Writing model

Read through the aims with the students. Remind them that each part of the *Writing* section will help to build their skills for the successful completion of the *Writing task*.

A Analyze

Students look at the brainstorm in response to the question, *What's your study space like?* They match the notes to the pictures.

ANSWERS
1 d **2** e **3** f **4** b **5** a **6** c

B Model

This section aims to introduce students to the idea of text cohesion—the way a text hangs together. Often, student writing is a series of sentences rather than a cohesive piece of communication.

Students read the instructions, and then read the sentences. Make sure students understand that the word *too* means *also*, *in addition*, or *as well*. Students complete the exercise. Ask students to think about why they have chosen the sentence they have—which fits better into the text? The sentences at the beginning of the text talk about what is on the desk. Then the sentence before the blank mentions what is on the wall. It would sound odd to go back to talking about the desk and makes more sense to continue talking about what is on the wall.

ANSWER
b

GRAMMAR

The verb *have*

Ask students to read *The verb have* box for homework before the lesson so that they are better prepared to understand your presentation. If possible, make a video recording of yourself presenting the grammar and upload it onto a hidden YouTube channel. Give the students the URL so they can watch it. In class, ask students questions to ensure they have understood the concept of what they read, e.g., *How many forms does the verb* have *have?* (two) *What are the two forms?* (have, has) *What words do we use to make it negative?* (don't, doesn't) *What words do we use to make a question?* (do, does) Reinforce this by conducting some drills. Repetition: *I have, you have, we have, she has*, etc.; Transformation: Make it negative: *We have a large window. We don't have a large window*, etc.; Question / Answer: *Do you have a photo of your closet? YES Yes, I have a photo of my closet*, etc. In each instance, start with a group drill, and then choose a few students to do some individual drilling.

1 Students complete the exercise alone, and then compare answers in pairs. When going over the answers, students read the entire sentence. As an extension, where possible ask the student to substitute the subject with a subject pronoun, e.g., *My teacher has a small office. She (or He) has a small office.*

ANSWERS
1 has **2** has **3** have **4** Does, have **5** has **6** have
7 Do, have **8** has

Exercises 2–5 could be done for homework to save class time for more productive work. Alternatively, do the first few questions of each exercise in class and assign the rest for homework. Go over answers in class the following lesson.

2 To help students complete this exercise, discuss question 1 together. Point out that there is a positive and a negative sentence in each question.

ANSWERS
1 don't have 2 has 3 doesn't have 4 doesn't have 5 don't have 6 don't have 7 doesn't have 8 don't have

3 To help students complete this exercise, show them how to decide which question word to use– *do* or *does*. Ask them to underline the subject and decide if it's singular or plural. If it's singular, use *does*; if it's plural use *do*. Refer them to the examples in the skills box above. Put students into pairs to ask and answer the questions, changing roles each time.

ANSWERS
1 Do Ken's walls have posters on them?
2 Does your office have a big window?
3 Does their room have blue walls?
4 Does Maria have a small dorm room?
5 Does your teacher have office hours from 1:00–2:00?
6 Do they have a class at 10:00?
7 Does Paul have a room on the third floor?
8 Do your parents have four bedrooms in their house?

4 Ask students to explain the mistake in each sentence or question when going over the answers, e.g., *Joe and his roommate, they* ***have***; ***Do you,*** *not does you*, etc.

ANSWERS
1 Joe and his roommate **have** a dorm with a big closet.
2 **Do** you have chairs in your room?
3 We **don't** have class on Friday.
4 **Does** Mr. Wilson have many students in this class?
5 Does your college **have** a lot of green space?
6 Sarah **doesn't** have a roommate this year.
7 **Do** you and your friends have fun in class?
8 Jake doesn't **have** a computer now.

5 Ask students to answer the questions using full sentences. In pairs, students ask and answer the questions. Ask several volunteers to read aloud their answers. If students are unsure about their answer, encourage them to ask you about it.

Extension activity

Conduct a "Find someone who" mingling activity. On the board, write *Find someone who* ... followed by a series of about ten prompts, e.g.:

has a pet.

doesn't have a car, etc.

Students copy the title and the list, leaving enough space below each prompt to write a yes / no question. They then stand up and ask other students the questions. When they find a person who, for example, doesn't have a car, they write his or her name down. The aim is to speak to many different students and to "find" a different person / name for each question.

WRITING

Writing skill

Writing sentences: adding information

The *Writing skill* section is an extension of what students did in the *Writing model* section, and it continues the skill of creating text cohesion. On the board, write the two sentences in the *Writing sentences: adding information* box. Read them to the students to help them notice that the repetition of *Tom's room has* ... doesn't sound good because the sentences aren't connected. Ask students what they could do to make the two sentences fit together and sound better. Cross out the repeating phrase, e.g., *Tom's room has a large desk. ~~Tom's room has~~ a comfortable chair.* Ask students what word could be added to make this a sentence (and). Direct students to the skill box to find two more ways the sentences could be combined. Draw students' attention to the comma that comes before *too*.

The position of *also* changes according to the verb. Compare: *It also has* ... *It is also* ... *She also studies* .... Draw students' attention to this rule: For most verbs, *also* comes before the verb and after the subject, but for the verb *be*, it comes after.

1 Ask students to work alone to combine the sentences using *and*. Ask students to check in pairs, and then check as a class.

> ANSWERS
> 1 I have a poster and a calendar on my wall.
> 2 Dan's room has two dressers and one closet.
> 3 My study space is in the corner and on the second floor.
> 4 Jim and his roommate have a large red chair.
> 5 Emiko's dorm is very big and sunny.

2 Students work alone to rewrite the sentences using the word at the end in parentheses. When checking, ask students if they remembered the comma before *too*. Check the position of the word *also*.

> ANSWERS
> 1 She also has a small desk lamp.
> 2 He has a table in front of the sofa, too.
> 3 Patricia's dorm is also on the third floor.
> 4 He has a big closet, too.
> 5 Paula's room also has three windows.

WRITING

Writing task

Brainstorm

Ask students to look at the picture of John's study space for 30 seconds, and then close their books and write down what they remember. With a partner, ask them to add to their lists. Ask the pairs to compare with other pairs to see if there is anything else they have missed. Have the class provide feedback and write the items on the board to help students with spelling the items.

> POSSIBLE ANSWERS
> desk, wall, shelves, laptop, flash drive, soccer poster, digital clock, calendar, printer, paper, highlighter pens

Plan

Students work alone or in pairs to plan their writing—what information they will include and how they will connect their sentences. Refer them back to the *Writing model* on page 56 if they need some ideas. They could compare their thoughts with another student pair to generate more ideas.

Write

Give students about 20–25 minutes of class time to write their paragraphs. Ask students to write 50–60 words about John's study space and to remember to use the key points, e.g., the use of the verb *have* and prepositions of place. Students then complete the *Writing task* in class.

Share

Students exchange paragraphs with their partner and underline any sentences they think can be connected with *and*, *also*, and *too*. To help with the peer review and to support the sharing stage, write guidelines on the board:

Does the paragraph describe John's study space?

Can any sentences be combined?

Are words spelled correctly? Are there capital letters and periods for each sentence?

Tell students to look at the checklist on page 189. They use the checklist to compare their writing in pairs and offer suggestions for improvement.

Rewrite and edit

Students read and consider their partner's comments and rewrite and revise their paragraph on a clean sheet of paper or via a word processor checking for errors, before turning it in. This could be done for homework. When giving feedback on students' work, you might consider giving recorded oral feedback using a free screen-capture app. Be sure to say what is done well in the work and give the student one or two targets to work on in future writing.

REVIEW

Wordlist

Students work in pairs or small groups to work through the *Wordlist*, checking that they all remember what each word or phrase means, how to pronounce it, and how it was used in the unit. Go through the list carefully with the class.

Vocabulary builder review

Students work through the sentences, check in pairs, and report back to the class.

ANSWERS
1 science **2** notebooks **3** every morning
4 highlighter pen

Unit review

Students work through the list alone to decide what they can and can't do. They discuss their answers in pairs, including what they remember from the unit about each point. Finally, open up the discussion to include the whole class. Pay particular attention to any boxes that the students didn't check. Explore with them ways of overcoming any remaining problems.

Extra research task

Link the topic of workspace with the type of workspace students will most likely be working in once they start a job in their field. For example, someone studying medicine might work in a lab, or in a doctor's office, or in a research facility. Assign the research task for homework and ask students to print out pictures of the kind of workspace they see themselves working in in the future. Ask them to prepare a mini-presentation that answers these questions: *What job do you want in the future? What does the workspace look like? Briefly describe the workspace. Why do you like this workspace?* Students can share their work in a number of ways—in class, put them into groups of four to present their future workspace. If class time is short, students can share in an online forum. To make sure students' posts are read by others, assign groups—each group member must read and comment on the other group members' posts.

4 MONEY

READING	Recognizing the topic
STUDY SKILL	Understanding percentages
VOCABULARY	Numbers
GRAMMAR	The simple present tense
WRITING	Using numbers in sentences

Warm-up

Draw students' attention to the picture and unit title to generate a discussion about money. If there is any current discussion about money in the news, you could raise that if appropriate. In a mixed-nationality class, ask students what the money (or currency) is in their country, and you could ask students to show each other the money from their country (suggest low-value currency). They might explain any people, images, or symbols on the money. You could also find out about which coins and bills students have, and if there are slang terms for money. For example, in the U.S., the coins are a penny (worth one cent), a nickel (five cents), a dime (ten cents), a quarter (25 cents), and a half dollar (50 cents). Dollar coins also exist, though they are not popular. Bills are $1, $5, $10, $20, $50, and $100. Slang terms for money in the U.S. include *bucks* and *dough—That sandwich costs five bucks. How much dough do you have?* If appropriate, ask students to take out their smartphones to look up the current exchange rate from U.S. dollars to the local currency. Ask students to turn off their smartphones and put them away for the remainder of the lesson.

Discussion point

Understanding information in graphs is a task students will have to do in many published exams. This unit helps students understand and be able to communicate about the data in pie charts.

Focus students' attention on the pie chart and the infographic. Check that students understand the categories, and allow dictionaries if needed.

Ask students to discuss question 1 with a partner. As the class gives feedback, make sure students use the sentence stem to give a complete sentence. Ask them if any of the figures are surprising. Since the infographic doesn't say where the data comes from, ask students where they think this data comes from.

Students discuss questions 2 and 3 in pairs. Refer them to the glossary to see the definitions of *more* and *less*. Note the phrase, *How about you?* (/'haʊwəˌbaʊʧu/) Encourage students to use this phrase as part of turntaking in conversation. (Practice it with a chain drill: Student 1: *I spend more on .... How about you?* Student 2: *I spend more on .... How about you?* Student 3: *I spend more on .... How about you?, etc.*) As the class gives feedback, tally the things most students like to spend money on and where they like to shop. Ask students to create a pie chart for the class's expenditure. Find out if anyone likes to *save* money. Ask if students have any sayings about money in their culture and see if they can translate them for the class.

Extension activity

Ask students to research how much they or families in their country spend on housing, food, etc. Use the categories from the infographic. Ask students to bring in a graph or pie chart later in the lesson when you start to cover the *Study skills* section.

VIDEO

Before you watch

Introduce the topic of the video and ask students to read the exercise and identify any new words. Write these on the board and discuss the meanings as a class. Then, ask students to complete the *Before you watch* section. Monitor and go through the answers with the class.

ANSWERS
1 d **2** c **3** b **4** a

While you watch

Play the video once. Ask the students to watch the video and complete the exercise. Play the video again so that students can check their answers. Go through the answers with the class.

ANSWERS
1 c **2** d **3** a **4** b

See page 108 for the video script.

After you watch

Put the students into pairs or groups and ask them to complete the exercise. Encourage them to use what they have learned in the video and the example answers to answer the questions. Go through the answers with the class.

READING 1

Money types

This text ties money types to personality. Money types are related to whether or not we are risk-takers or risk-avoiders, and if we are driven by the need for gratification or security. They could also be related to culture. Cultures with a long-term orientation tend to save money, whereas those with a short-term orientation tend to spend it.

A Vocabulary preview

1 Ask students to work in pairs to complete the exercise, using a dictionary if needed. Fast finishers can add this vocabulary to the class vocabulary box (see Teacher's Book page 21). Make sure students know the pronunciation of the vocabulary, especially *credit card* (stress on the first syllable of *credit* and on *card*) and *type* /**taɪp**/, not /**tip**/. Ask students how many of the words are nouns, adjectives, and verbs.

> ANSWERS
> **1** d **2** c **3** a **4** b **5** g **6** e **7** h **8** f

2 Students work alone to complete the exercise before comparing answers with a partner. As the class gives feedback, have volunteer students read the whole sentence. Ask students questions to personalize the vocabulary, e.g., *Is fruit a good gift? What type of fruit do you like? Do you have a credit card?* If appropriate, you could tell students this joke to help them remember the word *grow*: *Why is money like a flower? Because when you put it into the bank, it grows.*

Pay particular attention to spelling. Difficult words include *careful*, *dream*, *type*, and *worry*. Play "Snowman" with the class. On the board, draw lines for all the letters in the word, e.g., _ _ _ _ _ _ _. With books closed, students suggest letters that might be in the word. Write the letter in the correct space. If the letter is not in the word, write it on the board, and draw a big circle to represent the bottom of the snowman. Students continue to guess. For each wrong guess, draw more of the snowman: a smaller circle on top of the big one for the middle, and another smaller one for the head, two stick arms, two eyes, a nose, and a mouth (nine parts in total). The aim is to guess all the letters before the snowman is complete. "Snowman" is a useful activity that students can do in pairs to review vocabulary and spelling when they have an extra five minutes.

> ANSWERS
> **1** gift, type **2** save, grow **3** careful, credit card
> **4** dream, worry

Extension activity

Students create a page in their vocabulary notebooks on the topic of money. Things to include might be collocations (ask students to use the online Macmillan Dictionary to find collocations:). Ideas include: *spend/save money*, *big money*, *pocket money*, etc.; idioms or sayings (*money doesn't grow on trees*, *a penny saved is a penny earned*, *money makes the world go around*, etc.); other words for money (*bucks*, *dough*, *clams*, *bread*). Students can search online for words and expressions.

B Before you read

Write the sentence on the board: *I prefer to save / spend / give away my money.* Students complete the sentence for themselves, and then compare with a partner. As the class gives feedback, ask volunteers why they prefer to save, spend, or give away money. Do their parents have the same attitude towards money? Does the government want people to save or spend?

Point out that we can say *I save money* and *I spend money*, but we have to say *I give away money to someone or something*. Alternatively, we can say *I give away money*.

C Global reading

Recognizing the topic

Ask students why it's important to skim the text first and elicit *to understand the main idea*. Explain that *topic* is another way to say *main idea*. The topic is what it's about. Before asking them to read, ask students what they think the topic is in the reading *Money types*. (money)

1 Students read the question. Give them 30 seconds to skim-read the text to find the answer.

> ANSWER
> b

2 Students read the sentence. Ask them if they need to read the entire text to get the answers. (no) What do they need to read? (just the headings) Students skim-read the text again for 60 seconds and write the money types from the text headings under the pictures. When checking answers, make sure students understand that adding the *-er* to the verbs means *a person who* …, e.g., a *saver* is someone who saves money.

> ANSWERS
> **1** The Saver **2** The Giver **3** The Builder **4** The Spender

D Close reading

1 Ask students to read the text to identify which types of people do the things in the chart. It might be helpful for some students to underline or highlight where the answer is in the text. As the class gives feedback, ask students follow-up questions to lead to a deeper understanding of the text, e.g., *How do givers help others? What does one woman want to make happen with her money? Why don't spenders like to save money? Why don't givers ask for money back? Who worries about money more: people with a lot of money or people with a little money?*

ANSWERS
1 Givers **2** Builders **3** Spenders **4** Givers
5 Savers **6** Builders **7** Savers **8** Spenders

2 This exercise may be a bit more challenging for students because the answer isn't explicit in the text. Students have to apply what they know about the money types to the given situations. Students work alone to complete the exercise, and then compare in pairs.

ANSWERS
1 d **2** b **3** a **4** c

Extension activity

There is scope for an interesting discussion about the money types if your students are able and interested. Divide students into four groups. Each group has a different set of questions to encourage them to think more deeply and critically about the text. Group 1 (the spender): The text gives one reason that spenders like to spend money. Name two or more other reasons spenders like to spend money. Group 2 (the builder): The text gives one example of a builder. Give two more examples of builders. Group 3 (the giver): The text says that some givers give too much and they don't always think about what happens next. Think of two examples where giving money can be bad for the giver or the receiver. Group 4 (the saver): The text tells one good thing about savers and one bad thing. Give one more example of a good thing about saving and a bad thing about saving. Students regroup so that there is someone from each group to share answers. As the class gives feedback, ask students how true they think the money types are and if there are any other money types.

E Over to you

Note that the questions in the *Over to you* section require students to give reasons for their responses. Backing up opinions with reasons is an important academic skill. It challenges students to think more critically and demands that they expand their use of English. If students are struggling to say what they need to in English, give them a few minutes to think of their answers and write them down before putting them into pairs to discuss the questions. As the class gives feedback, give students lots of patience and support to encourage them to give reasons.

Extension activity

If you have a few minutes at the end of the lesson, wrap up with a "ticket out the door." Students have to hand something in before they are allowed to leave. For example, ask students to write a definition of *spender, builder, saver*, and *giver* on a piece of paper and hand it in before they leave. Another idea is for them to write down three things they learned in the lesson or something they didn't understand. A "ticket out the door" can have two purposes: First, it can consolidate the learning that took place, and second, it can help the teacher know if what was taught was learned.

STUDY SKILLS

Understanding percentages

Warm-up

If you asked your students to do the extension-activity research on expenses suggested in the extension activity following the *Discussion point*, students should bring in their pie charts here. Students compare pie charts in a mini-presentation to groups of two to three other students. To support the language needed to do this, write sentence stems on the board: *This pie chart shows how much money students spend in my country. … percent spend money on …*

Students read the *Understanding percentages* box for homework. In class, ask students if they remember what *percentage* means. Write *percentage* on the board, underlining *cent*. *Cent* is the Latin for 100; percentage means *part of 100*. Check that students understand the concept by asking questions: *What percent is one-half of a cake?* (50%) *What percent is one-fourth of a cake?* (25%) *What is the total percent in a pie chart?* (100%) Point out that in the sentence *John makes $400 …, makes* means *the amount of money he gets from his job*. A synonym, e.g., a word that has the same meaning as another word, is *earns*.

Do the math problem from the skills box with students on the board. Note: To calculate percentage, you need to divide the part by the whole. In the example, John makes a total of $400, so that is the whole. Fifty-six dollars is the part he saves. Divide $56 by $400 to get 0.14. Multiply that by 100 to get the percentage. 56/400 = 0.14 x 100 = 14%. (Another way of looking at it is to move the decimal over two places to get the percentage.)

Note that *percent* and *percentage* are both nouns, but we use them differently. We say, *What percentage* /pərˈsentɪdʒ/ *does John save? He saves 14 percent.* Students may have seen *percent* written as two words: *per cent*. This is the British spelling.

1 Ask students to calculate the percentages and complete the chart. Allow them to use the calculator function on their smartphones. If possible, bring in calculators for students to share, or ask them to work out the answers manually. As the class gives feedback, ask a full question and encourage a full answer, e.g., T: *What percent are from Brazil?* ST: *Thirty-five percent are from Brazil.*

ANSWERS
A 35% Brazil **B** 30% Mexico **C** 20% Japan **D** 10% China **E** 5% Oman

2 Focus students' attention on the information in the exercise. Students work out the percentages and draw a pie chart. As the class gives feedback, ask for full answers, e.g., *Sam spends 63% on housing.* Ask students what they think about Sam's expenses. Does he spend too much or too little on anything?

ANSWERS

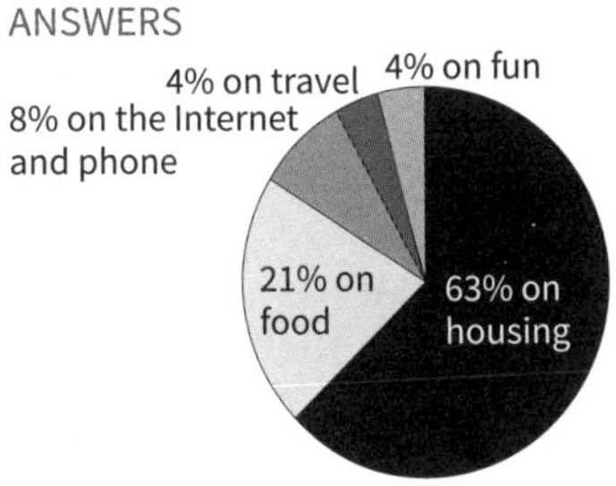

3 Ask students to work with a partner to answer the questions.

ANSWERS
1 James **2** Paul

Extension activity

If appropriate, have a class discussion about student spending. Do your students have a job or get an allowance? Do they pay for their own housing, food, etc.? What percentage do they spend on essentials such as housing, food, and Internet, and what percentage on things such as fun or clothes? Be aware that in some cultures, it's perfectly acceptable to talk about personal finances, while in others (such as the U.S.) it's taboo. Ask students if it's OK to ask in their culture, *How much do you make?*

READING 2

Daily spending

Warm-up

Ask students if they spend money every day or *daily*. If yes, what do they spend it on?

Ask students to come to the board and write some of their suggestions. Have a whole-class discussion on which items everyone spends on daily. Ask students to work out the highest and lowest percentage, i.e., what they spend the most on and what they spend the least on.

A Vocabulary preview

1 Students work alone to complete the exercise, and then compare in pairs. Fast finishers can add the words to the class vocabulary box. *Fast food* has stress on both *fast* and *food*: /ˈfæstˈfud/. *Gas* is /gæs/ not /gaːz/. Snack is /snæk/ not /snek/. Point out that *gas* also means a substance such as air that is neither a solid nor a liquid, and that in the U.K., they use the word *petrol* not *gas*. Note that *bill* and *rent* may be tricky to pronounce for some students. Raise awareness between the /b/ and /p/ sound to help students differentiate between the minimal pairs *bill* and *pill*, and the /r/ and /l/ sound to differentiate between the minimal pairs *rent* and *lent*. Remind students that the /p/ sound does not use the voice and that the tongue is pulled back in the mouth for the /r/ sound.

Write *bill / pill, rent / lent* on the board. Say each out loud. It's helpful if you over-exaggerate the mouth movements when you say them so that students can see the mouth shape when you say the words. Ask students to repeat the words. Say one of the minimal pairs; students point to the word you said. Ask students to write down the two sets of minimal pairs. In pairs, Student A says a word and Student B points to the word she or he heard. Then tell students to change roles.

ANSWERS
1 d **2** c **3** b **4** a **5** f **6** h **7** g **8** e

2 Students complete the exercise alone before comparing with a partner. As the class gives feedback, personalize some of the vocabulary with follow-up questions to the students, e.g., *Raise your hand if you like fast food. What fast food do you like? Do you eat it daily? What do you like to eat for a snack? Who pays the bill when you go out to eat?*

Pay particular attention to spelling. Difficult words include *daily* and *snack*. Repeat the "Snowman" activity suggested in on Teachers' Book page 41.

ANSWERS
1 cost **2** add **3** daily **4** snack **5** gas **6** bill
7 rent **8** fast food

Extension activity

If you have been building a class vocabulary box with the vocabulary word on one side of a card and the definition, example, or fill-in-the-blank sentence on the other side, ask students to use the cards to review vocabulary in pairs. Give each pair a number of cards. Student A takes a card, reads the definition, example, or fill-in-the-blank text and Student B says the word. Ask students to change roles. When they have finished with their set of cards, they exchange with another pair. Allow students who arrive early to class or who finish activities early to have access to the box to study vocabulary. In time, students will begin to use the cards to study without prompting from you.

If you are using a digital flash card set, use the app to host some team vocabulary competitions, encourage students to add to the set, and allow students to have access at home for review.

B Before you read

Students look at the layout of the text to answer this question. If you have been using a discussion forum, the layout will be familiar to the students.

ANSWER
a class website

C Global reading

Recognizing the topic

1 Ask students to read the questions before skimming the text so that they know what information they are looking for. See if they can predict the answer to the second question before reading. Give them 60 seconds to skim read.

ANSWERS
1 three **2** day **3** cell phone

2 If needed, give students another 60 seconds to find the information on how much each student spends a day. The answers are in the text and don't require students to do the math to calculate the amounts. Encourage students to find the totals quickly and not get distracted by the other numbers.

ANSWERS
1 c **2** b **3** c

D Close reading

1 This exercise presents information from the text in graphic form. Students should be able to figure out the answer without calculators by noticing that the rent for Marissa is 40% in the text, but allow them to do calculations if desired.

ANSWER
Marissa Carlson

2 Students work alone, and then compare answers in pairs. As the class gives feedback, ask students to make the false sentences true.

ANSWERS
1 T **2** T **3** T **4** F (He usually has his meals at home.)
5 F (She lives in a dorm.) **6** T

3 Ask students to try to do the exercise without looking back at the text. In this way, they have to use the context clues to decide which word fits. They can look back at the text to check their answers. As the class gives feedback, ask students if the money that Marissa, Brandon, and Celia spend is roughly the same amount they would spend on those things in their country or in the local country.

ANSWERS
1 rent **2** food **3** coffee **4** bus **5** dorm **6** car

E Over to you

Students discuss the questions in a group. As the class gives feedback, find out who spends the most or least daily. Make a list of ideas for ways to save money. You could extend the topic by asking whether your students think they should pay some of their bills (like Brandon) or if they should pay all of them (like Marissa and Celia), if parents should pay for their children while they are students, if students should get an allowance from parents so they can pay their bills without working, or if they should work while studying. Encourage impartiality. There is no right or wrong answer, and culture will play a large role in students' opinion about this topic.

Extension activity

Students create a five-to-seven-question questionnaire about daily spending, using the information from the unit to guide the questions. Agree with students who they will ask—they could ask another class or ask the wider student body. If appropriate, set up a pen-pal group with a class in another country (search *pen pal EFL* on the Internet). The questionnaire can either be written as a class or students can write it in groups. Each student should interview an agreed number of people to collect the data. In class, groups collate their data and report back to the rest of the class what they found.

VOCABULARY

Topic vocabulary

Numbers

Warm-up

Write numbers on the board in random order. The numbers should relate to you in some way as is appropriate for the culture—your age, the age of your children, your birthdate, any significant years (year of birth, year of marriage, etc.), number of countries you've visited, number of family members you have, etc. Tell students that the numbers all relate to you in some way, but that they must ask you questions to find out. Use a reformulation technique so that students can hear the right sentence structure or number, e.g., ST: *Nineteen nighty-six is year you daughter born?* T: *Is nineteen ninety-six the year my daughter was born? Yes, that's right.* If there is time in the class, ask students to write some numbers for their partner to guess.

Students might have some knowledge of numbers up to and over 100, but will most certainly need practice in pronunciation, punctuation, and speed of processing the number or saying it. Ask students to study the numbers in the *Numbers* box for homework and note down anything they have a question about. In class, important things to work on with numbers include:

The difference between 13 and 30, 14 and 40, etc. The stress falls on the second syllable for the teens (thirteen /θɜr'tin/) but on the first syllable for the tens (THIRty /'θɜrti/). Do some minimal pair work on these, working on comprehension and production.

Note the hyphen in numbers: twenty-one, twenty-two, thirty-six, ninety-nine, etc.

Years are said differently from numbers (nineteen ninety-six rather than one thousand nine hundred ninety-six. Although this unit focuses on numbers, students may want to know how to say years. 2017 is said in two ways: *twenty seventeen* or *two thousand seventeen,* but 2001–2009 would just have one way: *two thousand one, two thousand two*, etc.

Note the difference in the way large numbers are said in the U.S. vs. the U.K.: *three thousand two hundred ten* (U.S.); *three thousand two hundred and ten* (U.K.). The exception is with 101–109, which sometimes have the *and*: *a hundred and one.*

100 and 1,000 can be said as *a hundred, a thousand* or *one hundred, one thousand.*

Note the comma that separates the thousands from the hundreds: 1,000, 3,210, etc., and the ten thousands: 10,000. In some cultures, a dot (.) is used in place of a comma: 1.000, 3.210. If you teach students where a dot is the custom, this can be confusing. In English, a dot is used as a decimal point, e.g., 6.250 means *six and a quarter*, not *six thousand two hundred fifty* and is said *six point two five zero/oh.*

1 Students write the numerals from the words, and then compare answers in pairs. Student A says a number from the exercise, e.g., eighteen, and Student B points to that number. Ask students to change roles. Ask students to write any confusing numbers on a card for the vocabulary box. The numeral goes on one side and the word form on the other.

ANSWERS

1 800 **2** 12 **3** 6,202 **4** 77 **5** 14 **6** 105 **7** 3,200
8 563 **9** 18 **10** 25,000

2 In this activity, students practice saying numbers that can easily be confused. Draw their attention to the example dialogue below the table. This is a type of minimal-pair activity. Some difficulty is normal, but if students are struggling too much, stop the activity, drill the numbers, and then start the activity again.

Extension activity

Play "Numbers bingo." Students draw a 5 x 5 grid on a piece of paper. They fill in the grid with 25 different numbers—one number per square—using the numbers from Exercise 2. The teacher writes all the numbers from the table on separate pieces of paper and puts these into a hat or box. When students are ready, take out one piece of paper and read the number. If a student has the number on his or her grid, they cross it out. Continue in this way until someone has a row of five across, down, or diagonally. When they do, they shout *Bingo*! Be sure to check their answers against the numbers you have pulled out of the hat or box.

VOCABULARY

Vocabulary builder

Writing about numbers

Warm-up

Bring in one or more statements reporting figures from current news stories, e.g., *Over 50% of students live at home,* and write them on the board. Make sure they contain an approximation. Ask students why they think news stories and reports often use words like *over, around,* or *almost.* Do they ever see a news story or report that gives the exact figure? For example, *Today, 50.325% of students live at home.* (no) In general, when we report percentages, we don't usually give an *exact* number, we usually give an *approximate* /ə'prɑksɪmət/number.

1 Students work with a dictionary as needed to complete the exercise. Note that *almost, nearly, around,* and *about* are very close in meaning. *Almost* and *nearly* suggest that the actual number is slightly lower, so if something costs nearly $50, then it's not quite $50. *Around* and *about* could mean that the actual amount is either slightly lower or slightly higher. With *between,* you have to use two numbers. To check that students have understood the meanings and concept, ask some questions, e.g., *Give me a number that is almost* 50. (49) *What numbers are around 50?* (48, 49, 51, 52) *What number comes between 103 and 105?* (104) *Give me a number that is over 60.* (any number over 60) *What percent is a quarter?* (25%) *a third?* (33.3%) *Give me two ways to say one fourth.* (a quarter, 25%)

ANSWERS
1 b **2** a **3** d **4** c **5** h **6** g **7** f **8** e

2 Students work alone to circle the correct words in each sentence, and then compare answers in pairs. As the class gives feedback, have volunteers read aloud the complete sentence.

ANSWERS
1 about **2** between **3** one-fourth **4** over
5 exactly **6** around

3 Students work alone to match the underlined parts of the sentences to the correct numbers, and then compare answers in pairs. As the class gives feedback, have one volunteer read the original sentence and another read the sentence with the correct number in it.

ANSWERS
1 e **2** b **3** f **4** c **5** h **6** d **7** a **8** g

Extension activity

Ask students to look at the board with the coffee prices on it. Ask them to write three true sentences based on the information, e.g., *Cappuccino costs nearly $3. Macchiato is a little over $3,* etc. You could use this as their "ticket out the door" to check that they have the concept of approximations.

WRITING

Writing model

Read through the aims with the students. Remind them that each part of the *Writing* section will help to build their skills for the successful completion of the *Writing task.*

A Analyze

1 Give students time to study the information about the Peterson family.

2 Students choose the correct word according to the information in the chart.

ANSWERS
1 month **2** one-half **3** 10% **4** exactly **5** over

B Model

This is an exam-type exercise in which students must read the text and provide a suitable word that makes sense in context. In order to know which words to put in the blanks, students have to read ahead. For example, in number 2, students have to read the entire sentence in order to figure out what goes in the blank. Tell students to read the entire text before writing in any answers. Once they've read it to get the main idea of what the text is about, they will be better able to fill in the blanks with the appropriate words.

Note that we say, *The family spends...* but *They spend ....*

ANSWERS
1 month **2** one-half / half / 50% **3** $540 **4** exactly
5 over

Extension activity

For homework, students calculate the percentages for the Peterson family expenses. Students write sentences to describe the percentages, using vocabulary from the unit's academic word list where possible, e.g., *The Peterson family spends exactly half on rent*. In class, students compare sentences. Ask students how the Peterson family's expenses compare to theirs.

GRAMMAR

The simple present tense

Students read *The simple present tense* box for homework so they are prepared for the grammar presentation in class.

Warm-up

Ask the class to tell you some of the things they do daily, e.g., go to class, watch TV, etc. When you have a few ideas, ask students what they do once a week to generate a few more ideas. Do the same for once or twice a month. Point out that these are things they do *regularly*—daily, once a week, once or twice a month. Ask students what verb tense we use for talking about things we do regularly. (simple present)

Write the verb *spend* on the board and elicit the form:

Singular	Plural
I spend	we spend
you spend	you spend
he/she/it spends	they spend

Do a quick substitution drill with other verbs, including *cost* and *save*.

Draw students' attention to the irregular spellings of some verbs:

Do—he/she/it *does* (Example: *go*, *watch*, *teach*, and *finish* also follow this pattern. *Watch*, *teach*, *finish,* and *use* all have one syllable but gain a syllable when *-es* is added—/ˈwɑʧəz/, etc. This is because of the final sibilant sound [/z/, /ʧ/, and /ʃ/ in these cases]. Raise students' awareness to this pronunciation pattern.)

Worry—change the *y* to *i* and add *-es* he/she/it *worries* (Example: *study*, *cry*, *fly*, and *try* also follow this pattern.).

Note that *buy* does not change: he/she/it *buys*

Elicit the negative of spend:

I do not spend	we do not spend
you do not spend	you do not spend
he/she/it does not spend	they do not spend

Point out that in spoken and informal written English we use contractions: *don't* and *doesn't*.

Do a quick substitution drill changing the affirmative to the negative, ensuring that students are using the contracted form when speaking.

1 Students complete the activity alone, and then compare in pairs. If class time is short, do the first three items of each of the exercises in class and assign the rest for homework. As the class gives feedback, draw students' attention to the use of the simple present in the sentences: Is it a fact or something done regularly? For instance, the first sentence is a fact: This book costs $19.95. Sentences 3 and 4 could be a fact or something done regularly. The other sentences are fact.

ANSWERS
1 costs **2** doesn't save / does not save **3** buys
4 grows **5** don't spend / do not spend
6 don't worry / do not worry **7** doesn't have / does not have **8** use

2 Ask students to work alone and then check answers with a partner. This exercise is a little more challenging—students first choose the word that fits best in the sentence, and then decide which is the correct form of the verb to use. These sentences all use simple present to state a fact.

ANSWERS
1 like **2** has **3** costs **4** worry **5** live **6** grows
7 give **8** spends

3 Ask students to rewrite the sentences from Exercise 2 in the negative. Emphasize that they should write out the entire sentence and not just the verb forms. This written drill helps students internalize the context of the simple present. Once the answers are checked, put students in pairs. Student B has his or her book closed. Student A says an affirmative sentence, and Student B says the negative. Ask students to change roles and repeat.

ANSWERS
1 I don't like / do not like to spend money.
2 Sally doesn't have / does not have $400 in the bank.
3 Gas doesn't cost / does not cost a lot right now.
4 They don't worry / do not worry about money.
5 I don't live / do not live with my parents.
6 My money doesn't grow / does not grow in that bank.
7 My parents don't give / do not give me $25 a week.
8 David doesn't spend / does not spend a lot on rent.

4 Ask students to complete the exercise alone. This exercise personalizes the grammar. Students complete the sentences so that they are true for them. As the class gives feedback, ask volunteers to read their sentences and ask follow-up questions to learn more about your students.

Extension activity

Create a list of facts—some true, others false—using the simple present, e.g., *Animals don't see color, Everyone has 32 teeth, Birds that fly have hollow bones*, etc. Divide students into teams of three to four. Give them the list of facts—they have three minutes to choose which statements are fact and which are fiction.

WRITING

Writing skill

Using numbers in sentences

Students read the *Using numbers in sentences* box for homework. In class, write the sentences on the board to draw attention to grammatical items. Concept-check as you go along, e.g.,

Write: *There is one dollar on the table*. Ask: *Why There is?* Underline and circle: *There is one dollar …*

Write: *There are three dollars on the table*. Ask: *Why There are?* Underline and circle: *There are three dollars …*

Make sure students understand the difference between *make* and *save*. To *make* money is to receive it. We *make* money by working. To *save* money is to regularly put money into a bank or invest it so that you can use it later.

Spend: Note that we *spend* money in general, but we *spend* money on something.

Pay: Note that we *pay* bills and rent, but we *pay* for other things (pay for phone, Internet, dinner, books, etc.).

1 Students work alone to unscramble the sentences, and then compare in pairs. Students should write out the entire sentence in the space provided or in their notebooks. Make sure students check their work for capital letters and periods.

ANSWERS
1 Tom spends $6 on food.
2 This car costs $30,000.
3 Danni pays for gas.
4 She makes $1,200 a month.
5 The price of this computer is $699.
6 There are several dollars on the floor.

2 Ask students to read the sentences and correct the mistakes. This exercise helps students develop their editing skills. Students work alone before comparing in pairs. As the class gives feedback, students explain the mistake and correction.

ANSWERS
1 I save $80 a **month**.
2 There **are** three people in the classroom.
3 These two bus tickets **cost** $14.
4 We need to **pay our** rent today.
5 Jennifer spends $25 a week **on** fast food.
6 Kendra **makes $1,100 a week**.

3 Students write complete sentences to answer the questions. In pairs, Student A asks Student B the questions and Student B answers, trying not to read, but to remember the sentence. Ask students to change parts and repeat.

Extension activity

Work on collocations with *spend, spend … on, pay, pay for …, buy, make*, and *cost*.

At the top of their vocabulary notebook, students write *MONEY*. Down the left hand side, they write *spend money on*. They draw a circle around the phrase and three lines coming out from the circle. After each line they write a word or phrase that fits the collocation.

For example: *spend money on* – food
– rent
– coffee

Students do the same for the other verbs. Make sure students' collocations are correct. Possible answers:

Spend—money, a lot of money, $100 a month, nearly a third on, etc.

Spend money on—food, rent, coffee, clothes, fun, etc.

Pay—rent, bills, $100 a week, exactly half for, 25% for, etc.

Pay for—food, gas, tickets, etc.

Buy—a car, a ticket, fast food, etc.

Make—money, $25,000 a year, etc.

Cost—$3, money, a lot of money, etc.

WRITING

Writing task

Read through the *Writing task* with students. Then give some time for students to review the content of the unit and identify language and topics that will be useful for the *Writing task*.

Brainstorm

Students complete the exercise alone and compare answers in pairs.

ANSWERS
1 are **2** makes **3** one-third **4** 15% **5** over

Plan

Students work alone or in pairs to plan their writing, for example, by underlining any information they wish to use from the chart, including sentences from the *Brainstorm* section and deciding what will they include. They could compare their ideas with another student pair to generate more ideas.

Write

Give students about 20–25 minutes of class time to write their paragraphs. Ask students to write 60 words about the Stevens family and to remember to use the key points, e.g., the use of the simple present tense and numbers. Students then complete the *Writing task* in class.

Share

Students exchange paragraphs with their partner and decide if they have similar information and underline any information they think is incorrect. To help with the peer review, and to support the sharing stage, write guidelines on the board:

Is the information correct?

Are there any mistakes with the simple present tense?

Are words spelled correctly? Are there capital letters and periods for each sentence?

Tell students to look at the checklist on page 189. They use the checklist to compare their writing in pairs and offer suggestions for improvement.

Rewrite and edit

Students read and consider their partner's comments and rewrite and revise their paragraph on a clean sheet of paper or via a word processor, checking for errors before turning it in. This could be done for homework. When giving feedback on students' work, you might consider giving recorded oral feedback using a free screen-capture app. Be sure to say what is done well in the work and give the student one to two targets to work on in future writing.

REVIEW

Wordlist

Students work in pairs or small groups to work through the *Wordlist*, checking that they all remember what each word or phrase means, how to pronounce it, and how it was used in the unit. Go through the list carefully with the class.

Vocabulary builder review

Students work through the sentences, check in pairs, and report back to the class.

ANSWERS
1 three times a day **2** map **3** One-half **4** exactly

Unit review

Students work through the list alone to decide what they can and can't do. They discuss their answers in pairs, including what they remember from the unit about each point. Finally, open up the discussion to include the whole class. Pay particular attention to any boxes that the students didn't check. Explore with them ways of overcoming any remaining problems.

Extra research task

Ask students where they think is the most expensive country to live in. Brainstorm some ideas. What do they think is more expensive? Housing? Food? Healthcare? Group students into small groups. Each group chooses a country to research; it's OK if groups choose the same country, but it will be more interesting to have some variety. Each group must find out:

1. How much do people in that country spend on rent / housing?
2. How much do they spend on food?
3. How much do they make? (Pre-teach the word *salary*. Answer: a amount of money that you earn each month or year from your job)
4. Open choice: The group chooses one other category to report on, e.g., fast food, health care, etc.

Give them some help with search terms: *daily spending* (+ country name); *cost of living* (+ country name); *average salary* (+ country name); *How much does it cost to live in* (+ country name)? Another option is to provide students with appropriate URLs.

Once students have the information, ask them to create a pie chart and write a paragraph explaining their findings. Share the information on a class blog.

5 TASTE

READING	Reading for gist
STUDY SKILL	Improving your understanding
VOCABULARY	Food collocations
GRAMMAR	Using articles and adjectives with nouns
WRITING	Adding information using adjectives

Warm-up

Show students the unit title and picture on pages 80 and 81, and ask them to say what they think the unit will be about.

Ask students to read the glossary definition of the word *taste* on page 83, and then look at the pictures to say which foods taste good and which foods taste bad to them. Refer students to the infographic. It shows places to eat and foods people eat. Make sure students understand what *eat out* means. Give students a few minutes to understand the infographic, using dictionaries if needed. Ensure that students understand the concept, e.g., *Where would you find a food court?* (a mall) *Cafeteria?* (school, company). *Where do people like to eat out the most?* (restaurant) *What do most people order when they eat out?* (dessert). *Are there any results that surprise you? What country do you think this information comes from?*

Discussion point

Ask students to discuss the questions with a partner, using the sentence frames to help them get started. You could do this activity as a mill drill. Students stand up and ask at least three other people the questions, noting down their name and answers. As the class gives feedback, students report on what they said. Conduct an informal class survey and put the data on the board. Ask for a show of hands for where students like to eat out and what they order when they eat out.

VIDEO

Before you watch

Introduce the topic of the video and ask students to read the exercise and identify any new words. Write these on the board and discuss the meanings as a class. Then, ask students to complete the *Before you watch* section. Monitor and go through the answers with the class.

ANSWERS
1 d **2** b **3** e **4** a **5** c

While you watch

Play the video once. Ask the students to watch the video and complete the exercise. Play the video again so that students can check their answers. Go through the answers with the class.

ANSWERS
1 b **2** a **3** b **4** a

See page 108 for the video script.

After you watch

Put the students into pairs or groups and ask them to complete the exercise. Encourage them to use what they have learned in the video and the example answers to answer the questions. Go through the answers with the class.

READING 1

Food jobs

Warm-up

Elicit food jobs students know, e.g., *Who says hello at the door and takes you to your table?* (host / hostess) *Who brings your food to the table at a restaurant?* (server / waiter / waitress) *Who cooks the food?* (chef / cook) *Are there any other food jobs?*

A Vocabulary preview

If you find that some students regularly take a lot longer to complete the vocabulary exercises in class, suggest that they start Exercise 1 at home. Completing the *Vocabulary preview* at home will allow you to have extra class time to work on spelling and pronunciation and to do more activities to help students learn the vocabulary.

1 Students work alone, using a dictionary if needed. Drill pronunciation of the vocabulary. Difficult words include *chef* /**ʃef**/, not /**tʃif**/; *menu* /**'menjuː**/; *price* /**praɪs**/ not /**praɪz**/; *assistant* and *photographer* both have the stress on the second syllable: /**ə'sɪstənt**/, /**fə'tɒgrəfər**/. Point out that in contrast to photographer, photograph has the stress on the first syllable: /**'fəʊtəˌgræf**/. Tricky words to spell include *assistant*, *chef*, *photographer*, and *price*.

Students do not use articles to complete the exercise. Students will learn more about articles in the *Grammar* section later in the unit. Note that *to serve* is the full infinitive. In previous units, the base form (without *to*) has been presented.

ANSWERS
1 d **2** a **3** b **4** c **5** g **6** e **7** h **8** f

2 Ask students to complete the exercise alone before checking in pairs. As the class gives feedback, ask volunteers to read the entire sentence. In pairs, students quiz each other on spelling. Student A says a word from the *Vocabulary preview* and Student B writes the word down. Ask students to change roles and repeat.

ANSWERS
1 photographer **2** serve **3** menu **4** chef
5 magazine, price **6** assistant, company

Extension activity

Spelling in the round: Stand with students in a big circle. Say a word. The student to your left says the first letter of the word, the student to his or her left says the next letter, and so on. If a student says the wrong letter, they are "out" and must sit down. The student who is out chooses the next word, and the spelling continues from where they left off. Continue until you have one student left standing. If you have a large class, you can divide the class into several groups.

B Before you read

Students look at the pictures in the reading text and match them to what they show. Ask students if the pictures show food jobs, and if so, what job they think the pictures show.

ANSWERS
1 c **2** d **3** e **4** b **5** a

C Global reading

Reading for gist

Reading for gist is an important exam skill because students may need to read a text quickly to understand the main idea or main purpose. Gist reading is done quickly.

1 Focus students' attention on the *Reading for gist* box. Ask students if they think reading for gist is fast reading or slow, careful reading. (fast) Give students 30 seconds to skim-read the text for gist. Students circle the correct words in pairs. As the class gives feedback, raise students' awareness of the collocation *to do a job*.

ANSWERS
1 jobs **2** do **3** do **4** like

2 Ask students to skim the text quickly to find the job and underline it. They then write the job title in the space provided. The fifth job isn't explicit in the text—students have to infer the job title.

ANSWERS
1 food taster **2** food photographer
3 chef's assistant **4** food writer
5 food-truck owner / food-truck chef / food-truck driver

D Close reading

1 Ask students to work alone to complete the exercise, and then compare with a partner. As the class gives feedback, volunteers read the sentence, making sure to pronounce the third-person *-s*. Ask follow-up questions to check comprehension, e.g., *Why does Bert eat ice cream?* (His job is a food taster.) *Why does Jennifer make food look nice?* (so she can photograph it / so it looks good in the photographs) *When does Dan get to travel?* (when he does cookbook tours [A cookbook tour is when a chef writes a cookbook and then travels to different places to promote it. Often the chef will demonstrate how to cook something from the cookbook. The chef also signs the book for people who buy it.]) *Why does Tina need three desserts?* (because she writes about them for a magazine) *Who do you think Paul serves food to?* (people in the street)

ANSWERS
1 Bert eats ice cream. **2** Jennifer makes dishes look nice.
3 Dan writes emails. **4** Tina writes about desserts.
5 Paul serves food.

2 Ask students to choose *T* (True) or *F* (False) for each sentence. Put the answers on the board for students to self-check.

ANSWERS
1 T **2** T **3** F (She takes pictures for books, websites, and menus.) **4** F (She puts oil on meat.)
5 F (He doesn't help in the kitchen.) **6** T **7** T
8 F (She describes how the desserts taste and how much they cost.) **9** T **10** F (He serves Korean food on Tuesday. He serves Turkish food on Wednesday.)

E Over to you

Put students into groups of three or four to discuss the questions. Encourage them to respond to each other with phrase and follow-up questions. Write the phrases and question words on the board as prompts, e.g., *Yes, I think so, too. No, I don't think so. Why ...? What ...? Where ...? When ...? How ...?* Ask follow-up questions as the class gives feedback to elicit more information.

Extension activity

Refer students to the photographs of food at the bottom of page 84. Ask them if they ever take pictures of food and post them on social media. Find out if they know the dishes in the pictures. For homework, ask students to find a picture or description of food that they like to eat. It can be a photograph they take themselves or something they find online or on social media. They bring the picture to class to show other students and talk about what the food is and how it tastes. Alternatively, they can do the same activity using a photograph-and-voice-recording app, which they then share with the rest of the class or on the class blog.

STUDY SKILLS

Improving your understanding

Warm-up

Write the word *reading* on the board and ask students what they think of when they see that word. Write their ideas in mind-map format. Prompt them if needed, e.g., *Is it easy? Do you like reading? What kinds of things do you read?* Remind them that they have been working on reading skills. Ask them to say which ones (reading for gist, reading for main ideas, previewing, fast reading, skimming, recognizing the topic). Find out if they have any other ideas for how to make reading (in English) better. Write their ideas on the board.

Refer students to the *Improving your understanding* box. Give them five minutes to read the information and see if any of the ideas from the board are in the *Study skills* section. Add the three study skills to the board.

1 Ask students to read the instructions and make sure they understand what they should do, e.g., *What should you do first?* (Look at the title and picture.) *And then?* (Write a question.) *In b, how many sentences should you read?* (three) *In c, how many times should you read the text?* (twice) *What should you find out?* (Does it answer my question?)

Students work in pairs to complete the exercise. Ask students what they thought of the skills—did they make reading easier? Point out that when we read in our own language, we do these steps naturally. When we choose to read something informative, we are doing it because we want to find something out. We have a question in our mind that we want answered. Then, when we tell someone else about what we have read, we are showing our understanding of what we have read, and sometimes we have to read it again in order to explain it well.

ANSWER

a Students' own answers **b** Teddy's Kitchen restaurants
c Students' own answers

2 Ask students if they think the ideas from the *Study skills* section will help them when they do the next reading.

Extension activity

If students want to get good at reading, they need to read extensively. Graded readers are a helpful way for students to read outside of class at a level that is right for them. Find out if your institution has a set of graded readers, or if they would be willing to purchase a class set.

READING 2

Time for something new?

Warm-up

Divide the class into teams of three or four. On the board, write *Things you find in a restaurant.* On your mark, teams have three minutes to think of as many things as they can that they would find in a restaurant. Set the timer. Have students put down their pens when the buzzer sounds and exchange papers with another team. The other team decides if the items are actually found in a restaurant. Volunteers read aloud a few to class. The team with the most valid answers "wins."

A Vocabulary preview

1 Students complete the exercise alone, and then compare with a partner. As the class gives feedback, students add three more things to the list of things you find in a restaurant: *customer*, *dish*, and *staff*. Drill pronunciation. Tricky words to pronounce include *high* /haɪ/, mean /min/, and quick /kwɪk/.

ANSWERS

1 c **2** d **3** b **4** a **5** h **6** f **7** e **8** g

2 Students work alone, and then compare answers in pairs. Students quiz each other on spelling. Student A says a word from Exercise 1 and Student B writes the word down. Ask students to change roles and repeat. Tricky words to spell are *high*, *mean*, *quick*, and *staff*.

ANSWERS

1 fresh **2** dish **3** staff **4** quick **5** high **6** order **7** mean **8** customer

Extension activity

Write all the words that have double letters in them from the vocabulary sections in Units 1–5 on the board, e.g., *address, hobby, class, keep, dresser, roommate, messy, office, worry, add, bill, food, assistant*, and *staff*. Ask students what they all have in common. Students add a section to their vocabulary notebook with the head *Words with double letters*. They can add words to the list as they are introduced in upcoming units.

Students could also create a section for words that contain *ea*, e.g., *clean, meal, neat, dream*, and *mean*. Note the pattern in all of these words: *ea* has the sound **/i/**. There will be lots of these words in upcoming units—most of which follow the same pronunciation pattern.

Categorizing words in this way can help students remember the spelling.

B Before you read

1 Students read the instructions and complete the exercise. As the class gives feedback, do an informal tally with a show of hands. Ask follow-up questions to find out more, e.g., *Why is* where it is *important?*

2 Read the instructions to the students and ensure that they know what to do. Give them 30 seconds to preview the text. They answer the questions in pairs, using the sentence frame provided.

C Global reading

Reading for gist

Students have 60 seconds to skim-read the text. They choose the best answer and compare with a partner.

ANSWER

b

D Close reading

1 Refer students to the glossary and ensure that they understand the meaning of the three words there. Students then read the questions before reading the text. Avoid dictionaries at this stage. Students can re-read the text at home with dictionaries if needed.

ANSWERS

1 b **2** b **3** a **4** a **5** b

2 Ask students to complete the sentences with words from the text. In this exercise, students show their understanding of the reading by completing the sentences with an appropriate word. This exercise is a bit more challenging because the sentences are not exactly like the ones in the text. Ask students to underline the sentence in the text where they found the answer. To support lower-level students, put students into pairs with one lower-level student and one higher-level student.

ANSWERS

1 drinks **2** check **3** 22 **4** American **5** fish

E Over to you

Ask students if they think these restaurants are real. They are, in fact, all actual restaurants.

1 & 2 Students discuss the questions in groups of three, using the sentence frames. If you find that groups are dominated by one, talkative student, assign that student the role of insuring that each student in the group responds. Suggest prompts, e.g., *What do you think*, (name of person)? *Do you agree*, (name of person)?

Extension activity

Put students into groups to come up with an idea for an unusual restaurant. Put prompts on the board to guide them, e.g., *What type of place is it? (restaurant, café, etc.), What food is there? Who serves the food? What is different about it?*

VOCABULARY

Topic vocabulary

Food collocations

Warm-up

On the board, brainstorm some foods that go together. American examples include burger and fries; ice cream and cake; salt and pepper; rice and beans; spaghetti and meatballs; peanut butter and jelly; strawberries and cream. Be sure to include some combinations that are related to your students' culture, too. Ask why students think these foods go together. A possible answer is that they taste good together, or maybe it's just a common way of serving them. Use this as a lead-in to the idea that some words—collocations—go together, too.

There is no grammatical reason for collocations. Some words go together because that's the way they are said. A collocation mistake sounds odd. Just as some foods don't go together—*burger and jelly*—some words don't go together—*quick food*.

1 Ask students to work alone to complete the exercise. They should be able to pick out the words that are not collocations without needing a dictionary.

ANSWERS
1 menu **2** a dish **3** a menu **4** a chef **5** the price
6 a restaurant **7** the check **8** a customer

2 Ask students to unscramble the words to make sentences and write them in the spaces provided, ensuring they have a capital letter and period for each sentence. As the class gives feedback, students read the entire sentence.

ANSWERS
1 Let's try Turkish food.
2 Glen eats breakfast with his family.
3 That café serves great ice cream.
4 Jaime has a snack at 10:00 p.m. / At 10:00 p.m., Jaime has a snack.
5 I don't want to order a big meal.
6 I cook dinner every night. / Every night, I cook dinner.
7 Ken doesn't drink tea or coffee. / Ken doesn't drink coffee or tea.
8 I want to taste your dessert.

3 Students answer the questions in writing, using complete sentences. For question 5, refer students to the picture of the food court with different types of food being served. In pairs, Student A asks the questions and Student B answers, and then they change roles. If there is time, students change partners and repeat.

Extension activity

Show students how to find collocations in the dictionary. Show the entry for *eat* from the online Macmillan Dictionary: http://www.macmillandictionary.com/us/dictionary/american/eat

VOCABULARY

Vocabulary builder

Using adjectives

Warm-up

Bring in a piece of fruit or an item of food. Ask the students what it is, and then ask them to tell you more about it / to describe it, e.g., *What color is it? Is it big or small? How does it taste?* All the words used are adjectives. Ask students to compare two sentences about the food, e.g., *I eat an apple for lunch.* vs. *I eat a big, red, tasty apple for lunch.* Which is more interesting?

1 Students read the *Using adjectives* box, and then match the adjectives to their definitions, using a dictionary if needed. Drill the pronunciation. Note that, although *great* follows the same spelling pattern as *clean, meal, neat, dream, meat*, etc., its pronunciation is different: /greɪt/. In their vocabulary notebooks, students note down this pronunciation difference. Count the number of syllables in *expensive* (3); note that stress is on the second syllable.

ANSWERS
1 e **2** c **3** b **4** a **5** f **6** d

2 Ask students to complete the exercise alone, and then compare answers in pairs. As the class gives feedback, volunteers read the whole sentence. Ask students follow-up questions to personalize and help internalize the new vocabulary, e.g., *Where can you find low prices on food?*

ANSWERS
1 low **2** slow **3** expensive **4** large **5** great
6 boring

3 Ask students to match the adjectives to their opposites. Ask them to try matching without using a dictionary if they can. Ensure that they understand the concept of *opposite*, e.g., *Is* expensive *different or the same as* cheap? *Interesting* is a tricky word to pronounce—it looks like it should have four syllables, but in fact it has only three: /ˈɪntrəstɪŋ/. When spelling it, however, it is useful to think of it as four syllables: in-ter-est-ing. *Terrible* is another word with a double letter in it that students can add to their vocabulary notebooks, and *cheap* is another *ea* word with the pronunciation /i/.

> ANSWERS
> **1** c **2** d **3** e **4** a **5** f **6** b

4 Ask students to choose the correct word that makes sense in the given context. Students compare answers in pairs before going over the answers as a class. As the class gives feedback, ask students to say why the word is the best choice. For example, in number 1, *terrible* means the same as *really bad*, and in number 5, it's understood that there isn't a lot of time between classes, so the restaurant needs to be fast. In number 6, there is a contrast between the dinner prices and the lunch prices, so you need to use an opposite word. Check that students understand the idea of *high price* (expensive) vs. *low price* (cheap). Note that *high* and *low price* are collocations.

> ANSWERS
> **1** terrible **2** cheap **3** small **4** boring **5** fast
> **6** high

Extension activity

Divide the class into groups of six. Within each group are two teams—Team A and Team B—who will compete with each other. Pick out words from the class vocabulary set. One person from each Team A comes to the desk to see the word. Make sure they remember the meaning. They then go back to their group. They define the word, say the part of speech, give a similar word or opposite, or give an example so that the other students can guess the word. If Team A guesses, they get the point, but if Team B guesses first, they get the point. Repeat with students from Team B. Do this for five to ten words depending on class time. If you have a small class space or wish to make less noise, you could do the same activity, but in writing. The student who knows the word goes back to the desk and writes a definition, example, etc., and the two teams guess the word.

WRITING

Writing model

Read through the aims with the students. Remind them that each part of the *Writing* section will help to build students' skills for the successful completion of the *Writing task*. Before reading, ask students what the text is going to be about (a restaurant). Ask the class what information they think will be in the text.

A Analyze

1 Students read the list, and then read the model text. They put the items in the order they are mentioned in the text. As the class gives feedback, ask follow-up questions, e.g., *What is the name of the restaurant? Where is it?*

> ANSWERS
> **1** name of restaurant **2** what it serves **3** the meal size
> **4** the prices **5** the staff **6** what's good to order
> **7** what is not good about it **8** where it is

2 Ensure that students understand the meaning of *positive* and *negative* through concept checking, e.g., *Which word means* good? *What does* negative *mean?* Students complete the chart alone, and then check in pairs. Encourage them to write out their answers into the box rather than taking a short cut route by numbering the list and writing in numbers. Writing out the entire phrase will help them internalize the collocations and spelling. It might be helpful to think about who they think wrote the text—a student, or it could be a professor. Students and professors would most likely think that large dishes and low prices are positive things.

> ANSWERS
> **Positive things:** large dishes, low prices, friendly staff, great desserts, fresh food, cheap food
> **Negative things:** slow staff, where the restaurant is

3 Ask students to write their answers in full sentences, and then work in pairs with one student asking and the other responding. As the class gives feedback, ask volunteers for their answers. Check that they are using the third-person -s and pronouns (*It serves… His/her favorite food is … It's in a shopping mall …*).

> ANSWERS
> **1** American food **2** the cheeseburger
> **3** in a shopping mall (far from the / our college)

GRAMMAR

Using articles and adjectives with nouns

Articles can be problematic for students, especially for students whose language either doesn't use articles or uses them differently. Students can learn how to use them if they are helped to notice the way in which they are used in what they read, and also if they think about the rule being followed in examples.

Ask students to read the *Using articles and adjectives with nouns* box for homework so they are prepared for the grammar presentation in class. Ask them to come with questions they have about the grammar points. After your presentation, ask them if their questions were answered.

Explain the use of the articles *a/an*. Ask students *When do we use* a *and when do we use* an*? Can you give me an example?* It's important to emphasize here that we use *an* before a vowel sound. We say *a university,* but *an unusual food—university* starts with the consonant sound /j/ while *unusual* stars with the vowel sound /ʌ/.

Continue to explain when to use *a/an*. Break down the definitions of *singular* and *countable* in the *Grammar* box, e.g., *What is singular? Is it one thing or more than one thing?* (one thing) *What is countable?* (a noun that has a plural form; a noun you can add *-s* to). *Can you say three tables? Yes? Then it's countable. Can you say three foods? No. Food is uncountable.* Put a list of nouns from the *Grammar* box and exercises in this unit on the board. Students work in pairs to put them into two columns: countable and uncountable.

Countable	Uncountable
table	staff
customer	food
chef	bread
writer	meat
orange	money
dessert	Sushi
snack	

Move on to explain not specific vs. specific. On the board, write *a table / the table*. T: *When I say, "I eat at a table," do you know which table? No? Is it this one? That one? We don't know which one. It's not specific. But if I say you eat at the table over there, then it's specific. Do we know which table? Yes? That one over there. That specific table. Often we use* a *the first time, and then* the *when the thing is mentioned again: Dan has an assistant. The assistant works everyday.*

Explain when to use no article. On the board, write *Chefs don't make a lot of money.* Ask *Do we mean this or that chef? No? We mean all chefs, right? Chefs in general.* Write on the board *I don't eat meat.* Ask *Do I mean meat in general or specific meat?* (meat in general)

Focus students' attention on the last entry in the *Grammar* box and explain that adjectives go between the article and the noun. Elicit some more examples, e.g, *Ella's café is a friendly place.*

1 Ask students to complete Exercise 1 alone. In pairs, they compare and say which rule from the box above they used to decide which article to use. As the class gives feedback, check that they understand why the choice is correct by checking that they understand which rule is being followed.

ANSWERS

1 an [use *an* before a vowel sound; use *an* before a singular countable noun that is not specific]
2 The [use *the* before something specific—not just any price, but the price (specifically) of fish]
3 The [use *the* before something specific—not just any staff, but the staff here]
4 the, the [use *the* before something specific; note that you can't use *a* because *food* is non-countable]
5 Ø, The [no article for things in general; *the* for something specific]
6 Ø [no article for things in general]
7 the [use *the* for something specific]
8 Ø [no article for things in general]

2 Students work alone to complete the exercise, and then compare answers in pairs. Ask them to decide which rule they used to help them decide.

ANSWERS
1 The [use *the* before something specific; context is important here—if you are in a restaurant, then you mean menus for that restaurant, not menus in general]
2 a [use *a* before a singular countable noun that is not specific; we haven't said what kind of snack, it's just a general snack]
3 a [use *a* before a singular countable noun that is not specific]
4 the [use *the* before something specific]
5 an [use *an* before a vowel sound; use *an* before a singular count noun that is not specific]
6 the [use *the* before something specific; it's the check for our meal, not just any check]
7 Ø [no article for things in general]
8 Ø [no article before non-countable nouns; in this case, dessert is non-countable]

Explain to students the use of articles and adjectives with nouns. On the board, write *I want to go to a place.* Ask *Where can I put the word* cheap *in this sentence?* Write *I want to go to a cheap place*. Write *I want to go to an expensive place.* Ask students why it's *a cheap place* but *an expensive place* to help them notice that the article changes according to the word that follows.

3 Students add the correct adjective to the space before the noun.

ANSWERS
1 hard 2 soft 3 weak 4 strong 5 thin 6 thick 7 hot 8 cold

4 Ask students to rewrite each sentence by adding an adjective of their choice.

POSSIBLE ANSWERS
1 Please have some hot soup.
2 She takes great pictures of food. / She takes pictures of fresh food.
3 Let's go to the new café.
4 I want to order some fresh bread.
5 The cold juice is on the table.
6 The small restaurant is popular with students. / The restaurant is popular with Chinese students.

5 Ask students to correct the mistakes in the sentences. This exercise helps students learn to edit their own work by helping them to notice mistakes. Students work alone before comparing answers with a partner. As the class gives feedback, students say which rule they used to get the right answers.

ANSWERS
1 I try not to have **a snack** at night.
2 The food at **the Italian restaurant** is expensive.
3 The chicken at **the new chicken place** is great.
4 The menu here is **in five different languages**.
5 There is a problem with **the check**.
6 Tom works as **an assistant** to a food photographer.
7 **The thick noodles** at the Chinese café are great.
8 I want to have dinner at **a cheap place**.

Extension activity

As a way to review for the mid-term test, hold a grammar auction. First, create a list of 10–12 sentences, some with mistakes, and others without mistakes. You could use sentences from the units or write your own, but make sure the sentences review the grammar taught in Units 1–5. Put students into teams of four and ask them to think of a name for their team. Write the team names on the board. Every team starts with $1,000. Write $1,000 under each team name on the board. Give each team the list of sentences. They have about 15 minutes to look at the sentences and decide which sentences are good ones and which are not good ones, without looking in their books. When the auction begins, they will want to "buy" the good sentences. Start the bidding: *Who wants to buy sentence number 1? Who wants to start the bidding? One hundred dollars from Team Amazing. Any other bids? One hundred fifty dollars from the Blue Team …* When no one else bids higher, the team with the highest bid gets to buy the sentence. Keep track of who buys which sentence on the board and for how much—subtract the sale price from the total (this is also a good way to review numbers).

When all the sentences have been bought (or not bought), tell students which sentences are good. Teams that bought a bad sentence get a point subtracted. Teams that bought a good sentence gain a point. The team with the most money and most points wins.

WRITING

Writing skill

Adding information using adjectives

As a class, quickly brainstorm some adjective pairs from the *Vocabulary builder* section on Teacher's Book page 54. Ask students why we use adjectives (to make our sentences more interesting). On the board, write the examples from the *Adding information using adjectives* box without adjectives, e.g., *Sam is a chef. There is a café near here. I like that restaurant.* With books closed, ask students what adjective they could put into the sentences to make them more interesting. Ask students if the adjective goes before or after the noun (before).

1 Ask students to work alone to complete the exercise, and then compare answers in pairs. Ask fast finishers to write another sentence with three adjective choices on the board. As the class gives feedback, ensure that students understand why the adjective is the best choice for completing the sentence. Sometimes the reason is collocation, e.g., *quick snack*, *high prices*. Do the extra sentences (from fast finishers) as a class.

ANSWERS
1 quick **2** terrible **3** busy **4** large **5** high
6 third

2 Ask students to rewrite the sentences using an adjective in the box. Do the first sentence as a class so that students understand what to do. Students will need to understand the context in order to choose the right adjective. Ensure that they write out the sentences in full. As the class gives feedback, make sure they used the correct form—*a* or *an*—as well.

ANSWERS
1 I don't like strong coffee. I need to add water.
2 We need a large table. There are 15 of us.
3 One-Dollar sushi is a cheap restaurant.
4 Pizza Pit is a small place. It has four tables.
5 Jill is a great chef. Everyone loves her food.
6 Daniel is a terrible chef. No one eats his food.

3 Students complete the exercise alone, and then compare answers in pairs. Volunteers read aloud the sentences as the class gives feedback.

ANSWERS
1 famous **2** large **3** happy **4** Indian **5** interesting
6 expensive

4 Students write a sentence about their favorite restaurant, or, if they don't eat out, their favorite dish. Students read their sentence to three more students. You could also use this activity as a "ticket out the door"; students turn in their sentences to you as they leave the classroom.

WRITING

Writing task

Read through the task with students. Ask them to think about a restaurant they know or use an imagined one. Then give some time for students to review the content of the unit and identify language and topics that will be useful for the *Writing task*.

Brainstorm

Ask students to complete the exercise alone, but encourage them to help each other with ideas. If needed, monitor and assist as required.

Plan

Students work alone, or in pairs, to plan their writing; for example, what information they will include from the *Brainstorm* section and in what order. Refer them back to the model if they need some ideas. They could compare their thoughts with another student pair to generate more ideas.

Write

Give students about 20–25 minutes of class time to write their paragraphs. Ask students to write about 70 words about the restaurant and to remember to use the key points, e.g., the use of articles and adjectives with nouns. Students then complete the *Writing task* in class. As they write, observe their writing behavior. Are they using their plan?

Share

Students exchange paragraphs with their partner. Ask them to write down any questions they have about the restaurant in the space provided. To help with the peer review and to support the sharing stage, write guidelines on the board:

Are there adjectives to make the paragraph interesting?

Are words spelled correctly? Are there capital letters and periods for each sentence?

Tell students to look at the checklist on page 189. They use the checklist to compare their writing in pairs and offer suggestions for improvement.

Rewrite and edit

Students read and consider their partner's comments and rewrite and revise their paragraph on a clean sheet of paper or via a word processor, checking for errors before turning it in. This could be done for homework. When giving feedback on students' work, you might consider giving recorded oral feedback using a free screen-capture app. Be sure to say what is done well in the work and give the student one or two targets to work on in future writing.

REVIEW

Wordlist

Students work in pairs or small groups to work through the *Wordlist*, checking that they all remember what each word or phrase means, how to pronounce it, and how it was used in the unit. Go through the list carefully with the class.

Vocabulary builder review

Students work through the sentences, check in pairs, and report back to the class.

ANSWERS
1 tablet **2** slow **3** once a month **4** around

Unit review

Students work through the list alone to decide what they can and can't do. They discuss their answers in pairs, including what they remember from the unit about each point. Finally, open up the discussion to include the whole class. Pay particular attention to any boxes that the students didn't check. Explore with them ways of overcoming any remaining problems.

Extra research task

In groups of three or four, students research unusual restaurants like the ones in the Reading 2 text, *Time for Something New?* Using the questions in the *Writing* section as a guide, they prepare a poster presentation about the restaurant. Alternatively, they post the information on the class blog, along with pictures and the URL.

6 HEALTH

READING	Scanning
STUDY SKILL	Creative learning
VOCABULARY	Health collocations
GRAMMAR	Expressing frequency
WRITING	Joining sentences with *and* and *but*

Warm-up

Refer students to the picture at the beginning of the unit on pages 98–99 and introduce the idea of *health* and *healthy*.

Look at the infographic and ask *What makes us healthy? Is eating fast food healthy? Is walking good for our health?* Check that they understand *stressed*. Mime being stressed or allow students to look up the word in a dictionary.

On the board write *Drinking a lot of water = a good idea* and *Not exercising = bad idea*.

Ask students for other things that are good for your health to ensure that they understand the meaning of *health*.

On the board write *Exercise is good for your health. Exercise is healthy.* Tell students that one of these words is a noun and one is an adjective. Give them one minute to discuss in pairs which is which. Then ask them to tell you.

Discussion point

Students work in pairs to ask and answer the questions. Student A asks Student B the questions first. Then have students change roles.

When they have finished their discussions, ask each pair to take out a piece of paper and create a table with two columns. At the top of the first column, they write *Good thing to do for a healthy body*; in the second column they write *Bad thing to do for a healthy body*. Give them 30 seconds to write one idea in each column. They then pass the paper clockwise to another pair. Repeat so that the second pair now writes one more idea under each column. Pass the paper again and repeat the activity five or six more times. Ask volunteers to read their lists to the class.

As the class gives feedback, find out more about the students with follow-up questions, e.g., *Who drinks a lot of water? How much water do you drink? Who doesn't like exercising? Who walks a lot? What do you do for exercise?*

Extension activity

Work on building students' collocations vocabulary with *health / healthy*. Put students into pairs and allow them to find collocations in their paper or online dictionary, or with an online search (search *collocations with healthy / collocations with health* [NOTE: Give the online search option to stronger students].) Allow students five minutes to find one collocation with *health* and one with *healthy*. Write the information on the board as the class provides feedback, and give students time to copy the information into their vocabulary notebook or onto the class word-card set. Some examples include:

makes you healthy; is healthy; perfectly healthy; keep healthy; feel healthy

healthy body; healthy heart; healthy baby; healthy food; healthy lifestyle

good health; poor health; is good for / bad for your health; have health problems

Ask students to choose five collocations and write sentences using them.

VIDEO

Before you watch

Introduce the topic of the video and ask students to read the exercise and identify any new words. Write these on the board and discuss the meanings as a class. Then, ask students to complete the *Before you watch* section. Monitor and go through the answers with the class.

ANSWERS
1 e **2** d **3** c **4** a **5** b

While you watch

Play the video once. Ask the students to watch the video and complete the exercise. Play the video again so that students can check their answers. Go through the answers with the class.

ANSWERS
1 b **2** c **3** a **4** d

See page 108 for the video script.

After you watch

Put the students into pairs or groups and ask them to complete the exercise. Encourage them to use what they have learned in the video and the example answers to answer the questions. Go through the answers with the class.

READING 1

How healthy are you?

A Vocabulary preview

Valuable class time can be saved if students do the *Vocabulary preview* section for homework. This will free up time to do activities that practice spelling, pronunciation, and vocabulary retention, which are less easy to do at home without the input of the teacher. In class, ask students to compare answers before checking as a class, or provide the answers for students on the board for self-checking.

1 In class, ensure that students know the pronunciation of the new vocabulary and check that they have understood the meanings of the words. Note that *belong to* and *find out* are presented as two-word verbs; students will need to learn them as such. Note also that *pretty* has two meanings—one is the adjective form, *attractive*, and the other is the adverb form, *quite*. Check that students understand the two meanings. It is the <u>second</u> meaning, *quite* or *fairly* that is used in Exercise 2, number 1. Ask students to quickly identify one other word in the list that has at least two meanings (*point*—as a noun, it means a mark for counting; as a verb, it means to indicate with your index finger).

Ask students to add the word *pretty* to their list of words with double letters.

ANSWERS
1 c **2** d **3** b **4** a **5** e **6** f **7** g **8** h

2 Ask students to complete the sentences using the words from Exercise 1. Once answers are checked, reinforce the vocabulary through a contextualized whole-class vocabulary game. With books closed, give a context or a sentence to elicit the vocabulary word, e.g., *This is mine, it ____ me.* (belongs to) *I don't know when the homework is due, so I need to ____.* (find out)

In pairs, students review spelling. Student A says a word and Student B spells it (either in writing or orally). They then change roles.

ANSWERS
1 pretty **2** belong to **3** Several **4** gym **5** sport
6 point **7** without **8** find out

Extension activity

In pairs, students choose five vocabulary words from any unit already covered and write these words at the top of a sheet of paper. They then write a paragraph using all of the words they have at the top of the page, but leaving a blank space where the vocabulary word goes. Pairs exchange papers and complete each other's fill-in-the-blank texts. Lower-level students can write fill-in-the-blank sentences instead of fill-in-the-blank paragraphs. To increase the challenge, ask students to provide extra words as distractors.

B Before you read

Where a text comes from tells the reader a lot about the kind of information they will see before reading and sets expectations. For example, if a reader knows the text is from a textbook, they will expect first that it will contain information on a subject, and second that the information is true.

In pairs, students think about what kinds of reading texts they expect to find in magazines, textbooks, and newspapers. Ask to class to give feedback. Possible answers include **magazines**: articles, opinions, advertisements, questionnaires; **textbooks:** factual information about a subject (history, science, math, etc.), questions about a subject; **newspapers**: news (about sports, politics, finance, etc.), opinion (editorials). Ask students if they think they can believe the information they read in a magazine, newspaper, or textbook. The possible answer is that it will depend; some newspapers and magazines are more credible or believable than others. Textbooks will have gone through an editing process, so are likely to be credible.

Give students 20 seconds to preview the article and decide where the text is likely to be from.

ANSWER
in magazines

C Global reading

Scanning

Scanning a text differs from skimming in that the reader is looking for specific information rather than aiming to get a general idea. Tips for scanning include reading the question first so that you know what you are looking for, and looking for words or numbers that will answer the question.

Begin with a review of the skill of skimming. Write *Reading skill—skimming* on the board and ask students what they do when they skim. Possible answers include read quickly or read for the main idea. Ask students to read the *Scanning* box to find out firstly what scanning is, and secondly how it is the same as skimming.

Refer students to the exercise instructions. Ask them what words they will look for when they scan the text (sleep, sports, water, fast food). Give them 45 seconds to scan the text to find the question number for each topic.

Refer students to the photos showing three different exercises. Find out how many students can do a sit-up, a pull-up, and a push-up.

> ANSWERS
> sleep, Q9; sports, Q5; water, Q4; fast food, Q7

D Close reading

1 Students read the text and answer the questions for themselves. Support students as needed to understand the scoring rules. In pairs, students compare answers, asking follow-up questions. Write a few on the board to support lower-level students, e.g., *Which gym do you belong to or do you prefer exercising elsewhere? What sports do you play? Where do you run?*

As the class gives feedback, find out if the students agree with the results and the information in the survey. Ask volunteers to say why they agree or don't agree. If needed, ask questions to prompt responses, e.g., *Do you agree that you should drink six or more glasses of water a day? Is tea the same as water? Why is it not healthy to sleep more than eight hours at night?*

2 This exercise provides a model of how student notes taken from a text might look. Ask students if they ever take notes like this. This exercise is challenging because students have to apply the information in the text to the new format of notes. They also have to use a word for the blanks that makes sense in the context. If possible, pair lower-level students with higher-level students for this exercise. Note that at this point, students are not agreeing or disagreeing with the text, but are writing what the text says is healthy or not. This is an important distinction for academic work.

> ANSWERS
> **1** week **2** 6 **3** 30 **4** 2 **5** often **6** 10 **7** day **8** 6

E Over to you

Put students into small groups to discuss the questions. Encourage them to respond to each other with phrase and follow-up questions. Write the phrases and question words on the board as prompts, e.g., *Yes, me too. I think that … Why …?*

Ask students to write down their answers to the questions to turn in at the end of the lesson so that you can check the level of their responses. Ask higher-level students to write one or two questions they have for you related to health. Answer their questions in the next lesson.

Extension activity

Ask students to use the survey to interview five to ten people outside of class about health, e.g., friends, family, other teachers. They should reveal the scores to each person interviewed. They then create a pie chart of the results to bring to class and report on, e.g., *I interviewed ten people. Twenty percent are very healthy. Twenty percent are pretty healthy. Twenty percent are healthy, but can do more. Thirty percent should do more to get healthy.*

This activity could also be done using an online survey tool, which creates a graph of the data automatically.

STUDY SKILLS

Creative learning

Strong students often have a good set of study skills, while others have yet to develop the skills needed to be very successful at learning their subjects. This section will help those less-successful students by giving them some ideas for strategies. Stronger students will be valuable in sharing their learning ideas. For those students who feel they have good study skills, focus on the language they need to talk about it. For others, learning about the new skills may be enough.

Warm-up

On the board, write *learning*. Ask students to think about and discuss in pairs what *learning* means. Possible answers include *understanding*, *studying*, *to know information*, etc. Ask for a show of hands as to who thinks they are good at learning. If they think they are, encourage them by inviting them to share some of their ideas later in the *Study skills* section. If they think they are not, assure them that this section will help give them some ideas.

Write *creative* on the board before *learning*. Ensure that students understand the meaning of *creative* (involving a lot of imagination and new ideas). Ask students why it's a good idea to be a creative learner. Point out that we don't learn everything the same way, and creative learners try different things to help them learn.

1 Ask students to read the *Creative learning* box for five minutes alone and check the two ideas they think are best. On the board, write the sentence stem *I think number___ is best because* ... Students write the sentence and their reason. Once they have written at least one reason, ask students to find someone who did not check the same two ideas. They share why they chose the two ideas.

As the class gives feedback, discuss the ideas further. Three of the ideas involve writing and/or drawing something—there is a lot of evidence to suggest that writing helps us remember information. Writing also makes us think about how to make up things using our own words, and this mental process deepens the learning.

Ask students what kinds of imagined pictures would help them remember. Evidence suggests that mental images that are funny or extreme in some way (over-sized, brightly colored) can be memorable. For example, if you want to remember a shopping list—milk, butter, eggs—you might create a mental image of a huge white glass of milk that spills over and becomes bright yellow butter. Next to the butter are two brown eggs that suddenly crack open.

2 Ask students to look back at the Infographic on page 98, and use one of the ideas from the skills box to help them remember the information. For students who choose the first idea, you will need to provide some big sheets of paper. Students who want to use this idea can be put into a group to create the poster. Alternatively, put students into four different groups according to which idea they want to try. When finished, conduct a whole-class discussion of the strategies, what they did, and how students felt they worked.

3 Ask students to read and check the ideas they think are good ones to help them learn. Encourage them to think why they are good ideas in preparation for the next exercise.

4 Ask students to work with a partner. When they have finished their discussions, put students into groups of three to four, and give them one of the big sheets of paper. They write down three to five more ideas on the sheet and stick it to the wall. Each group presents their ideas to the rest of the class.

Extension activity

Students try one or more new ways from the *Study skills* section or from their peers to learn for a week—in any of their classes. They can do the learning strategy in their L1. They write about the experience in English on a class blog. They should write what they did, how they did it, and what they thought about it. For example: *I made a summary from my notes in science. I tried to think about a summary for another student to understand. It was hard to write. I read my notes many times. I think it was a good idea. I won't forget this science lesson.*

READING 2

Healthy habits

A Vocabulary preview

Ideally, students do the *Vocabulary preview* section for homework. In class, ask students to compare answers before checking as a class, or provide the answers for students on the board for self-checking.

1 Drill pronunciation. Difficult words to pronounce include *actually* /'æktʃuəli/ (three syllables, not four) and *hungry* /'hʌŋgri/ (two syllables, not three). *App* /æp/ and *spend* /spend/ could be tricky for some students who confuse the /p/ and /b/ sound. Students can add *actually* and *app* to their list of words that include a double letter.

> ANSWERS
> **1** a **2** d **3** b **4** c **5** f **6** h **7** g **8** e

2 With books closed, read the sentences aloud, and elicit the answers. Note that *cold* is also an adjective—*I have cold hands*, but in this case, *a cold* is a type of illness caused by a virus and is a noun. Note that *bad cold* is a collocation (we never say a *good cold*). Put students into groups of three and give each group one of the vocabulary words. The groups write a sentence with their word, but leave a blank where the word goes. Groups write their fill-in-the-blank sentences on the board. As a class, decide which words go into the spaces. Add the words to the class vocabulary box. Periodically use the cards in the box to review vocabulary.

> ANSWERS
> **1** cold **2** spend **3** hungry **4** at least **5** strong
> **6** sick **7** app **8** actually

Extension activity

Do a scavenger hunt review of *Vocabulary preview* 1 and 2 vocabulary. Put students into teams of three to four. Give them the following scavenger hunt as a handout. The teams have three minutes to find the answers in the two *Vocabulary preview* sections. To ensure that everyone participates, give them each a role: one is the writer, one or two are the finders, and one is the spelling checker.

1 Find two verbs that have two words. (belong to, find out)
2 Find two adverbs. (pretty, actually)
3 What kind of word is *without*? (preposition)
4 Find the opposites of these adjectives: *weak*, *healthy*. (strong, sick)
5 Find a word that can be a noun or an adjective. (cold)
6 Find three words that can have *a* before them but not *an*. (gym, point, sport, cold)

Students exchange papers with another team for checking. They make sure spelling is correct.

B Before you read

Warm-up

Write *healthy habits* on the board and check that students understand the meaning of *habits* (things you do regularly). As a class, quickly brainstorm some habits that are healthy.

Give students a minute to read the instructions, and then give them 30 seconds to skim-read the text and circle the correct words. Remind students that *gist* means main idea. As the class gives feedback, ask students what gave them the clue that it was from a magazine for students—was it the design or was it from the first line of the text?

> ANSWERS
> **1** magazine **2** students **3** four **4** habits

C Global reading

Scanning

Students first read the directions. Note that two of the options on the right will not be used. Set a timer for three minutes so that students scan quickly rather than reading carefully at this stage. As the class gives feedback, you may need to check that students understand the difference between *almost eight hours* in e and *eight or more hours* in f.

> ANSWERS
> **1** f **2** d **3** b **4** a

D Close reading

1 Students read the sentences, and then work alone to decide if they are *T* (True) or *F* (False). Note that frequency adverbs will be taught in the *Grammar* section, but if students are having problems, draw a simple scale on the board to show the difference between the adverbs in the exercise, or refer students to the scale in the *Grammar* section on page 111.

100%				0%
always	usually	sometimes	not often (or rarely)	never

Ask students to correct the false statements as the class gives feedback.

ANSWERS
1 T **2** F (He goes on Thursdays.)
3 F (She takes several thousand steps a day.) **4** T
5 F (She sometimes eats ice cream.) **6** T
7 F (He usually has a snack at night.) **8** T

2 Ask students to write the answers to the questions using complete sentences. In pairs, students compare answers with one student asking the odd questions and the other answering them. Student B then asks the even questions with Student A answering them.

ANSWERS
1 Sean plays soccer every day.
2 Sean plays basketball once a week.
3 Caitlyn thinks walking is the best way to stay healthy.
4 Jill watches sports on TV. / Caitlyn's roommate watches sports on TV.
5 Natalie rarely eats fast food.
6 Natalie tries not to eat desserts.
7 Antonio doesn't exercise.
8 Antonio doesn't get a lot of sleep.

E Over to you

As a way of varying the *Over to you* section, conduct it as a mingle activity. Ask students to make a 4 x 4 table on a piece of paper. They write *Name* across the top row, leaving the first column empty. In the first column, starting at the second row, they write the questions in the *Over to you* section. Ask them to find another student that they don't usually work with and ask them the questions, writing their name and their answers in the table. They repeat until they have interviewed three different people. Ask volunteers for answers to their questions as the class gives feedback.

Extension activity

In groups, students research the health habits of a person whom they admire, e.g., a sports person. Do they have any tips? Bring the tips to class to share or share them on the class blog.

VOCABULARY

Topic vocabulary

Health collocations

Warm-up

On the board, write *a bad cold*. Ask students what this is an example of to elicit *collocation*. Brainstorm some of the collocations from Unit 5, e.g., *cook dinner*, *drink coffee*, *eat a big meal*, *order a snack*, etc.

Students will have seen a number of collocations in *How healthy are you?* and *Healthy habits*. Ask them to look back at the texts to find a collocation with *tired*, *healthy*, *sick*, *cold*, *snack*, and *hungry*. Alternatively, give one for lower-level students to find and two or three for higher-level students, e.g., *feel tired*, *stay healthy*, *get sick*, *catch a cold*, *have a snack*, and *get hungry*. Write each of these on the board. Ask students if the combination is verb + noun or verb + adjective (verb + noun: *catch a cold*, *have a snack*; the rest are verb + adjective).

Students read the *Health collocations* box to find two more health collocations. Remind students that there is no grammatical reason for a collocation—the rules are determined by convention. If you speak the students' language, you may be able to find collocations in the L1 to hold up as examples.

1 Tell students they can use a dictionary if needed to complete the exercise, or they can choose the verb that sounds most natural to them. In choosing the most natural-sounding verbs, students are likely to choose the verb that they would use in their L1—this will give you an insight into the collocation used in students' L1. This type of contrastive recognition will help students learn the collocation. Note too that the noun in each is either plural or has an article.

ANSWERS
1 have **2** catch **3** have **4** play

2 Ask students to complete the exercise, and then check in pairs. After Exercise 2, students close their books. Review each collocation with a drill, e.g., T: *healthy habits*? STS: *have*. T: *tired*? STS: *feel*.

ANSWERS
1 feel **2** get **3** be **4** be

3 This exercise provides contextualized practice and could be assigned for homework if class time is short. Ask students to underline the verb that forms the first part of the collocation. Students add the collocations to their notebooks and to the class vocabulary bank.

ANSWERS
1 cold **2** sick **3** hungry **4** sport **5** stressed
6 tired **7** snack **8** habits

Extension activity

Students choose three collocations and write a sentence with each about themselves. One sentence should be false and the others true. In pairs, students read their sentences and guess which is the false sentence.

VOCABULARY

Vocabulary builder

Comparing actions

Warm-up

Each student writes down the number of hours they sleep a night on a clean piece of paper. They should write the number large so that everyone can see it. Ask students to stand up and form a line from the fewest hours of sleep to the most hours of sleep. Keep students in the line as you ask *Who sleeps more, (student name) or (student name)?* Introduce the new language: *So, (student name) sleeps more than (student name)*. Repeat with *less* and *less than* until students have the idea and sentence structure: *Student A sleeps more than / less than Student B*. Introduce *much* and *a lot more* or *less* by comparing students at the two ends of the line. Introduce *a little more / a little less* by comparing students with numbers very close together.

If your class is too large or your room is too small, ask for four volunteers to come to the front to form the line.

Give students some time to read the *Comparing actions* box. Check that students understand the concept and that they understand that this is the structure for comparing actions. Give a couple of sentences with different verbs and ask students what the action is in each.

1 For students who struggle with word order exercises, give them cut-up versions of Exercise 1 to physically unscramble. Students complete the exercise alone, writing out the sentences in full and ensuring that they complete each with a period.

ANSWERS
1 Gina studies more than Erica.
2 Brian sleeps less than Yousef.
3 Jennifer works much more than me.
4 William sleeps a little less than Randy.
5 Ava exercises a lot more than her sister.

2 Ask students to read each set of sentences and write one sentence comparing two actions in each set. Ask higher-level students to write each in at least two different ways. For example, number 1 has four correct options. It could be *Peter sleeps more / a little more than David*. Or *David sleeps less / a little less than Peter*. As the class gives feedback, offer all options as correct.

POSSIBLE ANSWERS
1 Peter sleeps (a little) more than David. / David sleeps (a little) less than Peter.
2 Tina's meal costs (a little) more than Layla's. / Layla's meal costs (a little) less than Tina's.
3 Kerry exercises (much / a lot) more than Diana. / Diana exercises (much / a lot) less than Kerry.
4 Oliver spends (much / a lot) less on gym classes than Adam. / Adam spends (much / a lot) more on gym classes than Oliver.
5 Trevor walks (much / a lot) less than Zac. / Zac walks (much / a lot) more than Trevor.

WRITING

Writing model

Read through the aims with the students. Remind them that each part of the *Writing* section will help to build their skills for the successful completion of the *Writing task*. Before reading, ask students what the text is going to be about (health habits). Ask the class what information they think will be in the text.

A Analyze

Refer students to the picture of Seth and Kevin. Ask students how old they think Seth and Kevin are and if they think they are healthy. Refer them to the list to the left of the picture. Students read the list, and then read the model to find out who each describes. Ask them if they are surprised that Seth looks so healthy!

ANSWERS
1 K **2** S **3** K **4** S **5** K **6** S **7** S **8** S

B Model

Ask students to read the model again to answer the questions.

ANSWERS
1 three times a week **2** eats fast food **3** some fruit

GRAMMAR

Expressing frequency

Warm-up

Give students a handout with the following questions, or write them on the board for the students to copy. Students can write two more questions in the space provided in the last two rows. Students ask at least three other people the questions. They write the person's name at the top of the column and their answers in the column next to the questions. As the class gives feedback, ask volunteers to tell the class about one of the people they interviewed. Use their answers as a springboard into the *Grammar* section.

Do you ever …	Name ____	Name ____	Name ____
sleep on the floor?			
drink coffee at night?			
exercise in the morning?			
play video games with friends?			
eat fast food?			
____ ____			
____ ____			

Use some of the information gained in the *Warm-up* to introduce the grammar of expressing frequency. For example, *Raymond said that Clara always sleeps on the floor. Is that right, Clara? Do you sleep on the floor every day?*

Ask students to close their books. Draw the frequency scale again from the *Healthy habits* text on the board.

100% ———————————————— 0%

always usually sometimes not often (or rarely) never

Elicit the six adverbs shown in the scale in the *Expressing frequency* box. Ask students where they think *hardly ever* fits in the scale. Point out that these adverbs are used when we ask the question *Do you ever …?* And that this is a yes / no question. Ask a couple of students a *Do you ever …?* question to provoke a yes / no answer with one of the adverbs on the board.

Ask students if they know another way to ask about how often someone does something to elicit *How often do you …?* Ask students how they would answer a *How often …?* question to elicit expressions such as *once a week, every day*, etc. Ask a couple of students a *How often …?* question to provoke an answer with a frequency expression. Ask students to open their books and refer them to the *Grammar* box to find more frequency expressions. Concept check: *Can we say "I exercise every month?"* (yes) *Can we say "I exercise twice month?"* (no) *What do I need to add?* (twice a month) *If I don't exercise, what can I say?* (I don't exercise at all. / I never exercise.)

Draw attention to the position of adverbs and expressions of frequency. The adverbs *always*, *usually*, *often*, *sometimes*, *hardly every*, and *never* come after the subject and before the main verb. *Sometimes* and *often* are more flexible and can come at the beginning or end of the sentence, as well. The expressions come after the main verb or at the beginning of the sentence, with the exception of *very much* or *at all*, which always come after the negative verb. Note that *hardly ever* and *never* are already negative, so they don't usually take a negative verb:

(✗) I hardly ever don't have a snack at night. / (✓) I never have a snack at night.

1 Ask students to work alone to complete the sentences with an adverb of frequency that makes the sentence true for them. In groups, they share their sentences. Encourage students to use the turn-taking phrase *How about you?* provided, so that the conversation is more natural.

Exercises 2, 4, and 5 can be done for homework if class time is short. Ensure that students understand what to do—allow them to do the first one or two of each in class, and the rest for homework.

2 Ask students to write out the question in full, ensuring that they include a capital letter and question mark. Support lower-level students by giving them cut-up sentences so that they can arrange them physically.

Conduct a substitution drill to ensure that students are using good question intonation and linking when asking the questions. They should link *how_often*. *Do you* can sound like **/djew/** in fast speech. Monitor students' use of intonation and remind them that intonation falls on the Wh- questions *How often …?* and rises on the yes / no questions *Do you …?*, e.g., T: *Go to the gym. How often*. STS: *How often do you go to the gym?* T: *Go to the gym. Do you*. STS: *Do you (ever) go to the gym?*

ANSWERS

1 How often do you go to the gym?
2 How often do you eat red meat?
3 Do you ever sleep in the library?
4 Do you ever drink coffee in class?
5 How often do you eat ice cream?
6 Do you and your friends ever play soccer?

3 Students work with a partner to ask each other the question. As the class gives feedback, ask volunteers to report on their partner to the whole class, ensuring that they switch the subject pronoun and add the third-person *-s* to the verb correctly.

4 Tell students to use the information in the schedule to write sentences. There is more than one possible answer, and in some cases, the frequency expression can change location. The answers below are possible answers only. Higher-level students can try writing a couple of different sentences for each.

POSSIBLE ANSWERS

1 Maria studies every day. / Maria always studies.
2 Maria runs with Jesse twice a week. / Maria sometimes runs with Jesse.
3 Maria plays tennis once a week. / Maria plays tennis on Sundays.
4 Maria often goes to the gym. / Maria goes to the gym three times a week.
5 Maria never plays basketball. / Maria doesn't play basketball at all.

5 Ask students to correct the mistakes in the sentences. This exercise helps students practice the skill of editing written work. For some students, it might help for them to say the sentences out loud in order to find the mistake. Lower-level students can be paired with higher-level students if they find this type of exercise too challenging. As the class gives feedback, revisit the rules to reinforce them.

ANSWERS

1 Paul **usually plays** tennis with his brother. (Frequency adverbs go before the verb.)
2 Megan runs **twice a week**. (*Twice a week* is a fixed expression.)
3 Rachel doesn't exercise **at all** / doesn't exercise **very much**. (fixed expression)
4 I **sometimes catch a cold** in the summer. / **Sometimes I catch a cold** in the summer./ I **catch a cold** in the summer **sometimes**. (Frequency adverbs go before the verb. *Sometimes* is an exception to this rule and can go at the beginning of the sentence or at the end.)
5 I **always feel** tired on Saturday morning. (Frequency adverbs go before the verb.)
6 How often **do you get sick**? / **Do you ever get sick**? (Choose one question or the other.)
7 Fouad **hardly ever** goes to the gym. (fixed expression)
8 Do **you ever** get hungry in the afternoon? (In a question, *ever* comes after the pronoun and before the verb.)

Extension activity

Students may need more practice with where to put adverbs and expressions of frequency. Divide the class into teams of three or four. Give each team the following sentences on a handout, or write them on the board. Some of the sentences are correct, but others are not. Teams must identify the incorrect sentences for 1 point and correct them for another point. If there is more than one way to correct the sentence, teams can get multiple points. They cannot use their books or notes. Don't give them too much time—keep time short to increase the energy.

1 Every day, Kevin goes to the gym. ✓
2 Kevin goes to the gym always. ✗ (Kevin always goes to the gym.)
3 Seth doesn't very much go to the gym. ✗ (Seth doesn't go to the gym very much.)
4 Seth never exercises. ✓
5 Kevin doesn't eat junk food at all. ✓
6 Very much Seth doesn't eat vegetables. ✗ (Seth doesn't eat vegetables very much.)
7 Seth three times a month goes for a walk. ✗ (Seth goes for a walk three times a month.)
8 Often, Kevin has a snack at night. ✓
9 Seth eats sometimes fruit. ✗ (Sometimes, Seth eats fruit. / Seth sometimes eats fruit. / Seth eats fruit sometimes.)
10 Kevin drinks usually coffee in the morning during the week, but on weekends, he drinks it hardly ever. ✗ (Kevin usually drinks coffee in the morning during the week, but on weekends, he hardly ever drinks it.)

WRITING

Writing skill

Joining sentences with *and* and *but*

Warm-up

Write this simple poem on the board:

I like coffee, and I like tea.

I like fast food, but it doesn't like me.

Ask students about the second line. Why doesn't fast food like me? (Possible answers include: it's not healthy, it makes me sick, it makes me fat, etc.)

Circle *and*. Ask students why *and* is used here to elicit that it gives more / additional information; both are the same—I like this and that.

Circle *but*. Ask students why *but* is used here to elicit that is gives different / contrasting information; *like* and *doesn't like* are different.

Ask students to write their own simple poem using the same structure. Share in pairs or as a whole class.

To understand this *Writing skill* section, students need to understand two things. First, they need to understand when to use *and* and when to use *but*. Second, they need to understand when the sentences being combined need a comma and when they don't.

Start with ensuring that students understand when to use *and* and when to use *but*.

On the board, write:

He eats a lot of fruit. He eats a lot of vegetables.

She's happy. She's a little tired.

Ask students to combine the sentences with either *and* or *but*. Which makes more sense in each case? Add the word to the sentences:

He eats a lot of fruit and he eats a lot of vegetables. (The second sentence gives more information.)

She's happy but she's a little tired. (The second sentence gives different / contrasting information.)

Next, show students how they can make the first sentence shorter—ask if there are words that repeat that can be taken out. Cross them out:

He eats a lot of fruit and ~~he eats a lot of~~ vegetables.

Do the same for the second sentence:

She's happy but ~~she's~~ a little tired.

In both of the sentences above, there is only one subject. Ask students to identify the subject and verb. Underline the subject and circle the verb:

He eats a lot of fruit and vegetables.

She's happy but a little tired. (Ensure that students understand that the 's in *she's* is the short form of the verb *is*—write it out in full if needed.)

Next, show students how to combine two sentences, keeping both subjects and verbs. Write the sentences below on the board and ask students to combine them with *and* or *but*:

I rarely eat fast food. My wife never eats it. ➤ *I rarely eat fast food and my wife never eats it.*

He wants to change. It's not easy. ➤ *He wants to change but it's not easy.*

Ask students if there is any repetition that can be crossed out. (no)

Underline the subjects and circle the verbs (include the adverb):

I rarely eat fast food and my wife never eats it.

He wants to change but it's not easy.

In the two examples above, there are two complete sentences, also called *independent clauses*. In this case, you need a comma before the *and* and *but*. (The grammatical term for this use of *and* and *but* is *coordinating conjunction*, but students do not need to know this terminology.)

I rarely eat fast food, and my wife never eats it.

He wants to change, but it's not easy.

1 Ask students to complete the exercise alone, and then compare with a partner. Ask them to underline the subject and verb in each of the sentences, cross out the words that they don't need to repeat, and then combine the sentences using *and*. They should write out the new sentences in full.

ANSWERS

1 Zoe plays tennis and volleyball. / Zoe plays volleyball and tennis.
2 Kenichi loves to watch and play sports. / Kenichi loves to play and watch sports.
3 They run in the morning and go to the gym in the evening.
4 This app shows where I walk and tells me my steps.
5 I drink a lot of water, and I don't eat a lot of meat.
6 She does 30 pull-ups and 50 push-ups every morning.

2 Ask students to underline the subject and verb in each of the sentences, cross out the words that they don't need to repeat, and then combine the sentences using *but*. They should write out the new sentences in full. As the class gives feedback, help students notice when they need the comma.

ANSWERS

1 Beth never exercises, but she stays pretty healthy.
2 I love to watch sports on TV, but I hardly ever play sports.
3 I sometimes eat meat, but I don't eat red meat.
4 Khadija has four meals a day, but she never snacks between meals.
5 I usually run on weekends, but I rarely run during the week.
6 Rory sleeps eight hours a night, but he's often sleepy in the morning.

3 Students work with a partner to complete the sentences, using their own ideas and including *and* or *but*. You could make this exercise the "ticket out the door" and collect the sentences for checking.

Extension activity

As a review, conduct a substitution drill using the sentences in the exercises or your own sentences. Books are closed. T: *This is your key. This is your information pack.* STS: *This is your key and your information pack*, etc.

WRITING

Writing task

Students read the *Writing task*. Ask them to think about where they might read a text that describes people's health habits. Possible answers include an online profile for a health website, a site that gives advice about healthy living, the college health clinic, etc.

Brainstorm

Students work in pairs to read the notes, underline the positive habits, and circle the negative ones. Note that there is room for disagreement here, and disagreements can be discussed. For example, Kath's favorite dish may be ice cream, but if she doesn't eat it every day, then it might not be a negative health habit. Discuss this with students and encourage them to put that information in their paragraphs if they wish.

ANSWERS

Positive habits

Emma: likes sports a lot, plays tennis twice a week, favorite dessert is fruit

Kath: runs several times a week, walks to and from college, sometimes eats fish

Negative habits

Emma: doesn't go to the gym, doesn't run at all, takes the bus to and from college, sleeps six hours a night

Kath: doesn't like sports very much, doesn't go to the gym, favorite dessert is ice cream, sleeps nine hours a night

Plan

Students work alone or in pairs to plan their writing; for example, they need to include at least one comparison. In thinking about how to begin, it might be helpful to think about their audience and reason for writing, i.e., who is the paragraph for and what is it trying to achieve? For example, if they are writing for a healthy lifestyle blog, they might focus on the positive habits of each student. Refer them back to the model on page 110 for support if needed. They could compare their ideas with another student pair to generate more ideas.

Write

Give students about 20–25 minutes of class time to write their paragraphs. Ask students to write 75–80 words and to remember to use the key points, e.g., expressions of frequency and combining sentences using *and* or *but*. Students then complete the *Writing task* in class.

Share

Students exchange paragraphs with their partner and decide if they have one suggestion to improve it. To help with the peer review and to support the sharing stage, write guidelines on the board:

Is there at least one sentence that compares Emma and Kath?

Are there any sentences that can be combined with and *or* but?

Are there capital letters and periods for each sentence?

Tell students to look at the checklist on page 189. They use the checklist to compare their writing in pairs and offer suggestions for improvement.

Rewrite and edit

Students read and consider their partner's comments and rewrite and revise their paragraph on a clean sheet of paper or via a word processor, checking for errors before turning it in. This could be done for homework.

When giving feedback on students' work, you might consider giving recorded oral feedback using a free screen-capture app. Be sure to say what is done well in the work and give the student one or two targets to work on in future writing.

REVIEW

Wordlist

Students work in pairs or small groups to work through the *Wordlist*, checking that they all remember what each word or phrase means, how to pronounce it, and how it was used in the unit. Go through the list carefully with the class.

Academic words review

Students work through the sentences, check in pairs, and report back to the class.

ANSWERS

1 boring **2** more **3** folder **4** over

Unit review

Students work through the list alone to decide what they can and can't do. They discuss their answers in pairs, including what they remember from the unit about each point. Finally, open up the discussion to include the whole class. Pay particular attention to any boxes that the students didn't check. Explore with them ways of overcoming any remaining problems.

Extra research task

Students create a three-to-four slide PowerPoint or a one-page PDF based on a healthy lifestyle web-quest task. Each group must find one new piece of information online related to these topics:

1 food
2 exercise
3 lifestyle or sleep

They can find information about what is or is not healthy. Using complete sentences, they must write what it is and why it is or isn't healthy. Under the information, they should include the URL that they found it in. They should also include pictures or graphs in their PowerPoint or PDF.

Encourage students to find information that is not well known—a new food type or surprising information based on new research.

7 PLACES

READING	Finding information in a text
STUDY SKILL	How helpful are your notes?
VOCABULARY	Places in a town
GRAMMAR	Modifying adjectives
WRITING	Expanding notes into sentences

Warm-up

Start the topic by getting students to think and talk about their "happy place." A happy place is somewhere you go that makes you feel happy and relaxed. If you have a happy place, start by telling the students about it. Where is it? Why is it your happy place? What do you do there? How often do you go there? Bring in a picture if possible. Next, ask students to think about their happy place. Put them into pairs to talk about their happy place, and allow them to show a picture of it from their smartphone if appropriate. Ask volunteers to tell the class about their happy place.

Discussion point

Refer students to the picture at the beginning of the unit. Ask them if the place pictured looks like a happy place to be. Ask students where they like to spend time with friends on campus as a lead-in to asking where students generally eat lunch. Brainstorm some ideas on the board. Refer students to the infographic showing where students at Lakewood College spend their lunch break, and ask students to discuss the figures in comparison with their own campus. Write a couple of example sentences on the board for support, e.g., *More / fewer students eat (in the cafeteria) at our school. I think 40% of our students eat (on the sports field) at our school.* In pairs, students write at least one sentence comparing Lakewood with their school. Have the class provide feedback.

This is also a good time to check that students remember how to talk about percentages. Ask students to say how many Lakewood students eat in the cafeteria, at the snack bar, etc.

You could also ask students to notice the prepositions in the infographic as a way of reinforcing the preposition work done in Unit 3. Ask them to circle the prepositions *in*, *at*, *on*, *by*, and *in front of*. Ensure that they understand that *by* means the same as *next to*.

Before putting students into pairs for the *Discussion point*, ensure that they understand the difference between *town* and *city* (city—a large important town; town—a place where people live and work that is smaller than a city). As a way of varying the *Discussion point* activity, and if permitted, use a student-response app to collect the data after the discussion.

Extension activity

Students create an online survey to find out about the students' preferences at their school. They can use the same topic—where do you spend your lunch break? Or choose a topic that is more relevant to them. Help them choose a question that will get information about places on campus to fit into the topic of the unit. There are many free, online survey tools that are easy to use and students will have a social network they can access to get the results.

VIDEO

Before you watch

Introduce the topic of the video and ask students to read the exercise and identify any new words. Write these on the board and discuss the meanings as a class. Then, ask students to complete the *Before you watch* section. Monitor and go through the answers with the class.

ANSWERS
1 b **2** a **3** d **4** e **5** c

While you watch

Play the video once. Ask the students to watch the video and complete the exercise. Play the video again so that students can check their answers. Go through the answers with the class.

ANSWERS
1 park **2** sun **3** phone **4** good

See page 108 for the video script.

After you watch

Put the students into pairs or groups and ask them to complete the exercise. Encourage them to use what they have learned in the video and the example answers to answer the questions. Go through the answers with the class.

READING 1

Favorite neighborhoods

The word *neighborhood* looks difficult to pronounce and even more difficult to spell. Start by teaching the meaning. Drill pronunciation /ˈneɪbərˌhʊd/ and break down the word into segments to help with spelling: neigh-bor-hood. Point out that the *gh* is silent. (Other words that follow this pattern include *weigh* and *straight*.) Ask students if they know who their neighbors are to help fix this word in their memory.

Check that students understand the word *favorite*, and ask for examples of their favorite food, favorite place to eat, etc. Check pronunciation: /ˈfeɪv(ə)rɪt/ not /ˈfeɪv(ə)raɪt/.

A Vocabulary preview

1 Ask students to match the words with their definitions and compare answers. If necessary, allow students to use a dictionary. Students can do the *Vocabulary preview* exercises for homework if time is short. Note that *traffic* is another double consonant word students can add to their list of words with double letters. Fast finishers can add the words to the class vocabulary box. Drill pronunciation. Difficult words include *crowded* /ˈkraʊdəd/ not /ˈkrəʊdəd/, *museum* /mjuˈziəm/, and *popular* /ˈpɑpjələr/.

Pay particular attention to spelling. Ask students to close their books and put the words on the board with the vowels missing. Students work in pairs to reconstruct the words, and then check in their books.

ANSWERS
1 c **2** a **3** d **4** b **5** g **6** h **7** e **8** f

2 Ask students to work alone to complete the sentences, and then compare answers in pairs. Ask pairs to write a silly story that contains at least six of the words. Explain that sometimes silliness helps us to remember. Exchange stories with another pair and ask volunteers to read theirs to the class.

ANSWERS
1 market **2** traffic **3** park **4** neighborhood
5 wide **6** crowded **7** popular **8** museum

Extension activity

Teach students the "look, say, cover, write" method of learning how to spell. First, they look at the word, and then they say it. They then cover up the word and write it down without looking. They should do this three to four times over the course of a few days—not all at once. Revisiting the word after a lapse of time is more effective than trying to learn the spelling in the short term.

B Before you read

Put students into pairs to discuss the questions. If possible, ask students to prepare some information about popular neighborhoods before class, or bring a picture of one. It may be possible for them to search *popular neighborhoods in ... (+ their town or city)* to find out more information. Brainstorm what makes neighborhoods popular with different types of people. For example, what makes a neighborhood popular with students? (cafés, places to go, parks, etc.) With families? (good schools, supermarkets, etc.).

C Global reading

Scanning

Ask students if they remember what they do when they *scan* a text. After they have read the task, give them two minutes to scan it and write the answers. After checking answers, give them some time to look at the pictures and discuss whether or not they have been to these places.

ANSWERS
1 Ueno, Tokyo **2** Gràcia, Barcelona
3 Bellas Artes, Santiago

D Close reading

Finding information in a text

Finding information in a text is an important skill both in terms of general reading skills and for reading more efficiently for exams. Often students feel they need to understand everything in the text they read, but more often than not, they only need to understand the part that gives them the information they need.

1 Students read the *Finding information in a text* box. To help students practice this skill, ask the whole class to scan the text for the word *cafés*. When they have found it, they raise their hand. Ask the first person who raised their hand to say which neighborhood cafés was mentioned in. Scan once more to see if it is mentioned again, with students raising their hand when they have found it. Do this for *markets* and *museums*, and then allow students to scan on their own to find the rest. Set a time limit of 60 seconds or less for students to complete this exercise. The hand-raising activity will let you know who are the fastest scanners and will encourage slower ones to scan more quickly rather than taking a lot of time reading.

ANSWERS
1 Gràcia, Bellas Artes 2 Ueno, Bellas Artes
3 Bellas Artes 4 Gràcia 5 Ueno, Gràcia, Bellas Artes
6 Ueno 7 Bellas Artes

2 Ask students to circle the correct answers. Students should continue to use the skill of finding information quickly when doing this exercise. As the class gives feedback, note that for question 1, *overseas visitors* is not mentioned, but *tourists* is. *Young people* is not the right answer because the text says that the market is popular with them, not the neighborhood. For question 4, students need to understand that *low prices* suggests that the neighborhood is *pretty cheap*.

ANSWERS
1 overseas visitors 2 crowded 3 is no traffic
4 pretty cheap 5 two

3 Students scan to find the authors' favorite places. For homework, ask students to re-read the texts and underline all the vocabulary words from the *Vocabulary preview* section.

ANSWERS
1 the night market 2 Park Güell 3 the fish market

E Over to you

Students discuss the questions in groups. Ask students to work with two people they don't usually work with for the discussion. Ask volunteers for their responses in plenary. Help the class discussion by asking students if they agree with what was said by another student or if they have anything to add. Encourage students to give reasons for their responses.

As a "ticket out the door," students write their answers to the *Over to you* questions. Alternatively, ask students to answer the questions in an online class-discussion forum.

Extension activity

For homework, students make a short video blog about their favorite place in town or on campus. Ask students to go to their favorite place and use their smartphone or tablet or other recording device to record themselves talking about it. They can describe it or say why they like it. They then upload their videos onto the class blog and each student watches at least three of the videos. To ensure they watch each other's videos, ask them to write a short summary of the three videos they watched. Alternatively, watch them in class.

STUDY SKILLS

How helpful are your notes?

Warm-up

Prepare a mini-lecture (5–10 minutes) on any topic you feel you can talk about. In addition, prepare a set of notes from the lecture that you think are a good example of "good notes."

Give your lecture and ask students to take notes. When you are finished, students compare their notes. Ask students how helpful they think their notes are—could they use them to study with? Are they clear and organized?

Show students the notes you prepared. How do your notes compare with theirs? Point out that there is no right or wrong way to take notes, but that some ways are more helpful than others.

1 You may need to pre-teach some language before students do the activity: *main idea*, *clear*, *missing*, *key details*, and *organized*. Allow students to use dictionaries if needed.

If students have started attending lectures, ask them to bring in some of their notes to show other students. If not, they can use their notes from your English classes, or the notes they took from your mini-lecture. Students read the *How helpful are your notes?* box. Then they complete the exercise, using the notes they brought in as the object of their evaluation. Alternatively, ask them to evaluate each other's notes using the evaluation criteria.

As the class gives feedback, see if you can find students who think their notes or their peer's notes are very good. Find out what makes them good. Pass them around for others to see. Emphasize that notes are a personal thing, and what works for one student may not work for another. Often it's the act of writing the notes that aids learning. There are, however, some tips that students can use to take better notes.

2 Students compare with a partner and discuss how to improve notes. Students may lack the language to discuss how to improve notes, so if appropriate, allow them to use their mother tongue. To aid this discussion, write some discussion prompts on the board:

1 How can you make notes easy to read or understand?

2 How can you make main ideas and details clear?

3 What is a good organization for notes?

4 Why is it important to put notes in your own words?

3 Students work in pairs to read the tips and decide if they are easy or difficult to do. Ask them to add two more tips. As the class gives feedback, each pair of students shares their tips. Write them on the board for the benefit of the other students. Be prepared to spend some time on this section—find out what difficulties students have and see if anyone can give tips to help.

Ask students to choose one or two tips they want to try for a week. After a week, get feedback from the students. Did they try the tips? Did they help improve their notes?

Extension activity

If you find that students are not very good at taking notes or don't know what good notes look like, find some examples online to bring into class, or ask students to do some online research to find examples of clear, well-organized notes.

READING 2

A greener Seoul

Write the title of the text on the board and ask students what they think it means. Tell them that *greener* in this context has two meanings. They are going to find out what the two meanings are in this section.

A Vocabulary preview

Ask students to complete the *Vocabulary preview* exercises for homework, using a monolingual dictionary website to find the definitions and listen to the American pronunciation of each word (e.g., www.macmillandictionary.com/us).

1 Ask students to match the words with their definitions, and then compare answers in pairs. Drill pronunciation. Difficult words to pronounce from the spelling include *air* /er/, *beautiful* /ˈbjutɪf(ə)l/, *once* /wʌns/, *tourist* /ˈtʊrɪst/, and *temperature* /ˈtemp(ə)rəˌtʃʊr/. Note that *temperature* has three syllables, not four.

Students can add the word *cool* to their list of words with double letters.

With books closed, write the words on the board, but this time, take out the consonants, leaving spaces where the consonants should go. Pairs try to reconstruct the words with a five-minute time limit. Ask student to open their books to check the spellings. Encourage them to use the "look, say, cover, write" method at home to learn the spelling.

ANSWERS
1 c **2** a **3** d **4** b **5** h **6** f **7** g **8** e

2 Write the answers on the board for students to self-check. In pairs, students test each other on the words. Student A closes his or her book. Student B reads a definition. Student A says the word. Change roles and repeat. Fast finishers can review words from the *Vocabulary preview* from *Reading 1* or choose words from the class vocabulary box.

ANSWERS
1 air **2** temperature **3** cool **4** tourist, drive
5 capital, once **6** beautiful

Extension activity

On the board, write this list of adjectives from this and previous units: *beautiful, cool, capital, crowded, expensive, great, large, popular.* All of these adjectives collocate with *city*. Ask students to choose three or more combinations and describe them, e.g., *a beautiful city—a city with many parks and green spaces*. Note that descriptions will vary according to personal opinion.

B Before you read

Students look at the places in pairs and decide which every town or city needs. They should give reasons for their choices. Ask pairs to find another student pair to discuss their choices. In the new group of four, students agree on one other thing not listed that every city or town needs. As the class gives feedback, volunteers say why they think cities need or don't need each. Ask each group what they decided every city or town needs.

C Global reading

Skimming

Students read the three topics, and then have one minute to skim the text to find the topic.

Find out if any of your students have been to Seoul. When they read the text more closely, ask them to find information that they didn't know about the city.

ANSWER
c

D Close reading

1 Ask students to read the questions before reading the text to find the answers. Give them a time limit for the activity so that they use the reading skill of scanning for information. Students compare answers in pairs. In whole-class discussion, ask students to read the sentence where they found the information for the answer. They can underline or highlight it. This will help lower-level students who may be having a hard time finding the information. For number 4, the answer isn't explicitly stated, and some inferencing is needed. The fact that "all the people walking in this part of the city" is "great for the cafés, restaurants, stores, and other businesses" suggests that the answer is b.

ANSWERS
1 a **2** b **3** c **4** b

Finding information in a text

2 Ask students to scan the text to find the numbers to complete the sentences. In pairs, they read the sentences, concentrating on saying the numbers correctly. As the class gives feedback, make sure students are saying numbers correctly and review numbers as needed.

Refer back to the question of the two meanings of *green* in the context of the article. See if students can recognize that green means the color— the park in Seoul is green because of the grass and trees. Green in this context also means good for the environment—the park is good for the environment because of the plants and areas for wildlife as well as the reduction in the number of cars.

ANSWERS
1 ten / 10 **2** 11 **3** 730 **4** 22 **5** 0 / no **6** 1.4%
7 Three / 3

E Over to you

Students discuss the questions in a group, using the sentence stems as prompts.

Extension activity

Students research to find a café, market, museum, park, restaurant, store, or area in Seoul. Students choose one of the places and do an Internet search to find (1) the name of a good place for tourists to go, and (2) why it is a good place for tourists to go.

VOCABULARY

Topic vocabulary

Places in a town

Warm-up

Do a quick brainstorm of places in a city. On the board, write *places* vertically down the left-hand side. Give students three minutes to work in pairs to try to think of places that contain the letters—the words don't have to begin with the letters. Do one or two together as a model. A completed example would look something like this:

Park
Library
mArket
Café
musEum
storeS

1 Ask students to match the words to make places collocations. Refer them to the pictures in Exercise 2 if needed to aid understanding of the new vocabulary.

ANSWERS
1 b 2 c/g 3 d 4 a 5 g/c 6 h 7 f 8 e

2 Ask students to complete the sentences with places from Exercise 1. This activity reviews prepositions of place while practicing the new vocabulary. Drill the pronunciation of the places. Ensure that students are stressing both words in the collocation and not just the second word, e.g., *ART CENter*, not *art CENter*. Concept check with the whole class, e.g., *Where can you go to see famous paintings? If you want to travel to another place, where do you go? Where can you go to send a letter?*

ANSWERS
1 The gas station is behind the bus station.
2 The post office is inside the shopping mall.
3 The movie theater is next to the fitness center.
4 The art museum is across from the department store.

3 Students discuss the questions in a group, using the sentence stems as prompts.

Extension activity

Using different-colored board markers, draw a city on the board, describing it as you go along. *In my city, there is a long river* (draw a winding river in blue). *Along the river there is a big park and lots of apartments* (draw the park in green and the apartments in black). Continue drawing and adding places. *There is a movie theatre next to the park, and across from the movie theater there is a fitness center.* Every so often, stop and ask students where something is. *Where is the movie theater?* Ask students to work in pairs to draw their city—real or imagined—describing it to their partner. An alternative is to draw the basic city plan, but get students to put in the places. Give them sticky notes with places written on them, and ask them to stick them up on the board to create the city. Students then write a description based on what they have created.

VOCABULARY

Vocabulary builder

Describing the number of things

In this section, students learn to quantify things, both in exact numbers and in approximations. At this stage, it is not important that students differentiate between an approximate number and a quantifier. They should, however, be sure to use plural nouns and note carefully when they need to use *of—thousands of, lots of,* etc.

Warm-up

Ask the whole class questions to elicit numbers, e.g., *How many cafés are there on campus? How many cafés are there in the city? How many restaurants? How many cars?* Make sure you ask about things that are easily counted and things that you would have to approximate. Highlight this difference, e.g., *You said there are three cafés. Is that an exact number? What about millions of cars? Is that an exact number or an approximate number?*

Refer students to the *Describing the number of things* box to find three ways to describe the number of things. Check that students understand the difference between *exact* and *approximate*. *Three cities: Do we know how many? Several fountains: Do we know how many? Not really.* Several *is more than two but could be as many as ten or more. We don't know exactly.* You could introduce another common approximation: *dozens of.* Note that a dozen is twelve. *Dozens of* would be a smaller number than *hundreds of.* Note that there is no difference between *lots of* and *a lot of.*

1 Ask students to circle the larger number in each pair. Remind students that *both* means *two*. Another expression meaning *two* would be *a couple of.* We might use *a couple of* when we aren't being exact: *There are a couple of cafés in town*. We use *both* when there are two things we are referring to: *Both cafés are good.*

Check students' pronunciation, paying particular attention to the linking of the final /z/ sound in *hundreds, thousands*, etc., to *of*: *hundreds of* /ˈhʌndrədzəv/.

> ANSWERS
> **1** four **2** several **3** many **4** a lot of
> **5** thousands of **6** millions of

2 Students unscramble the sentences, writing out the new sentence in full. For students who struggle with this type of exercise, cut up the sentences for them so that they can move the words around to form the sentences. In checking, ask students if they have included a capital letter and period. Ask concept-check questions to ensure students understand the meaning, e.g., *Do we know how many older people live in Gràcia?* (no) *Is it a large or small number?* (large)

> ANSWERS
> **1** Many older people live in Gràcia.
> **2** Gràcia has some great restaurants.
> **3** Several stores in Umeno sell Japanese clothes.
> **4** Millions of people live in Tokyo.
> **5** There are a lot of universities in Bellas Artes.

3 Ask students to read the questions. Pair up lower-level students with higher-level students for support.

> ANSWERS
> **1** My city has two bus **stations**.
> **2** **Thousands** of people live in my neighborhood.
> **3** **A lot of** people visit the park every day.
> **4** There are several **colleges** in my town.
> **5** Many **tourists** come to the capital every year.
> **6** The fitness center costs **hundreds of dollars** a month.
> **7** I need to buy **some** clothes today.

WRITING

Writing model

Read through the aims with the students. Remind them that each part of the *Writing* section will help to build students' skills for the successful completion of the *Writing task*.

A Analyze

Refer students to the mind map. Ask them if they ever take notes like this, i.e., using a mind map to help them plan what they want to write about. Mind maps are a quick and effective way to get ideas down on paper quickly. You can write what comes to mind without having to think about sentence structure or grammar. Later, the mind map can be organized into a plan.

Students look at the mind map and underline all the places. As the class gives feedback, help students recognize the branching. Ask them what else they might write for *on my street, businesses,* or *near my house.*

> ANSWERS
> my street, lots of houses, my house, a school, small park, movie theater, restaurants, fitness center

B Model

1 Students read the model and answer the questions. As the class gives feedback, ask students what information in the paragraph tells them that Sunnyville is a good place to live (pretty interesting, everyone is very friendly, nice restaurants, nice fountain, I like my neighborhood).

> ANSWERS
> Sunnyville is a good place to live.
> One problem the author mentions is that the fitness center is too crowded.

2 Ask students to read the model text again to decide which sentences are true. Ask students to correct the incorrect sentences. As the class gives feedback, draw students' attention to how the writer begins and ends the paragraph. They start with a general statement about where they live, and then finish with a comment about why they like the neighborhood. The rest of the information in the paragraph comes from the mind map.

ANSWERS
Students check the following items: 1, 2, and 4

Extension activity

Books are closed and students are in pairs. Give each pair a copy of the model text. They must use the information in the model to re-create the mind map. After five minutes, students compare their mind map with the one in the book. This activity encourages students to focus only on the key information that needs to go into the mind map.

GRAMMAR

Modifying adjectives

Students read the *Modyifying adjectives* box for homework so that they are ready for your presentation in class.

Warm-up

Books are closed. On the board write, *My English class is __________ interesting*, leaving a space between *is* and *interesting*. Ask students what word you can add to that sentence if you really love your English class to elicit *very* and *really*. Write both in the space, one below the other in a vertical column. Ask students what word they could use if they think it's interesting, but they only like it, not love it, to elicit *pretty*. Write *pretty* under the other words in the vertical column. Ask them what they could say if they don't really like it to elicit *not very* and *not … at all*, and write these on the board under *pretty*. Ask students if you can say *My English class is too interesting.* What makes it sound unusual? (*Too* is usually used with adjectives with a negative connotation. *Interesting* has a positive connotation, so it sounds odd to say that the class is *too interesting*, meaning "more interesting than is necessary." Its use here would make the sentence sound ironic.) Ask students if you can say *My English class is not interesting enough*. (yes)

Refer students to the *Modifying adjectives* box and ask them to underline or highlight the modifiers and adjectives in the examples. Ask them which two have the adjective in the middle rather than after (*not* + adjective + *at all; not* + adjective + *enough*).

1 Ask students to work alone to rewrite the sentences in full, and then compare answers in pairs.

ANSWERS
1 The people in this neighborhood are very friendly.
2 The night market gets really busy around 10:00 p.m.
3 That restaurant has pretty good desserts.
4 My college isn't very expensive.
5 The cafés in this neighborhood are not nice at all.
6 The art museum is too crowded on weekends.
7 The streets around here aren't wide enough.
8 This neighborhood is really famous for its Italian cafés.

2 In this activity, students rewrite the sentences using the word in parentheses so that it means the same thing as the originals. This is a challenging exercise, so allow students to work in pairs and support them as needed. After checking, do a substitution drill, e.g., T: *It's too cold. Hot*. STS: *It's not hot enough*. T: *It's not big enough.* Small. STS: *It's too small.*

ANSWERS
1 This café is not quiet enough.
2 That table is too small for us.
3 You're not old enough to see that movie.
4 The river is too cold to swim in.

3 Ask students to work alone to find the mistakes and correct them. As the class gives feedback, volunteers read aloud the corrected sentence.

ANSWERS
1 There are three **really old** fountains in the park.
2 The fish in the market is **too expensive**.
3 The park next to the college is **not very big** / is **very small**.
4 You can get **pretty good** ice cream at that store.
5 The people in the neighborhood are not friendly **at all**.

4 Ask students to rewrite the sentences using modifiers and making it true for them. This exercise could be done for homework. Alternatively, use is as a "ticket out the door." Lower-level students could choose just three items to complete while higher-level students could write an additional two of their own. Students share their sentences in pairs, and volunteers share one of their sentences with the class.

5 Put students in pairs to answer the questions, and then tell them to join with another pair to ask and answer them. If time allows, students write one to two more questions to ask each other.

Extension activity

Students write a description of a place. Other students guess where it is. It could be a city or country, or it could be a place in a city such as a restaurant.

WRITING

Writing skill

Expanding notes into sentences

Warm-up

From the class, elicit two verbs, two nouns, two adjectives, and two modifiers. Write these on the board. Put students into groups of three. Each group uses the words on the board to write one sentence using all the words. They will have to add other words. The sentences can be silly, but should be grammatically correct. Challenge higher-level students to write a long sentence. After five minutes, students read their sentences to the rest of the class.

Students read the *Expanding notes into sentences* box. Ask students why notes are generally not in complete sentences. Possible answers include the need to write down information quickly, or the fact that thinking about the grammar of a sentence can distract your mind from what you are trying to write.

1 Ask students to complete the exercise alone, before comparing answers with a partner. Ask fast finishers to write their answers on the board so that other students can check.

POSSIBLE ANSWERS

1 There are two nice stores on my street.
2 My neighborhood has a big park.
3 The subway is next to a fountain.
4 The fitness center is behind the bus station.
5 My street has a great Japanese restaurant.
6 The shopping mall is too crowded.
7 There is an interesting sculpture near my house.
8 The highway is not wide enough.

2 Ask students to look back at the mind map notes on page 128. Working alone, they write three sentences using the notes, and then compare in pairs. Volunteers read one of their sentences to the class. If possible, collect students' sentences for checking.

3 In this activity, tell students to use a note-taking style and not to write complete sentences. They should use the notes in Exercise 2 as a model for what is expected. You could use this activity and the next one as the "ticket out the door."

4 Ask students to use the notes from Exercise 3 to write two sentences.

WRITING

Writing task

Students read the *Writing task*. Ask them to think about where they might read a text that describes a neighborhood. One possible answer might be a promotional blog that encourages people to move there.

Brainstorm

Students create a mind map about their neighborhood. If it is helpful, ask them to imagine that they are going to write a short article about their neighborhood for the school blog or newsletter to send out to new students. Note that not all neighborhoods have a name, so students can just write *my neighborhood*, or they could describe its location instead. Students share their mind map with their partner and advise each other on any missing information.

Plan

Students work alone or in pairs to plan their paragraph. It might help them to number the notes so they can remember what order they want to talk about each item. They should write notes from the mind map similar to the notes they wrote in the *Writing skill* section.

Write

Give students about 20–25 minutes of class time to write their paragraphs, using the model on page 128 if needed. Ask students to write 80–90 words and to remember to pay attention to the use of modifiers. Students then complete the *Writing task* in class.

Share

Students exchange paragraphs with their partner and decide if they have one suggestion to improve it. To help with the peer review, and to support the sharing stage, write guidelines on the board:

Does the paragraph begin with a general sentence about the neighborhood?

Does the paragraph talk about some things in the neighborhood?

Does the paragraph say what the writer likes about the neighborhood?

Are there adjectives and modifiers?

Are there capital letters and periods for each sentence?

Tell students to look at the checklist on page 189. They use the checklist to compare their writing in pairs and offer suggestions for improvement.

Rewrite and edit

Students read and consider their partner's comments and rewrite and revise their paragraph on a clean sheet of paper or via a word processor, checking for errors before turning it in. This could be done for homework. Encourage students to include some pictures. When giving feedback on students' work, you might consider giving recorded oral feedback using a free screen-capture app. Be sure to say what is done well in the work and give the student one or two targets to work on in future writing.

REVIEW

Wordlist

Students work in pairs or small groups to work through the *Wordlist*, checking that they all remember what each word or phrase means, how to pronounce it, and how it was used in the unit. Go through the list carefully with the class.

Vocabulary builder review

Students work through the sentences, check in pairs, and report back to the class.

ANSWERS
1 every day **2** between **3** hundreds of **4** less

Unit review

Students work through the list alone to decide what they can and can't do. They discuss their answers in pairs, including what they remember from the unit about each point. Finally, open up the discussion to include the whole class. Pay particular attention to any boxes that the students didn't check. Explore with them ways of overcoming any remaining problems.

Extra research task

Groups do a research project about a famous neighborhood with the aim of convincing the other students to go there for a vacation. In their project they should include:

- the name of the neighborhood
- why it is famous or popular
- some of the places in the neighborhood
- who lives there (e.g., famous people if applicable)
- any other information
- why the other students should visit this neighborhood.

Students publish their work with pictures on a class blog. Ask students to rate each other's neighborhoods with a five-star rating system to see which neighborhood is the most attractive.

8 PLANS

READING	Identifying text types
STUDY SKILL	Using a planner
VOCABULARY	Days, months, and time
GRAMMAR	Simple present for future; *will* for intentions
WRITING	The language of emails

Warm-up

Choose three to four quotations about planning, and put them on the board or on a handout. Some suggestions are below. Ask students to read the quotes and discuss them in a group. Which one(s) do they agree with? Find out if they know any quotes related to planning.

A goal without a plan is just a wish.—Antoine de Saint-Exupéry

By failing to prepare, you are preparing to fail.—Benjamin Franklin

Plans are nothing; planning is everything.—Dwight D Eisenhower

We have a plan for life but sometimes, life has a different plan for us.—Saji Ijiyemi

Always, always have a plan.—Rick Riordan

Discussion point

Refer students to the picture and infographic. Give them some time to process the information, using the images to understand the new vocabulary. Drill the pronunciation of the tools so that students are confident using them. Ask students if there are any other time-planning tools they can think of and write them on the board.

In pairs, students discuss the questions, using the sentence frames for support. As the class gives feedback find out by a show of hands how many students like making plans and how many don't. Ask them if it's OK to have a plan for some things but not for others.

Extension activity

If you haven't done so already, create a class calendar with the plan for the unit that includes homework and other due dates. You can post this online for students to access.

VIDEO

Before you watch

Introduce the topic of the video and ask students to read the exercise and identify any new words. Write these on the board and discuss the meanings as a class. Then, ask students to complete the *Before you watch* section. Monitor and go through the answers with the class.

ANSWERS
1 b **2** d **3** a **4** e **5** c

While you watch

Play the video once. Ask the students to watch the video and complete the exercise. Play the video again so that students can check their answers. Go through the answers with the class.

ANSWERS
1 F (iHub opened in 2010.) **2** T **3** T **4** T

See page 108 for the video script.

After you watch

Put the students into pairs or groups and ask them to complete the exercise. Encourage them to use what they have learned in the video and the example answers to answer the questions. Go through the answers with the class.

READING 1

TechQuest Conference

Warm-up

Introduce the topic with a mingling activity. On a handout, or on the board, write the following questions:

Do you use technology? What technology do you use?

Do you play video games? Which ones?

Do you meet with other people to talk about games or technology? Where?

(Your own question) ______________________

As the class gives feedback, ask volunteers to share some of their findings. Ask students if they have been to gaming conferences or conventions such as Comic-Con. (Different countries have different versions of gaming and technology conferences.) The glossary on page 137 gives a definition of a conference.

Write the text title on the board and ask students to guess what it means. Any students who are gamers will probably know what a *quest* is, or you could project the definition on the board from www.macmillandictionary.com/us. Come up with a class definition of a "TechQuest Conference." A possible answer is a large meeting where people talk about technology.

A Vocabulary preview

1 Ask students to complete the exercise for homework, or have them work alone to match the words and definitions, and then compare in pairs. On the board, write *information*, *invitation*, and *interested*. Tell students that two of these words have four syllables and one has only three. Give them 30 seconds to discuss which is which. Drill the stress pattern of each with a humming exercise. Instead of saying the word, hum the stress pattern, asking students to repeat: *information* = mmm mmm MMM mmm; *invitation* = mmm mmm MMM mmm; *interested* = MMM mmm mmm. Hum one of the words and ask students to guess (*invitation* and *information* have the same stress pattern, but *interested* is different). Show the stress pattern of *social media* in the same way: mmm mmm MMM mmm mmm. Ask students to practice in pairs for one minute. Write one of the words on the board and ask the class to spell it in chorus. Erase one letter. The class spells the full word again. Continue to erase letters (randomly) until the class can spell the entire word without it on the board. Ask students to write it on their paper or reconstruct it as a class on the board.

ANSWERS
1 d **2** a **3** c **4** b **5** f **6** g **7** e **8** h

2 Ask students to work alone to complete the exercise. Put the students in pairs, and have one student read the sentence, while the other provides the missing word. Draw students' attention to the use of *in* after *interested* and give some examples of when to use *in* and when not to on the board, e.g., *I am interested in gaming. Are you interested in joining the group? No, I'm not interested. Yes, I'm interested.*

ANSWERS
1 join, online **2** invitation, date **3** social media, interested **4** pleased, information

Extension activity

Students write the vocabulary words on slips of paper or card—one word per slip. They put these facedown on the table between them. Set a time limit of one minute. Student A takes a slip and gives a definition or example. Student B guesses the word. See how many definitions Student B can guess in one minute. Change roles and repeat. This is a good activity to do frequently as a way of reviewing vocabulary.

B Before you read

Identifying text types

Warm-up

Understanding different text types is an important critical-thinking skill. If possible, bring in a few examples of different text types: advertisement or flyer, email, newspaper, etc. Otherwise, write the text types on the board. Ask students what the purpose of each is. For example, an advertisement's purpose is to get you to buy something whereas a newspaper's purpose is to relate the news. Ask students why understanding purpose might be important. One possible answer is that it helps the reader know how to interpret the information. An advertisement will make something look good to convince you to buy it whereas a news article about the item will just give information with less bias. You would probably trust a news article about something more than an advertisement, for example.

Give students a few minutes to read the *Identifying text types* box. The text says how you might identify an advertisement and an email. Ask students what a social-media page might include. Point out that *ad* is short for *advertisement*.

1 Students read the task, and then have 30 seconds to skim-read the text to find out the text type.

ANSWERS
d an invitation

2 Students read the task, and then scan the text for the information.

ANSWERS
Students should check: a title, several headings, several pictures, several web links

C Global reading

Students read the task then skim the text for the information. To support lower-level students, ask them to circle where they found the information in the invitation.

ANSWERS
1 a web page **2** Tech Talk **3** invites **4** learning

D Close reading

1 Ask students to read the questions, and then read the text to find the answers. Pair up lower-level students with higher-level students for support. As the class gives feedback, ask for the full answer instead of just the letter.

ANSWERS
1 c **2** a **3** b **4** c

Finding information in a text

2 Ask students to read the questions, and then read the text to find the answers. As the class gives feedback, ask volunteers for the answers and review how to say the date. Dates are spoken and written differently. The month comes before the day (6/30 = June 30th) and sometimes Americans even say the dates as numbers, *since six thirty* rather than *since June 30*th.

ANSWERS
1 May 5 **2** Dubai World Trade Centre **3** three
4 Friday, May 6

E Over to you

In small groups, students discuss the questions. See if the group can come to a consensus on question 2. For question 3, ask students to add a talk title that they would find very interesting.

Use this topic as an opportunity to find out students' views on using technology in the classroom. Are there any technological tools they think should be used more or used less? Students may have some very good suggestions for apps or sites that could help in their learning. Take the best suggestions and try them out.

Extension activity

Stage a mini-debate about the use of technology in learning. Divide the class into opposing sides. Each side thinks about the reasons for or against technology in learning in the classroom. In a large class, divide students into smaller groups. Give them 15 minutes to prepare their arguments. Re-group the students so that there are six people in a group—three for and three against for the debate. If you are concerned about noise levels, the debate could be held in a class forum. Decide on a procedure for the forum, e.g., *Present your argument, read the other arguments, comment on each argument giving reasons why you agree or disagree.*

STUDY SKILLS

Using a planner

Students already know the word *plan* from the beginning of the unit. Ask them what they think a *planner* is and brainstorm some types of planner. Possible answers include, e.g., a paper-based planner (or journal, diary), a planner app, reminders on a smartphone, etc.

A good way to start this section is with the first discussion question from exercise 2. This will help students who don't use a planner be more receptive to learning this study skill. You could add the question, *What do other people say when you forget things?*

Ask students to read the *Using a planner* box. Tell them to put a check next to the things they do. As the class gives feedback, ask students who put a check next to an item and why they do this.

1 Ask students to read the planner, and then complete one for themselves. In pairs, students compare planners to see if they have any activities in common (other than this English class). As the class gives feedback, ask students which parts of the planner they think are the most important or if there is any information they would add or leave out.

2 Students discuss the questions in a group. As the class gives feedback, get some suggestions from students about the best planner to use. Make sure students give reasons why their planner works for them.

Extension activity

Give each student a page from a planner that lists the days Sunday–Saturday, and the times 1:00– 23:00. Alternatively, draw this on the board for students to copy. Students put events into the planner. They must have at least one event every day and at least ten different events. Events can be repeated. They shouldn't show their planner to anyone. Put students into groups of about six. Tell them they need to arrange a time to meet with everyone in the group for a group conference. Put sentence frames on the board to support lower-level students: *Can you meet on … at … ? No, sorry, I am busy. What about … at … ? Yes, I'm free then.* Discourage them from showing each other their calendars so that they have to speak to each other in order to make plans.

READING 2

Will you speak at TechQuest?

A Vocabulary preview

1 Students complete the exercise for homework, or have them work alone to match the words with their definitions, and then compare in pairs. Note that *book* is used as a verb here. *Professor* is another word with double consonants to add to the list. Difficult words to pronounce include *probably* /'prɑbəbli/ (3 syllables), *document* /'dɑkjəmənt/ not /'dɑkumənt/, and *world* /wɜrld/. Students may have heard the term *earth*. *Earth* refers to the planet in general, while we use *world* to include the people on it.

> ANSWERS
> **1** b **2** d **3** a **4** c **5** f **6** h **7** g **8** e

2 Ask students to complete the exercise and compare answers with a partner. As the class gives feedback, ask volunteers to read the entire sentence with the correct answer. Concept-check that students have understood the meaning of the words, e.g., *What can you book?* (tickets, a hotel, etc.) *Name three companies. Name three things that are free on campus.*

> ANSWERS
> **1** free **2** probably **3** book **4** world **5** professor
> **6** company **7** document **8** describe

Extension activity

Review the vocabulary from the unit with a quick team scavenger hunt:

Find a word that can be a noun or a verb. (book)

Find four adjectives. (free, interested, online, pleased)

Find an adjective that collocates with *in*. (interested *in*)

Facebook, Snapchat, WhatsApp, and LinkedIn are all examples of what? (social media)

Find two verbs that fit this sentence: You need to _____ your interest in technology to _____ this group. (describe, join)

B Before you read

Identifying text types

Ask students some questions about TechQuest to help them recall, e.g., *What is TechQuest? When is it? Where is it? How many speakers do they have?* Refer them to the picture on pages 141–142. Working in pairs, students describe the picture in one or two sentences.

Students read the instructions and then skim-read the text in five seconds to find the text type.

> ANSWER
> a

C Global reading

Ask students to read the instructions and then scan the text in 60 seconds to complete the information.

> ANSWERS
> **1** 25 **2** speak **3** asks questions **4** 5

D Close reading

Refer students to the glossary of terms and ask them to underline the words in the text. To revisit vocabulary, students highlight or underline the words from the *Vocabulary preview* section.

1 Ask students to read the task. They then read the emails and number the events in order. To support lower-level students, ask them to put a star next to where they find the information in the text. As the class gives feedback, ask *What happens next?* to elicit a full answer.

> ANSWERS
> **1** Khalid asks Claire to speak at the conference.
> **2** Khalid gives the dates for the conference.
> **3** Claire says she is interested in speaking at the conference.
> **4** Claire asks Khalid when he wants her to speak.
> **5** Khalid asks Claire to send him the title of her talk.
> **6** Claire attaches a document to her email.

Finding information in a text

2 Students work alone to find the answers, and then compare in pairs.

> ANSWERS
> **1** an invitation **2** Dubai **3** travel **4** ABC Games
> **5** speakers **6** 4:00 **7** Khalid **8** airport

E Over to you

Students discuss the questions in a group, using the sentence frames as prompts. For question 1, they should make a list of the examples that support their view. For question 3, they look at the questions below and decide which are important for Claire to know the answers to. Ask them to write a question they think Claire should ask. As the class gives feedback, ask students if they think it's normal for emails to become less formal. It may be usual in some cultures while in others the level of formality may remain high, and in others, the level of formality may be low from the beginning.

Extension activity

Ask each student to take out a piece of paper. They are going to exchange "email correspondence" with their partner. At the top, they write, *To: (partner's name); From (their name); Subject: invitation*. Each person writes a short invitation. They then pass their paper to their partner. They read their partner's "emails" and reply. They must write a response and a question. They pass their paper back, and read and respond to the "email" and include another question. This continues a couple more times until they have agreed on a time and a place to meet or have agreed not to meet at all.

VOCABULARY

Topic vocabulary

Days, months, and time

Warm-up

Do a quick review of days, months, and times:

What are the weekdays?

What are the weekend days?

What months are spring, summer, fall, and winter months?

What time is it now? (Write times on the board or use a large clock and review how to tell time.)

Refer students to the *Days, months, and time* box to find out which word—*in*, *on*, or *at*—is used with days, months, and times. Note that we say *in* + month, but if there is a specific date, e.g., the fifth, then we use *on*.

1 Students write the days of the week in the right order. Note that in U.S. culture, Monday is the first day of the week, but in other cultures, Sunday is the first day. Wednesday is a tricky word to spell because the *d* is silent. Ask students to "look, say, cover, write" to practice the spelling of the days of the week. Remind students that days are always capitalized.

ANSWERS
1 Sunday **2** Monday **3** Tuesday **4** Wednesday
5 Thursday **6** Friday **7** Saturday

2 Students write the months in the correct order. They practice spelling with "look, say, cover, write." Remind students that in the U.S., the month goes before the date, so that August 2 is 8/2 and not 2/8. Remind students that months are always capitalized.

ANSWERS
1 January **2** February **3** March **4** April
5 May **6** June **7** July **8** August **9** September
10 October **11** November **12** December

3 Ask students to complete the sentences. Ask them to try to complete them without looking at the rules. After their attempt, they can look at the rules to check.

ANSWERS
1 at **2** on **3** on **4** in **5** on **6** on **7** on **8** on
9 in **10** at

Extension activity

Write some important dates, days, and times on the board in a random order. Write the dates in number format, e.g., 7/7. Students guess why the dates and days are important, e.g., STS: *July seven(th) is your birthday.* T: *Yes!* STS: *Saturday is the day you were born.* T: *No, something I always do.* STS: *You go shopping on Saturday.* T: *Yes!* STS: *Six forty-five is when you get up.* T: *No, it's in the evening.* STS: *When you get home?* T: *Yes!* Put students in pairs to repeat the activity.

VOCABULARY

Vocabulary builder

Degrees of possibility

Warm-up

Write a list of future predictions on the board or on a handout. In pairs, students decide if they think these things will happen, if they aren't sure if they will happen, or if they are sure they won't happen. Each pair writes one more prediction they are sure will happen and one they think maybe will happen. Pairs compare lists with other student pairs. As the class gives feedback, volunteers share their thoughts. On the board, write three columns, e.g., *Will happen (100% sure), Will happen (80% sure), Maybe will happen (50–50 chance), and Won't happen (0% chance).* As a class, put the predictions in the columns.

Example future predictions:

Robots will help us in our house.

We will have cars with no drivers.

People will not eat meat.

We will have flying cars.

Everyone will learn online.

There will not be any paper books.

There will not be any money, there will only be cash cards.

Use the results of the *Warm-up* to introduce the degrees of possibility in the *Degrees of possibility* box. For the "100%-sure" column, introduce the terms *sure*, *certain*, *definitely*, and *certainly*. T: *Are we sure this will happen? Are we certain? Yes, we are sure; we are certain. It will happen. It will definitely happen. It will certainly happen.* On the board, add *definitely* and *certainly* to one of the sentences in the column. Write: *We are sure / certain this will happen.*

Do the same for the remaining columns. Then help students create a summary of rules with examples. Students copy the rules into their notes.

1 Ask students to unscramble the words to make sentences. For lower-level students, cut up the scrambled sentences so that they can re-order them manually. Ask students to follow the rules they have just copied into their notes and use the notes in the skill box to help them.

ANSWERS
1 I will probably go to the cafeteria today.
2 The library is definitely closed tomorrow.
3 I am certain I can watch TV tonight.
4 I will possibly see my grandparents this weekend.

2 Ask students to answer the questions so that they are true for them. Pair lower-level students with higher-level students for support. Monitor and check their answers.

Extension activity

Use the theme of future trends to practice using the adverbs of possibility. Give pairs of students six to ten slips of paper. They write future predictions—one per slip—using *will* or *won't*. Alternatively, create a set of ten future predictions for each pair of students. Students put the slips facedown between them. Students take turns taking a slip and reading it, and then inserting (*definitely*, *certainly*, *probably*, or *possibly*). If students have written their own, they can exchange with another pair to repeat. Students then choose five and write them out. This could be turned into a poster project depending on time.

WRITING

Writing model

Read through the aims with the students. Remind them that each part of the *Writing* section will help them to build their skills for the successful completion of the *Writing task*.

A Analyze

Working alone, students read the questions and then read the model to find the answers. They compare in pairs before giving feedback to the class.

ANSWERS
1 Mr. Sloane 2 before June 11 3 the Grand Hotel

B Model

Students circle the correct words, and then compare answers in pairs. As the class gives feedback, volunteer students read the sentence where they found the information. Encourage students to underline the information in the text if needed.

ANSWERS
1 Puebla University 2 September 14 3 conference
4 airport

GRAMMAR

Simple present for future; *will* for intentions

Students read the *Simple present for future;* will *for intentions* box for homework so that they are ready for your presentation in class.

Warm-up

Ask students about events that are upcoming on campus, e.g., T: *Is anyone going to the game tonight? What time does it start?* Reformulate students' responses to include the present tense, e.g., T: *So it starts at 7?*

Review the form of simple present, using the board to write examples. Ask the students questions to ensure their understanding of the concept, e.g., *When do we add -s?* (with he, she, and it) *When do we say doesn't / don't?* Do a substitution drill, e.g., T: *The conference begins on May 5. Make it negative.* STS: *The conference doesn't begin on May 5.* T: *Make a question.* STS: *Does the conference begin on May 5?*

Review the form of *will*. Ensure that students don't add the third-person *-s* when using *will*. Do a substitution drill as with the simple present. Note that it's more natural to use the contraction in spoken English, e.g., *I'll*, *He'll*, etc.

Ask students which of the two forms we can use to talk about the future (both). Ensure that students understand that the simple present is used for future meaning when it's a scheduled, timetabled event. Ask students to underline the part of each sentence in the *Grammar* box that shows that the event is timetabled or scheduled. (*on May 5, on May 7, until 11:00*)

Students already understand that they use *will* for future. They now get a deeper understanding of how *will* is used for intended events in the future. Ensure that students understand the meaning of *intend* (http://www.macmillandictionary.com/dictionary/american/intend).

1 Ask students to complete the sentences alone, and then compare in pairs. As the class gives feedback, ask students when each thing happens to emphasize that this tense is used for scheduled events. For number 5, check the spelling of *goes* (not *gos*).

> ANSWERS
> **1** begins **2** gets **3** starts **4** doesn't end **5** goes
> **6** arrives **7** doesn't start **8** arrive

2 Refer students to the timetable next to the questions about the conference. Ask them to answer using complete sentences. This exercise also reviews prepositions. Refer students back to the presentation of prepositions on page 144 if needed.

> ANSWERS
> **1** The conference starts on April 18.
> **2** Talk 1 begins at 9:00.
> **3** Lunch ends at 1:00.
> **4** People ask questions at 4:00.

3 Ask students to complete the exercise alone. Then in pairs, students take turns to ask and answer the questions. This activity could be used as a "ticket out the door."

Exercises 4 and 5 could be done for homework.

4 Ask students to complete the sentences. Ask them to read the whole sentence when checking answers.

> ANSWERS
> **1** will call / 'll call **2** will book / 'll book
> **3** won't go / will not go / 'll not go **4** will go / 'll go
> **5** will stop / 'll stop **6** will invite / 'll invite
> **7** won't pay / will not pay / 'll not pay
> **8** will answer / 'll answer

5 As a way to vary this exercise, ask students to write their sentences on slips of paper. Put students into groups of three or four. Students put all their sentences into a hat or box and mix them up. One student takes out a slip and reads it. The group members must guess whose sentence it is.

WRITING

Writing skill

The language of emails

Warm-up

Write the following questions on the board. Students discuss in small groups, and then give feedback to the class. Find out who has the most email addresses, who sends the most emails, and who receives the most emails. For question 5, talk a little about informal vs. formal emails. Students will be learning about writing formal emails in this section.

How many email addresses do you have?

How often do you send emails?

How many emails do you receive a day?

Who do you email the most?

Is an email to your friend different from an email to your teacher? How?

Students read the *The language of emails* box. Check that they understand the concept of why emails are short with clear language and where the reason for writing is usually located.

1 Students may need some help understanding some of the terms—*greeting*, *identifying*, *stating*, and *signing off*. Allow plenty of time and the use of dictionaries. Fast finishers can help other students. If possible, give students an email template. In pairs, students use the information in the exercise to reconstruct the email.

> ANSWERS
> **1** f **2** b **3** j **4** g **5** i **6** c **7** d **8** e **9** h
> **10** a

2 Ask students to unscramble the phrases. As the class gives feedback, point out that these phrases don't vary much, i.e., they are fixed phrases. Students can learn and use them as they are. Note that *Thanks for ...* is less formal than *Thank you for ...*. Ask students to look back at the reading text on pages 141–142 to find one more way to sign off (*Best wishes*), and one more way to open (*Hello*).

> ANSWERS
> **1** Please see attachment. **2** All the best,
> **3** Thanks for your email. **4** It's on Friday at 3:00.

3 Ask students to read the email and put the sentences into the correct places. Note the way Sun-hee Kim signs off. Students can add this to their list of options.

> ANSWERS
> **1** b **2** a **3** d **4** c

WRITING

Writing task

Read through the *Writing task* with the students. Allow some time for students to review the content of the unit and identify language that will be useful for writing their email.

Brainstorm

Students work alone to brainstorm the details of their email.

Plan

Students work alone to plan their email. Ask them to number the information to help them put it in the right order and to decide what to include from the *Brainstorm* section. They should refer back to the parts of an email in the *Writing skill* section, Exercise 1, page 149.

Write

For this first draft, students use the email template in the book. Give students about 20–25 minutes of class time to write their emails, referring to the model on page 146 if needed. Ask students to write about 80 words in their email and to remember to use the key points, e.g., the use of the simple present tense for future, *will* and *won't* for things you plan to do, and to use the phrases and sentences from the language of emails. Students then complete the *Writing task* in class.

Share

Students exchange emails with their partner for peer review. Ask students to refer back to the parts of an email on page 149 and check that all the parts are there. They should check that the phrases for each section are correct.

Tell students to look at the checklist on page 189. They use the checklist to compare their writing in pairs and offer suggestions for improvement.

Rewrite and edit

Students read and consider their partner's comments and rewrite and revise their email. Ideally, they would write the email using their email account and email you their final version. In this case, provide them with a suitable subject line, e.g., *Job skills for the future invitation.* Check that they have used the right email convention and phrases. Email them back your comments and suggestions. Be sure to say what is done well in the work and give the student one or two targets to work on in future writing.

REVIEW

Wordlist

Students work in pairs or small groups to work through the *Wordlist*, checking that they all remember what each word or phrase means, how to pronounce it, and how it was used in the unit. Go through the list carefully with the class.

Vocabulary builder review

Students work through the sentences, check in pairs, and report back to the class.

> ANSWERS
> **1** probably **2** printer **3** large **4** several

Unit review

Students work through the list alone to decide what they can and can't do. They discuss their answers in pairs, including what they remember from the unit about each point. Finally, open up the discussion to include the whole class. Pay particular attention to any boxes that the students didn't check. Explore with them ways of overcoming any remaining problems.

Extra research task

In groups, students go online to find a new invention that they think will be very popular or which will change life for most people. They create a flyer that includes:

- a picture of the invention
- what it's called
- what it does
- how / why it will change life or be popular.

Students can post their flyers up on the class blog or print them out to bring to class to share.

9 JOBS

READING	Highlighting and annotating text
STUDY SKILL	Writing a résumé
VOCABULARY	Jobs
GRAMMAR	*Like, would like, be like*
WRITING	Supporting your writing by giving reasons

Warm-up

As a class, brainstorm jobs on the board. Ask students to think about jobs they know and jobs their friends or family members have. Once you have a number of jobs on the board, ask students which ones require a degree or qualification, experience, or special skills. Circle these. To apply for a job, students need a résumé, which is what they will learn to write in this unit.

Discussion point

Refer students to the picture and ask them what kind of jobs there are in this environment. (Possible answers: metal workers, builders, engineers, welders, etc.). Ask students what they think they would need to do to get a job like this. Pre-teach the word résumé and ask students what information they think a résumé contains. Note that résumé is pronounced /'rezuˌmeɪ/ not /rɪ'zum/. Sometimes you might see the word written with an accent over each *e*: résumé.

Ask students to read the infographic. Check that they understand *networking* (http://www.macmillandictionary.com/dictionary/american/networking). Explore each tip in a little more detail. For example, talk about how to connect with other people though career-specific social networking sites, or how to get some experience to put on a résumé. Spend some time discussing number 5; students may not have thought about what others can see about them, but assure them that employers will look for them online to find out more about them. Encourage them to think carefully before posting things. Assign them the task of doing an Internet search on themselves to see what comes up.

The process for searching for a job differs from country to country, so ask students to find out if the process is different in their country, maybe by asking an older relative who is working.

Ask students to discuss the questions with a partner.

Extension activity

Students go online to find information about two or three companies in the field they plan to go into. Suggestions for what information to find include, e.g., where the main company's headquarters are, how many employees, what they do, etc.

VIDEO

Before you watch

Introduce the topic of the video and ask students to read the exercise and identify any new words. Write these on the board and discuss the meanings as a class. Then, ask students to complete the *Before you watch* section. Monitor and go through the answers with the class.

ANSWERS
1 c **2** d **3** e **4** b **5** a

While you watch

Play the video once. Ask the students to watch the video and complete the exercise. Play the video again so that students can check their answers. Go through the answers with the class.

ANSWERS
1 F (He used to be a banker but now he is a farmer.)
2 T **3** T **4** F (The plants grow in a shipping container under artificial light.)

See page 108 for the video script.

After you watch

Put the students into pairs or groups and ask them to complete the exercise. Encourage them to use what they have learned in the video and the example answers to answer the questions. Go through the answers with the class.

READING 1

Looking for a job

A Vocabulary preview

Students can complete the *Vocabulary preview* exercises for homework if time is short.

1 Students match the words with their definitions. Drill pronunciation, especially the stress pattern of the multi-syllable words: *education*, *experience*, *full-time*, *manager*, *part-time*, *program*. Use the humming activity from the Teachers' book, page 83.

Practice spelling. Write the word on the board and ask the class to spell it in chorus. Erase one letter. The class spells the full word again. Continue to erase letters (randomly) until the class can spell the entire word without it on the board.

Note that *experience* is always singular in this context: *I have a lot of experience in cooking.* / *I have a lot of work experience.*

> ANSWERS
> **1** c **2** d **3** b **4** a **5** h **6** g **7** f **8** e

2 Ask students to complete the sentences with the words from Exercise 1. Show students collocations with *full* and *part-time*, e.g., *work full-time/part-time* and *have a full-time/part-time job.*

Put students into pairs or small groups and ask each pair to take out a sheet of paper. Give each pair a different vocabulary word which they write at the top of the page. They then write a sentence with that word. Pairs pass their paper to another pair. Each pair now has a piece of paper with another word and a sentence. They write another sentence with that word and pass the paper to a different pair. Continue in this way until each piece of paper has eight sentences with the one word and each pair has written eight sentences—one with each vocabulary word.

> ANSWERS
> **1** part-time **2** skill **3** experience **4** education
> **5** full-time **6** manager **7** goal **8** program

B Before you read

Students discuss the questions with a partner, and then volunteers give feedback about some of their ideas to the class. Ask students what some of the positives are to working while studying and what some of the negatives are. Be culturally sensitive to the issue of working while studying. In some cultures, students' sole job is to study, and working just for work experience would not be seen as desirable.

C Global reading

Identifying text types

1 Students quickly skim the reading to find the answer. As the class gives feedback, ask students a few more questions about the text, e.g., *Where would you find job advertisements like these? What headings are in the résumé?*

> ANSWERS
> three, résumé

2 Students skim the text to find the answer. As the class gives feedback, discuss the reason why travel writer is the best job for Katie. (Possible answer: She is already a Spanish teacher [Sept. 2016–Present]. Her work experience involves writing and photographic experience. She has IT skills including Photoshop®. Her hobbies involve writing and travel. She can read and write English and Spanish. She doesn't have three to five years of experience since finishing her degree to qualify for the professor role.) Ask students which job looks the most interesting to them (if any).

> ANSWER
> travel writer

D Close reading

Highlighting and annotating text

Students learn the skills of highlighting and annotating. By a show of hands, find out how many people write notes when they read a text. Do they do this only in English class? What kinds of things do they write? Refer students to the *Highlighting and annotating* box to find out (1) what highlighting is and why it is useful, and (2) what annotating is and what the three ways to annotate are.

1 Ask students to work alone to practice highlighting important information. (If they don't have highlighter pens, encourage them to get some. In the meantime, they can underline the information.) In pairs, they discuss why they chose to highlight certain information. As the class gives feedback, ask volunteers why they highlighted the information they did.

2 Working alone, students annotate the text. In pairs, they compare annotations. Higher-level students can help lower-level students with their annotations. As the class gives feedback, volunteers say what they annotated and why.

3 Ask students to read the text and answer the questions.

> ANSWERS
> **1** full-time **2** company **3** Colorado **4** six **5** has
> **6** two **7** two languages **8** can

E Over to you

Students discuss the questions in a group. As the class gives feedback, ask each group for their idea of a good interview question and write these on the board. Find out if there are any questions that are not allowed in their country, e.g., questions about age, race, religion, disability, marital status, national origin, pregnancy are all illegal questions in the U.S. Ask each group to make a list of what should go on a resume. Find out if there are any cultural differences in resumes. For example, in some countries, a photograph is required.

Extension activity

Students look online for some example résumés. They print one out that they like the look of and bring it to class. In pairs, they explain why they like the way it looks or the way it is formatted. Pair up again and repeat two or three times so that students get a wider exposure to résumé style and preferences. As the class gives feedback, ask students if there was anything that all the résumés had in common and if there is anything they have learned about a good résumé (Possible answers: clear layout, easy to read, not too long, it gives you an idea of who the person is, etc.).

STUDY SKILLS

Writing a résumé

With books closed, ask if students can remember what the headings were on Katie's résumé. Write these on the board. Students look back at the résumé on page 155 to see if they remembered them all. Brainstorm some of the things that you might put for each, e.g., for *Education*, you would put high school and college, but probably not elementary school. You also would put any courses you have taken outside of school and any qualifications you have.

Students read the *Writing a résumé* box. Ask them why they think the names, addresses, and dates for education and experience are important.

1 Ask students to check the ways of getting work and life experience that are possible for them. Then have them work with a partner to compare and discuss. Ask pairs to list one or two more ways of getting life or work experience. Possible answers include organizing a fundraising event or participating in a volunteer abroad activity.

2 Tell students to work alone to rank the interview questions, and then compare in pairs. Find out which questions students think would be difficult to answer and why. Students might need help thinking about what skills they have that would be useful to an employer.

Ask students to think about why employers ask these questions, e.g., what is it they want to find out. Give them a few minutes to discuss in pairs or groups of three, and then have the class give feedback. (Possible answers: Employers want to get to know who you are to see if you will fit into the company. They want to know if your goals fit their offer because if not, then you are unlikely to be happy in the job. With work experience and young people just starting out, employers don't expect a lot of work experience, but may want to see that you have some initiative. The skills show that you have something to offer and hobbies give insight into you as a person.)

Ask students if there are any other questions an employer might ask or if there is any other information they might put on a résumé. One possible addition might be *awards*.

3 Students work alone to complete their résumé. This could be done at home, with students typing their answers to produce an actual résumé. In class, students take turns conducting an interview, using the questions in Exercise 2.

Extension activity

Here are some suggestions for extension activities. Allow students to choose which one they would prefer to do.

- Students find out about local jobs from the newspaper or an online jobs search. There may be a local, job-search website they can subscribe to and get notifications of job openings. Students choose a job and write a résumé to fit.
- Students research to find out about opportunities for volunteering. The career center on campus would be a good place to start.
- Students find an online profile builder such as LinkedIn and begin to build their professional profile.

READING 2

Tell me about your job

A Vocabulary preview

Students can complete the *Vocabulary preview* exercises at home if time is short.

1 Students match the words with their definitions. Difficult words to pronounce include *choose* /tʃuz/ (note the /z/ sound makes the /u/ long) and *pass* /pæs/. Students add *pass* to their list of words with double consonants and *team* to their list of *ea* words. With books closed, say one of the vocabulary words and ask students if it is a noun, verb, adjective, or adverb.

You could introduce the noun form of *choose—choice* /tʃɔɪs/ and of *safe—safety*, or encourage higher-level students to find these word forms.

ANSWERS
1 b **2** d **3** a **4** c **5** g **6** f **7** e **8** h

2 Ask students to complete the sentences with the words from Exercise 1.

ANSWERS
1 forest **2** choose **3** pass **4** fire **5** alone **6** safe **7** outside **8** team

Extension activity

In pairs, students choose five or six words from either *Vocabulary preview* 1 or 2. They write a sentence with the word, but leave a blank space where the word should go. When they have written their fill-in-the-blank sentences, they pass their paper to another pair. Pairs should try to put the right word into the blank without looking in their books, but could use their books for support if needed.

Warm-up

Students interview each other about their working preferences.

Give each pair a handout with the following questions, or write them on the board. They take turns interviewing each other.

Do you like to work …

- alone or in a team?
- inside or outside?
- in the forest or on the beach?
- days or nights?
- with animals or people?
- part-time or full-time?
- as a manager or an employee?
- at home or in a company?

Your perfect job would be … (Students supply the answer.).

B Before you read

Put students in pairs with someone they don't normally work with to discuss the questions. As the class gives feedback, find out if anyone would like to be a forest ranger, flight attendant, or film editor.

C Global reading

Scanning

Students read the instructions, and then quickly scan the text to find one thing each likes and dislikes. Students compare answers in pairs.

POSSIBLE ANSWERS

1 **Likes**: working outside, working with people and animals **Dislikes:** working alone
2 **Likes:** to travel and go to some interesting places **Dislikes:** working on weekends, crowded planes
3 **Likes:** working with other people **Dislikes:** working long hours, low pay.

D Close reading

Highlighting and annotating text

Draw students' attention to the word *degree* in the text. Ask for a show of hands who is working towards getting a degree.

1 Students highlight what each person does.

POSSIBLE ANSWERS

Marcy: I look for any fires in the forest. I teach people. I sometimes work with groups of people.
Alex: I answer questions, help people with their bags, and serve food and drinks on planes. I also help keep people safe.
Lily: I look at the film one second at a time. I choose what to use and what not to use. I put the film together in an office.

2 Ask students to work alone to read and find out who does each of the things listed, according to the text. They then think about who else might also do these things. As the class gives feedback, ask volunteers to say why they think the other people do the things listed. For example, it's likely that Marcy has to answer questions from the people she teaches or the groups she works with.

ANSWERS

1 Alex (and Marcy) **2** Marcy (and Alex) **3** Lily (and Alex) **4** Alex (and Marcy) **5** Lily **6** Marcy **7** Alex **8** Marcy

3 Students answer the questions according to the information in the text. As the class gives feedback, encourage volunteers to use full sentences.

ANSWERS

1 They need to pass a test.
2 Because he often works on weekends.
3 Most people are nice, but sometimes they aren't friendly.
4 They usually need a degree.

4 Annotations are a personal thing, so students should annotate in a way that is useful to them. A reaction could include an exclamation mark if information is surprising, or might be a question or comment. Students compare annotations and say why they annotated in the way that they did. Support lower-level students by guiding them with questions, e.g., *Is there a new word you want to remember? Is there any surprising information or information that you want to remember? Is there any information that you want to find out more about?*

E Over to you

Ask students to discuss the questions in small groups. Ask them to rank, in order of importance, the four things listed in question 2. Are there any things that they would add to the list?

Extension activity

Organize a speaker (or group of speakers) to come to the class to talk about their job. You can often find local professionals who are willing to share some of their time. It could also be someone from within your organization. Ideally, the person would speak English, though it isn't crucial that they present in English—maybe just answer the students' questions in English.

As a class, write an invitation, using the skills learned in Unit 8. Students should prepare some questions ahead of time to ask the speakers about their jobs.

If you can't get a visitor to come into the classroom, you might be able to organize a VOIP call with a visitor instead.

VOCABULARY

Topic vocabulary

Jobs

Warm-up

Ask students what your job is to elicit *teacher*. Write this on the board. Ask students what a teacher does and write their ideas on the board, e.g., grades papers, helps students, plans lessons, etc.

1 Refer students to the pictures on page 162 and ask them what each picture shows. Check and drill pronunciation, and then ask students to write the job under the correct picture. Tricky words to pronounce include *chef* /ʃef/, *coach* /koʊtʃ/, *musician* /mjuˈzɪʃ(ə)n/, and *tour guide* /tʊr gaɪd/. Practice the stress patterns of *photographer*, *receptionist*, *musician*, and *police officer*. *Officer* is another word with double consonants for students to add to their list. Note that the job titles are not capitalized.

ANSWERS
1 musician **2** tour guide **3** police officer **4** artist
5 nurse **6** farmer **7** doctor **8** receptionist

2 Ask students to work alone to match the job with the action. As the class gives feedback, check that students are pronouncing *teaches* with two syllables. Note that the -*s* sounds like a /z/ after voiced sounds (*draw*, *clean*, *care*, *grow*, *play*, *bring*, *answer*, *show*) and like an /s/ after voiceless sounds (*cook*, *take*, *keep*).

In pairs, students test their memory for the jobs. With books open, Student A asks for the name of the job. Student B has the book closed and says the name of the job, e.g., ST A: *Who cooks food?* ST B: *A chef.* ST A: *Correct. Who draws or paints?* Have students change roles. For a bigger challenge, ask higher-level students to write one more thing each person does in their job, and use these in the activity described above.

ANSWERS
1 c **2** a **3** b **4** d **5** g **6** h **7** f **8** e **9** j
10 l **11** i **12** k

3 Tell students to work in pairs to complete the exercise. As a follow-up, ask students to create a table with three columns—Works in a restaurant, Works in a hospital, and Works in an office. They list the jobs in the correct column. Higher-level students write where the other people work (Possible answers: artist—studio; coach—school or sports facility; farmer—field or outside; musician—studio; photographer—studio or outside; a tour guide— outside.).

POSSIBLE ANSWERS
a restaurant: a chef
a hospital: a nurse, a doctor (a dentist)
an office: a receptionist (a police officer)

Extension activity

Put students into pairs to form a team, and then put pairs together to form competing teams. Give each team a set of cards with the names of jobs on one side. These should be put facedown in the middle. One person from Team A takes a card and mimes the job for the others. If their partner guesses, they get the point, but if the other team guesses, they get the point. Repeat with a person from Team B miming the job. To increase the energy, give teams a time limit, which they keep themselves. The teams have one minute to guess the job. Another variation is for the teams to try to guess as many jobs as they can in one minute.

VOCABULARY

Vocabulary builder

College jobs

Warm-up

Write this quote on the board: *Choose a job you love, and you will never have to work a day in your life.—Confucius.* Ask students to discuss in pairs what they think this quote means, and then have the class give feedback. Ask students if they think they could love a job working at the school.

1 Ask if students can quickly name a few academic jobs before asking them to complete Exercise 1. *Dean* is another *ea* word students can add to their list. Drill pronunciation and check that students are using the correct stress patterns for *career counselor*, *lab technician*, and *teaching assistant* (Both words are stressed in each case.). Difficult words to pronounce include *lecturer* /ˈlektʃərər/ and *technician* /tekˈnɪʃ(ə)n/.

Pay particular attention to spelling. With books closed, write the words on the board, leaving out the vowels. Say the words aloud. Students write the words out in full. Increase the energy by turning this into a team competition.

> ANSWERS
> **1** c **2** d **3** a **4** b **5** g **6** h **7** f **8** e

2 Ask students work alone to circle the correct words, and then compare in pairs. Students write their own sentences with the words and add them to the class vocabulary bank.

> ANSWERS
> **1** dean **2** lecturer **3** researcher **4** lab technician
> **5** career counselor **6** teaching assistant **7** tutor
> **8** librarian

3 Refer students to the picture. What do they think it shows? (Possible answer: a student talking to a career counselor) Students work in small groups to answer the questions. Put one student in charge of asking the questions and leading the discussion. This student should encourage everyone to answer. Provide sentence frames if needed, e.g., *What do you think, (Alexander)? Do you agree with him, (Marco)?*

Extension activity

In pairs or small groups, students find out the names of the dean, librarian, and career counselor at their institution. Ask them to find three more academic jobs, a definition, and the name of who does them. They can find the information on the institution website or ask around.

WRITING

Writing model

Read through the aims with the students. At the end of the *Writing* section, students revisit the aims and self-assess if they have learned them. Remind them that each part of the *Writing* section will help to build their skills for the successful completion of the *Writing task*.

A Analyze

On the board, write: *What kind of job would you like to have?* Ask students to think about the question. Remind them of the quote by Confucius (page 95 in the Teachers' Book).

Refer students to the model. Ask them where they think the text comes from. Have they ever posted comments on a web page? Why would *Education Matters* be interested in what kind of job people want?

Ask students to work alone and read the model. Remind them of the skill of highlighting. Students highlight the information. Students compare answers in pairs before giving feedback to the whole class.

> POSSIBLE ANSWERS
> **Two things the student is interested in:** art and computers
> **The job the student would like to have:** a graphic designer
> **Three reasons why the student would like the job:** they like to paint and draw; they love to make designs; a graphic designer can work with a lot of other people.

B Model

1 Remind students what annotation means. Then ask them to add the annotations listed to the correct place in the model. Pair up lower-level students with higher-level students for support.

> POSSIBLE ANSWERS
> **skills:** computer skills, use several computer programs
> **degree:** I would like to get my BA degree in graphic design …
> **where to study:** … at the University of Art & Design in Helsinki, Finland.
> **where to work:** I would like to work for a large design company in Europe.

2 Ask students to add one more annotation to the model, conferring with their partner if needed.

GRAMMAR

Like, would like, be like

Students read the *Like, would like, be like* box for homework so that they are ready for your presentation in class.

Warm-up

Bring in a picture of a person engaged in some sort of activity. Pass it around for students to see if it is small, and then stick the picture to the board. Create a backstory for the picture, e.g., *This is a picture of a friend of mine. In the picture, you can see her with her hat and hiking boots on. She's at the top of a very big mountain and she's smiling.* Ask students what they think her life is like. Write their ideas on the board under *Her life is ….* Ask students what they think she likes to do and doesn't like to do. Write their ideas on the board under *She likes to …* and *She doesn't like to ….* Tell them she doesn't have a job right now, but she is thinking about what job she would like to have. Ask students what job they think she would or wouldn't like and write their ideas on the board under *She would like to be… / She wouldn't like to be….*

Use the information on the board to introduce the three ways *like* is used. Draw students' attention to the difference between *like to do* and *would like*, e.g., *Does she have a job yet? No. But she would like a job, right? She likes to … Is this always true about her?* (yes). Ask individual students *What do you like to do?* to elicit *I like to….* Switch to *What would you like to do this weekend / this summer/ in the future?* to elicit *I would like to / I'd like to / I wouldn't like to ….* Draw students' attention to the fact that the answer to *What's … like?* must include an adjective. Ask individual students questions with *What's … like?* to elicit adjectives. Ask students what the short form of *would like* is. Refer them to the *Grammar* box to find the answer (*She'd like*).

1 Ask students to work alone to circle the correct words in the conversations, and then compare answers in pairs. As the class gives feedback, ask volunteers to say why they chose the answer they did.

ANSWERS

1 Do you like **2** like **3** would you like **4** like
5 Would you like **6** don't like **7** like **8** like
9 would like

2 Students match the sentence halves. Note that it is possible to use *like* in answer a to finish 2, 4, and 6, but number 6 only works with answer a. As the class gives feedback, volunteers read the full sentences.

ANSWERS

1 b **2** c **3** f **4** d **5** e **6** a

3 Ask students to work alone to correct the mistake in each sentence. Remind them that being able to find the mistake will help them edit their own work and make them more independent. In pairs, students take turns asking and answering the questions.

ANSWERS

1 Do you **like** to use a computer?
2 What **is** the pay like at your job?
3 I **don't** like to work with numbers.
4 What company **would you like** to work for?
5 I **wouldn't / would like** to be a professor.
6 What is your new job **like**?
7 Where **would** you like to work someday?
8 Our office manager doesn't **like** to work on weekends.

4 This exercise could be used as a "ticket out the door." Students write the answers in complete sentences.

Extension activity

Students paste a picture of a person onto a piece of paper. Around the picture, they write a few sentences about what the person *likes*, what he or she *would like*, and about what he or she *is like*. This could also be done as a recording using an app, or could be done as an online project.

WRITING

Writing skill

Supporting your writing by giving reasons

Warm-up

Ask students if they have ever been around a two-year-old child. What question do two-year-olds ask a lot? (They ask *Why …?)* Explain that even at a young age, we want to know the reasons for things, and giving reasons is also important in academic work. Ask students what word we use for giving reasons (*because*).

On the board, write *I like my job because I love to travel*. Ask students which part of the sentence is giving the reason, and then underline it. Write *I often work weekends, so I don't see my friends a lot*. Again, ask students to identify the reason and underline it. Circle the words *because* and *so*.

1 Ask students to read the *Supporting your writing by giving reasons* box, and then match the sentence halves. They underline the part of the sentence that gives the reason. Point out that when you use *because*, the reason comes after, but when you use *so*, the reason comes before. This distinction will help students who are having problems identifying which part of the sentence is the reason.

ANSWERS
1 d **2** e **3** f **4** a **5** c **6** b

2 This exercise may be challenging for some students who aren't able to identify which part of the sentence is the reason. Support lower-level students by first asking them to underline the part of the sentence that gives the reason. Another way to help is to ask Why …?, e.g., *Why would Jared like to be a tour guide? Why does Sam work nights and weekends? Does it make sense to ask "Why is Sam a police officer?" and answer "because he works nights and weekends"?* (no).

ANSWERS
1 because **2** so **3** so **4** because **5** so
6 because **7** so **8** because

3 Ask students to work alone, circle a word, and complete the exercise with their own ideas. Students then share their sentences with a partner. Monitor and check answers. This activity could be done as a "ticket out the door," and will show you if students have grasped the concept of giving reasons.

WRITING

Writing task

Read through the *Writing task* with the students. Explain that thinking about the job you would like to have can help you create goals / plans. Everyone has to ask themselves these questions at some point (and sometimes at many points) in their lives. Thinking about this now will also help in future interviews. Allow some time for students to review the content of the unit and identify language and topics that will be useful for the *Writing task*.

Brainstorm

The *Brainstorm* may work better if students think about the questions at home and come to class with ideas. Put students into pairs to ask and answer the questions. Help students think about their skills and experience—sometimes students think they have none, but it's often the case that they simply don't recognize them. (Note: More work will be done on skills in Unit 10.) Refer them back to the work they did in the *Study skills* section on page 157. Reassure students that even if they don't have the skills or experience now, they can take steps to build skills and get experience.

Plan

Students work alone or in pairs to plan their paragraph. To give them a sense of purpose for writing, tell them to imagine that the career counselor or possible employer will be reading the paragraphs. Having a sense of the audience will make the writing more meaningful. Ask them to look back at the *Brainstorm* section and include some of their answers to the questions. They could compare their ideas with another student pair to generate more ideas.

Write

Give students about 20–25 minutes of class time to write their paragraphs, referring to the model on page 164, if needed. Ask students to write about 90 words and to remember to use the key points, e.g., the use of *like* and *would like*. Students then complete the *Writing task* in class.

Share

Students exchange paragraphs with their partner for peer review. Ask them to highlight three things in the text they like and annotate the text with a question for their partner to answer. In pairs, they say why they liked what they highlighted.

Tell students to look at the checklist on page 189. They use the checklist to compare their writing in pairs and offer suggestions for improvement.

Rewrite and edit

Students read and consider their partner's question and rewrite and revise their paragraph on a clean sheet of paper or via a word processor, checking for errors before turning it in. This could be done for homework. Collect both the draft and final version to see what comments and edits students made.

REVIEW

Wordlist

Students work in pairs or small groups to work through the *Wordlist*, checking that they all remember what each word or phrase means, how to pronounce it, and how it was used in the unit. Go through the list carefully with the class.

Vocabulary builder review

Students work through the sentences, check in pairs, and report back to the class.

ANSWERS
1 librarian **2** calendar **3** definitely **4** lecturer

Unit review

Students work through the list alone to decide what they can and can't do. They discuss their answers in pairs, including what they remember from the unit about each point. Finally, open up the discussion to include the whole class. Pay particular attention to any boxes that the students didn't check. Explore with them ways of overcoming any remaining problems.

Extra research task

Video résumés (or video CVs) are a popular way for job seekers to get themselves noticed. Ask students to research how to create a video résumé or CV, and create one using the information they wrote in their paragraph. Share these on a class blog.

10 SKILLS

READING	Organizing information into a chart
STUDY SKILL	Checking your paragraphs
VOCABULARY	Collocations related to skills
GRAMMAR	*Can* for ability and possibility
WRITING	Writing paragraphs

Warm-up

Give each student a handout with the following mingle activity, or write it on the board for them to copy. Students talk to as many people as possible. When they find someone who says "yes," they write their name next to the relevant item, and then move on to talk to someone else. Ideally, they should end up with ten different names. Support lower-level students by giving them the sentence frames needed to ask the questions, e.g., *Do you like …? Are you …?* Students can add their own question at the bottom of the questionnaire.

Find someone who …	Name
likes to solve problems or puzzles.	
is good at sports.	
likes to study with friends.	
is good at explaining things to other people.	
is a fast learner.	
is good at remembering information.	
is good at writing.	
is a good cook.	
likes to give presentations.	
is good at following instructions.	
is good at / likes ______________	

Discussion point

Refer students to the photo on page 171. Ask them what they think the person likes doing or is good at doing and what skills he has. Students read the infographic. In pairs, students think of a job where the skills would be useful.

Students discuss the questions. Encourage them to give reasons for their opinion in question 1. For question 2, pre-teach *people skills*, e.g., someone who is good at working with others, understanding them, communicating effectively, etc. For question 3, conduct a poll using a polling app, online survey, or write the six skills on the board. Ask students to come up and check the ones they are skilled at. Students count the results and work out the percentages.

VIDEO

Before you watch

Introduce the topic of the video and ask students to read the exercise and identify any new words. Write these on the board and discuss the meanings as a class. Then, ask students to complete the *Before you watch* section. Monitor and go through the answers with the class.

ANSWERS
1 e **2** d **3** c **4** a **5** b

While you watch

Play the video once. Ask the students to watch the video and complete the exercise. Play the video again so that students can check their answers. Go through the answers with the class.

ANSWERS
1 sports **2** teacher **3** afternoon **4** work

See page 108 for the video script.

After you watch

Put the students into pairs or groups and ask them to complete the exercise. Encourage them to use what they have learned in the video and the example answers to answer the questions. Go through the answers with the class.

READING 1

Children and their skills

Ask students what skills children have and if they are different from the skills adults have. Which skills do children need to learn to become adults?

A Vocabulary preview

Students can complete the *Vocabulary preview* exercises at home if time is short.

1 Ask students to match the words and phrases with their definitions. In class, students compare answers. Note that there are two more *ea* words for students to add to their list, but the *ea* in *idea* has two syllables instead of one, making *idea* a three-syllable word. (*Real* is one syllable.) *Throw* is tricky to pronounce—the tongue is forward for the /θ/ sound, and then moves quickly back for the /r/ sound. Ensure that students are saying /θroʊ/ and not /θru/. Note that *try out* is a two-word verb that can be separated, e.g., *He wants to try out the new idea. He wants to try the new idea out.* With the pronoun, the verb must be separated, e.g., *He wants to try it out.*

In pairs, students test each other. Student A has the book closed and Student B reads the definition for Student A to supply the answer. Change roles and repeat.

Students practice the "look, say, cover, write" method to learn spelling. Repeat this again at least twice during the course of the unit.

> ANSWERS
> **1** c **2** b **3** d **4** a **5** e **6** h **7** g **8** f

2 Ask students to complete the sentences, and then compare answers in pairs. Brainstorm common collocations with some of the words. Possible answers include, e.g., *during*—the lesson, my studies; *future*—in the future; *idea*—a good / great/ bad idea; *improve*—improve a skill, improve quickly / slowly (you could also teach the noun form—*improvement*— to make a lot of improvement, a great improvement); *remember*—something, to do something; *throw*—a ball, something on the floor, something away; *try out*—something new.

> ANSWERS
> **1** improve **2** during **3** remember **4** try out **5** real **6** idea **7** throw **8** future

B Before you read

Previewing

Remind students how to preview a text, e.g., look at the layout, the title, and headings. Refer them to the glossary for new words that will come up in the text. At this stage, they aren't reading the text, just previewing it.

> ANSWER
> (See *Global reading*.)

C Global reading

Students skim the text quickly to see if their prediction is correct. After checking, ask students if their professors provide an online summary of lectures such as the one in the reading text. Why might they do this? Possible answers include to give to students who missed a lecture or to highlight the important points of the lecture for students to remember. Point out that lecture summaries don't replace the information gained from attending the lecture where it's possible to ask questions and where the teacher may give more information than they put into the summary.

> ANSWER
> a

D Close reading

Organizing information into a chart

1 Students read the text and highlight key information. To support students in this, talk about some of the things they might highlight in the first paragraph. Ask students what they think key information is—the name of the researcher? The dates? The summary of the lecture? Ask students to justify their decision.

Students compare what they highlighted with a partner. If they highlighted different things, they should explain to their partner why they felt the information was important.

Ask students how easy they would find it to study from the lecture summary. Would they use it as it is or do something different? Refer students to the *Organizing information into a chart* box. Check students' understanding of the concept by asking why putting information into a chart is a good idea.

2 Ask students to now add information from the text to the chart. Students can work in pairs for this, and may wish to re-create the chart in their notebook to give themselves extra writing space. Ask fast finishers to put the information on the board.

> POSSIBLE ANSWERS
> **Stage 1** 0 to 2: understand what they can see, feel, throw, or put things in mouth; understand things not in front of them (8 months); begin to understand language (2 years)
> **Stage 2** 2 to 7: their use of language improves; they begin to understand words, numbers, and pictures; can remember information and talk about things not in front of them; tell stories that are not real; start to ask questions (age 4)
> **Stage 3** 7 to 11: think about other people more; understand why things happen; begin to think like a scientist; can solve problems by trying out new ideas
> **Stage 4** 11 to 15: think in an abstract way; use symbols; think about different ways to do things; think about what is possible in the future

3 Ask students to match the sentence halves. Point out that the five sentences make a short summary. Find out when students have to summarize information in writing or orally (e.g., on exams, in research papers, to a professor to show they have understood something, etc.). Students reorder the sentences to write the summary in the space provided.

ANSWERS
1 c **2** a **3** e **4** b **5** d
Correct order for summary: 2, 3, 5, 1, 4

E Over to you

Ask students to discuss the questions in small groups. At the end of their discussion, ask them to write a short summary (one summary per group) of the discussion, e.g., *We think you can learn … as a child. We think it's best to learn … when you are …,* etc.

STUDY SKILLS

Checking your paragraphs

Pre-teach the term *topic*. Ask students what they talked about with their friends prior to class—the weather? School? The news? Other friends? Point out that these are all *topics*. Ask students how they start a conversation about a topic,e.g., would you come up to your friend and say, "He's OK now, though." No, you wouldn't because your friend wouldn't know what you were talking about. So, you would need to start with a topic sentence, e.g., "Did you hear that Dan had an accident on his bike?" This is true with speaking or writing— you need a topic sentence to lead into what you are going to say.

Refer students to the *Checking your paragraphs* box. When they have read the skills box, ask them why it's important to be able to check your own paragraphs. Some students think it's the teacher's responsibility to check, but one of the skills students need in higher education is independence from the teacher, so they need to be able to check their own work before handing it in. Discuss each tip in the checklist. Sometimes it's helpful if you re-read a paragraph a few hours after writing it—this can help you notice where edits are needed. Ensure that students understand what *link* means.

1 Ask students to read the paragraph and write the topic. Support struggling students by asking *What's the paragraph about?* Students highlight the topic sentence. Note that the topic sentence is usually the first sentence in a paragraph.

ANSWERS
Topic: my nephew Jason
Topic sentence: My nephew Jason is seven years old.

2 Students put the checklist tips into practice. They cross out the sentence that is not needed. As the students give feedback, ensure that they understand why it is not needed—it sounds out of place because the paragraph is talking about what Jason is good at—science and sports, and the sentence about a job interrupts that topic. Also, we wouldn't expect a seven-year-old to have a part-time job, so it's an odd thing to say in this topic about Jason.

ANSWERS
Cross out sentence: He doesn't have a part-time job.

3 Ask students to check where the sentence fits best.

ANSWER
After: He also is good at music.

4 Students choose which two sentences to combine using *and*. Note that they should be two sentences that are already together. As the class gives feedback, make sure students have a comma if needed.

5 Students rewrite the paragraph with the changes. This could be their "ticket out the door."

READING 2

The people I know

Warm-up

Ask students to write down the names of one or two people they are close to, e.g., friends or family. Ask *What are they like?* Students write a few adjectives or phrases to describe what they are like. In pairs, they share their descriptions. Ask volunteers to share with the class. Ask questions related to what the students have said that will also lead into the topic, e.g., *You said your friend works hard. Do you think she has clear goals? You said your brother never gets stressed. Is he a calm person?*

A Vocabulary preview

Students can complete the *Vocabulary preview* exercises for homework if time is short.

1 Ask students to match the words with their definitions. In class, students compare answers, and then check as a whole class. *Accountant* is another word with double consonants to add to the vocabulary bank, and *leader* is another *ea* word. If students have a *jobs* section in their notebooks, they can add *accountant* to that, too. Note that the *l* in *calm* /kɑm/ and the w in wrong /rɔŋ/ are silent. Ask students which two words on the list rhyme (care and share). With books closed, say the word. Students repeat and then say if the word is a noun, verb, or adjective. Practice spelling. Write a word on the board. Students look for ten seconds. Ask *How many letters?* Students dictate the spelling to you as you rewrite the word.

> ANSWERS
> **1** d **2** a **3** c **4** b **5** f **6** h **7** g **8** e

2 Ask students to use words from Exercise 1 to complete the sentences. They then compare answers with a partner and test each other. Student A has the book closed, and Student B reads the sentence, pausing where the blank is. Student A says what word goes in the blank. Change roles after four words.

Ask students questions to elicit the new vocabulary words, e.g., *What kind of person needs an accountant? What do you do when you are hurt?*

> ANSWERS
> **1** hurt **2** wrong **3** leader **4** accountant **5** share
> **6** fact **7** calm **8** care

B Before you read

Students quickly read the title and headings and look at the pictures. Ask students what kind of text this is (magazine article) and the type of magazine they think it is from (business magazine). In pairs, students look up the words in a dictionary. Drill pronunciation. Draw students' attention to the verb root of each word—*inspect, give, protect, supervise*. Do a quick drill to practice pronunciation: T: *Who inspects?* STS: *Inspectors*, etc.

Students predict what the text will say about each by matching the type with a description.

> ANSWER
> (See *Global reading*.)

C Global reading

Skimming

1 Students skim the text to see if their predictions were correct.

> ANSWERS
> **1** b **2** d **3** c **4** a

2 Ask students to skim the text again to decide if any of the descriptions fit them. Ask volunteers to say which and in what way.

D Close reading

1 Ask students to read the description of each type in the text and highlight positive things about each type and underline negative things.

> POSSIBLE ANSWERS
> (See answers for Exercise 2.)

Organizing information into a chart

2 Remind students of the organizing-information-into-a-chart skill they learned in *Children and their skills*. Students complete the chart. As the class gives feedback, encourage volunteers to give complete sentences, e.g., *Inspectors have clear goals … They are good with details. A good job for an inspector is …*, etc.

> POSSIBLE ANSWERS
> **1** **Positive:** have clear goals and work hard to meet them, good with details **Negative:** don't always work well with different people / ideas **Possible jobs:** accountants, web designers
> **2** **Positive:** good people skills, work well on a team **Negative:** sometimes not good at solving problems **Possible jobs:** nurses, salespeople
> **3** **Positive:** they are good listeners, they are good at understanding other people **Negative:** they can forget about their own work **Possible jobs:** teachers, librarians
> **4** **Positive:** they are always fair, they are born leaders **Negative:** they can sometimes hurt others **Possible jobs:** managers and business people

3 Ask students if the four types are completely different or if they share some similarities. In pairs, students find two types to fit each description.

> ANSWERS
> **1** Inspectors, Protectors **2** Inspectors, Givers (Protectors can remember details about other people.)
> **3** Givers, Protectors **4** Inspectors, Supervisors

E Over to you

Give students a few minutes to think about the answers to the questions before putting them in groups to discuss. Some students may be reluctant to talk about themselves. Point out that in a job interview, they will need to have confidence to describe themselves, so this is good practice.

VOCABULARY

Topic vocabulary

Collocations related to skills

Warm-up

Ask students if they remember what a collocation is (from Unit 5). Put students into teams of three or four. Write the word *play* on the board. Give teams three minutes to think of collocations with *play*. Exchange papers to check with one team reading aloud another's collocations. A correct collocation gets 1 point. Half points are given at the teacher's discretion. Example answers include, e.g., *play + (the) piano, (the) guitar, a game, a musical instrument, soccer, football, see a play, act in a play, play with toys*, etc.

Ask students what kind of skill playing the piano is—a life skill or a work skill (or both). Refer students to the *Collocations related to skills* box to find two more collocations related to skills. Ask students what part of speech *play*, *give*, and *write* are. The collocations in this section are all verb + noun.

1 Ask students to look at the pictures and write the correct collocation beneath them. After checking answers, students close their books. Call out the verb and have the students say the noun in chorus. Note the stress pattern. Both main words in the collocation are stressed, e.g., *cook a meal, drive a car*. For multi-syllable words, the stress falls on the first word and the stressed syllable of the second word, e.g., *give a presentation, solve problems, follow instructions*.

ANSWERS
1 drive a car **2** use a computer **3** cook a meal
4 give a presentation **5** manage money **6** lead a team
7 follow instructions **8** solve a problem

2 Ask students to complete the exercise alone, and then check in pairs.

ANSWERS
1 lead a team **2** follow instructions **3** use a computer
4 solve a problem **5** drive a car **6** cook a meal
7 manage money **8** give a presentation

3 Ask students to decide whether the skills from Exercise 1 are work skills, life skills, or both. In pairs, students justify their choices, e.g., *"Give a presentation" is a work skill because you usually give a presentation in a company. "Cook a meal" is a life skill unless you are a chef.*

POSSIBLE ANSWERS
Work skills: give a presentation, lead a team
Both: use a computer, manage money, follow instructions, solve problems, drive a car
Life skills: cook a meal

VOCABULARY

Vocabulary builder

Describing people

Warm-up

Bring in some pictures of well-known people that the students are likely to know. Hold up the pictures and ask *What's he / she like?* to elicit some adjectives. Stick them on the board to use later.

1 Ask students to match the adjectives with their definitions. Drill pronunciation. Note the stress pattern of *easygoing*. The *ea* in *creative* has two syllables to make a three-syllable word, e.g., *cre-a-tive*. *Funny* is another double consonant word to add to the word bank of doubles. Ensure that students don't confuse the words *quiet* and *quite*. *Sociable* has three syllables, not four, e.g., /ˈsoʊʃəb(ə)l/. Students use the "look, say, cover, write" method to practice spelling. They should do this at least two more times over the course of the unit.

ANSWERS
1 c **2** b **3** d **4** a **5** g **6** h **7** f **8** e

2 Students work alone to choose the correct adjective, and then compare answers in pairs.

ANSWERS
1 creative **2** funny **3** friendly **4** sociable **5** fair
6 polite **7** easygoing **8** quiet

3 Ask students to answer the questions alone. They should not just give a yes / no answer, but should give reasons for their opinion. In pairs, they take turns asking each other the questions and giving answers.

WRITING

Writing model

Read through the aims of the *Writing* section with the students. At the end of the section, students revisit the aims and self-assess if they have learned them. Remind them that each part of the *Writing* section will help to build students' skills for the successful completion of the *Writing task*.

A Analyze

1 Ask students to read the interview questions and notes. Point out that in notetaking, you don't have to write complete sentences. Refer students to the model paragraph. They highlight the information in the notes that the writer includes in the model. Ask students why they think the student didn't use all the information from the notes in her or his paragraph.

ANSWERS
(See answers below in Exercise 2.)

2 Students put the highlighted notes in the order the writer includes them in the model.

ANSWERS
Number the notes as follows:
1 people find her friendly, sociable
2 violin (in college band)
3 soccer, basketball, volleyball (leader)
4 yes, both
5 add very large numbers in her head

B Model

1 Students underline the topic sentence in the model. Ask students why this is a good topic sentence —does it tell us what the paragraph is going to be about? (Yes, we know that we are going to read about Suchin's skills.)

ANSWERS
My classmate Suchin is a very friendly and sociable person and has some interesting skills.

2 Students circle information about Suchin that the writer includes that is not in the notes. Ask students why they think the writer included this information—does it make the paragraph feel more complete?

POSSIBLE ANSWERS
I think Suchin can be a very good accountant or banker someday. It's clear that she has many useful skills and abilities.

GRAMMAR

Can for ability and possibility

Students read the *Can for ability and possibility* box for homework so that they are ready for your presentation in class.

Warm-up

Ask students if they have heard of a Venn diagram and if they understand what it means. (a drawing of circles that cross over each other, showing features shared by different sets [= groups of numbers]). Then draw a Venn diagram on the board. At the top of one circle, write *humans* and at the top of the other, write *robots*. Ask the students what goes in the middle (both). In pairs, students think of abilities a human has, a robot has, and both have. Give students a few minutes to write their ideas, and then share them with another pair. Get some ideas from each pair and write them on the board.

Introduce *can* and *can't* with the students' ideas, e.g., *So, a human can write a song, but a robot can't write a song. Both a human and a robot can play chess.* Be sure to use the reduced form of *can* in the sentence (/**kən**/) so that students get used to hearing it. Write your example sentences on the board. Underline *can / can't* + the verb. Ask students what the long form of *can't* is (cannot). Point out that we often use *cannot* in formal writing, but *can't* is more common in speaking and informal writing.

Ask students to make a yes / no question with the example and write it on the board, e.g., *Can a robot write a song?* Point out that to make the yes / no question, you just flip the subject and *can*: *A robot can* ➜ *Can a robot ...?* Do a substitution drill with some of the other ideas from the warmer, e.g., T: *Humans and robots can play chess.* STS: *Can humans and robots play chess?*

Ask students to think of a question with *What* and *can* and write it on the board, making corrections as needed, e.g., *What games can robots play?* If needed, show how the words change place from the statement to the question: *Robots can play games* ➜ *What games can robots play?* Conduct a substitution drill to practice this, e.g., T: *Humans can write songs. What.* STS: *What songs can humans write?*

Ask students if you have been talking about *can* for ability or *can* for possibility (ability). Point out that ability is related to skills. Possibility is for things that may happen, but we aren't sure if they will happen or not. Write, e.g., *I am able to, I know how to = I can. I'm not able to, I'm unable to, I don't know how to = I can't. It's possible for me to = I can. It's impossible for me to = I can't.*

1 Students work alone to find the mistakes, and then compare answers in pairs. As the class gives feedback, ask students to say why it's a mistake (see reasons below). This will help students internalize the rules.

ANSWERS
1 Mike can **go** to the library at 6:00. (Use the base form of the verb.)
2 What time **can you** come to our study group? (Word order in questions: *can* + subject + base verb)
3 Kevin **can't** play soccer today. (Needs apostrophe ['])
4 Can Jessica **speak** another language? (Use the base form of the verb.)
5 Adam can **be** very unfriendly sometimes. (Use base form of the verb.)
6 Where can we **put** our book bags? (Use base form of the verb.)
7 These notes **can't** be right? (Spelling mistake)
8 I think **you can** do anything you want in life. (Word order in statements: subject + *can* + base verb)

2 Ask students to work alone to rewrite each sentence in full. Compare in pairs. As the class gives feedback, ensure that students are pronouncing *can* with the reduced form.

ANSWERS
1 I can't speak French. 2 I can help you study.
3 Rachel can't use a computer. 4 Ben can join your club.
5 Pete and his wife can't meet us.
6 We can't follow these instructions.

3 This exercise could be challenging for some students, so provide cut-up questions for some students to reorder manually if needed. Students should write out the questions in full.

ANSWERS
1 What can you cook? 2 Can you solve problems easily?
3 Can you manage money well?
4 Where can students study at your college?
5 Can your best friend drive a car?
6 What can you use a computer to do?

4 Ask students to work with a partner. Student A asks Student B the questions from Exercise 3 and writes down Student B's answers. Then change roles and repeat. Student pairs compare answers.

5 This could be done for homework or in class as a "ticket out the door."

WRITING

Writing skill

Writing paragraphs

The way a text in English is organized may differ from the way texts are organized in other languages, and students may not be aware of this difference. English is very linear and follows a pattern of main idea, supporting ideas, and a conclusion. This structure can seem overly simplistic to students from cultures that take a different approach. In some cultures, for example, it's not considered very sophisticated to state the topic—the writer writes around the topic and the reader infers it. It's worth raising students' awareness to any differences in text organization. Ask students if this structure is the same or different in their language.

On the board, write *How is a paragraph organized in English?* Find out what students already know, and then refer them to the *Writing paragraphs* box to remind them about checking paragraphs.

1 Ask students to work alone to decide if the statements are *T* (True) or *F* (False). Compare answers in pairs. Discuss any incorrect answers in more depth to raise student awareness of their expectations regarding paragraph structure.

ANSWERS
1 T 2 T 3 F (It is usually near the beginning of a paragraph.) 4 T 5 F (The concluding sentence usually ends the paragraph.)

2 Ask students to read the paragraph and follow the instructions. Compare answers in pairs before the class gives feedback.

ANSWERS
Mainly about and topic sentence's main idea: Children … when they are 11 to 15 … think in an abstract way.
Concluding sentence: They have a deeper understanding now of what is right and what is not.

3 Students put the paragraph in order. As the class gives feedback, discuss the omitted sentence and why it doesn't fit.

POSSIBLE ANSWERS

1 My aunt has several skills and can do many interesting things.
2 She can speak or understand several languages, such as Spanish and Portuguese.
3 She is very funny, and can make people laugh easily.
4 She can also do many things at the same time, and is always calm.
5 All of these things help her in her job as a nurse.

Extra sentence: She is sometimes tired and quiet.

4 Students re-write the paragraph, changing the sentences to make it about someone they know.

WRITING

Writing task

Read through the task with the students. Ask students when they might have to talk about another person's skills and abilities. Examples might be, e.g., before presenting them with an award, when introducing them before they give a speech or presentation, when introducing them to another person. Allow some time for students to review the content of the unit and identify language and topics that will be useful for the *Writing task*.

Brainstorm

Students read the questions. Higher-level students can write some of their own questions. In pairs, they take turns interviewing each other and making notes about what the other person has said.

Plan

Students work alone or in pairs to plan their paragraph, e.g., by looking back at their *Brainstorm* section and deciding what information they want to include, the order of the sentences they want to write about it, and writing a topic sentence.

Write

Give students about 20–25 minutes of class time to write their paragraphs, referring to the model on page 182 if needed. Ask students to write about 100 words about a classmate and to remember to use the key points, e.g., to include a topic sentence and concluding sentence, to ensure all the sentences support the topic sentence, and to pay attention to the use of *can*. Students then complete the *Writing task* in class.

Share

Students exchange paragraphs with their classmates for peer review. They should decide if the paragraph describes them well. Students can use the checklist on page 189 to support their review, and they should annotate the paragraph with one or two questions or comments. They should use the checklist to compare their writing in pairs and offer suggestions for improvement.

Rewrite and edit

Students read and consider their partner's questions and comments and rewrite and revise their paragraph on a clean sheet of paper or via a word processor, checking for errors before turning in. This could be done for homework. Collect in both the draft and final version to see what comments and edits students made.

REVIEW

Wordlist

Students work in pairs or small groups to work through the *Wordlist*, checking that they all remember what each word or phrase means, how to pronounce it, and how it was used in the unit. Go through the list carefully with the class.

Academic words review

Students work through the sentences, check in pairs, and report back to the class.

ANSWERS

1 researchers **2** sociable **3** creative **4** expensive

Unit review

Students work through the list alone to decide what they can and can't do. They discuss their answers in pairs, including what they remember from the unit about each point. Finally, open up the discussion to include the whole class. Pay particular attention to any boxes that the students didn't check. Explore with them ways of overcoming any remaining problems.

VIDEO SCRIPTS

Unit 1: Self

NARRATOR: People think Norway is a happy country. Cecilia lives in Norway. She says it's nice when the weather is good.

CECILIA, SPEAKING (ENGLISH): Especially in the spring I think because then it's bright and light and the heat is coming. Then we are happy.

NARRATOR: Some people also think *Denmark* can be the number one happy country.

STIG, SPEAKING (ENGLISH): It's difficult to compare, but I find most people there are satisfied with their day-to-day life so yes, why not?

MARIA, SPEAKING (ENGLISH): I think Norway is happier than Denmark because they have more money.

NARRATOR: ... People in Denmark and Norway say they are happy – so these two countries are doing something right.

Unit 2: Family

NARRATOR: It is the day before Chinese New Year. This day is very important in China. Zheng Luo, from Beijing, says this is a time for food, family, and friends.

ZHENG LUO, SPEAKING (CHINESE): We make dumplings and buy all the decorations we need and put them up in our home. Then on New Year's Day, we go around to visit our family and friends at their houses.

NARRATOR: There is a lot to do before the celebrations can begin. This is a market. People buy fireworks here.

NARRATOR: Before New Year's Day people buy food. They cook a special meal for their friends and family. Everyone wants to have a great New Year.

Unit 3: Study

NARRATOR: This is a hotel. It's in Georgia, in the mountains. It is special. Rooms are in big metal boxes called "containers".

NARRATOR: You can see the mountains from every window.

NARRATOR: This is Iraki Eristabvi. He says that people want to stay in his hotel. They think it's interesting and comfortable.

NARRATOR: All rooms have one or two beds. They have big windows, wardrobes, and desks.

NARRATOR: If you can put a hotel in big metal boxes, can you use them for a study space?

Unit 4: Money

NARRATOR: It is a cold winter's day here in the city of Prague, in the Czech Republic. This is the Czech National bank.

NARRATOR: These people are learning about money. The bank uses computers to compare notes and coins.

NARRATOR: Marek Petrus works for the Czech National bank. He says you can use a computer or a tablet to see more information about a real note.

MAREK PETRUS, SPEAKING (ENGLISH): The application allows users to view bank notes and coins of the Czech currency in detail on their mobile devices.

NARRATOR: You can move the image of the note on your screen. This helps you to see every part of it.

NARRATOR: A real note has something called a watermark. If the watermark on your note is not correct, you know there is a problem with your money!

Unit 5: Taste

NARRATOR: Here in Egypt, people go to the food carts to buy "ful medames". "Ful" is a dish made with beans.

NARRATOR: Some new restaurants in Cairo also serve Egyptian dishes like "ful".

NARRATOR: But people who work at the food cart say their food is really the best.

RAMADAN, SPEAKING (EGYPTIAN ARABIC): This is what we do and nobody can do it like us. We cook it right here. We cook it differently.

NARRATOR: Cairo Kitchen is a new restaurant in Cairo. Nadine Bashir is the owner.

NADINE BASHIR, SPEAKING (EGYPTIAN ARABIC): What makes us different is how we serve our food. We are a kitchen, you come inside you can choose what you want to eat from the kitchen.

NARRATOR: Which is the real Egyptian food then – the one from a street cart or the one from a new restaurant?

Unit 6: Health

NARRATOR: This is a robot show. It's in Tokyo, in Japan. There are many robots in Japan. This robot, called Taizo, is showing people how to exercise.

NARRATOR: One in four people in Japan is more than sixty-five years old. Robots like Taizo can help them stay healthy.

NARRATOR: At the exhibition, a man is wearing a robot suit called HAL. It can make people stronger and help them walk.

NARRATOR: This is Paro. Yukitaka Kawaguchi talks to people about it. He says Paro doesn't need much time or money.

YUKITAKA KAWAGUCHI, SPEAKING (JAPANESE): It is hard for old people to take care of pets. They are too expensive. They buy this robot and really like it.

Unit 7: Places

NARRATOR: Every park has benches for people to sit on.

NARRATOR: But this bench, in Boston, a city in the U.S., is special.

NARRATOR: It's called a Soofa. It charges your phone. The benches get their power from the sun. You use a cable to connect to the bench. Then you wait for your phone to charge – easy!

NARRATOR: Every Soofa bench uses the internet, so it can tell the company when it gets energy from the sun, and when people use the bench.

NARRATOR: Mark Woods is visiting Boston. He thinks it's good that Soofa uses solar power.

MARK WOODS, SPEAKING (ENGLISH): I think that having a space that is solar powered, which is great for green energy, is really the wave of the future in terms of cities providing services to people.

NARRATOR: Soofas are good for the environment and fun to use. Do you want to have one in your city?

Unit 8: Plans

NARRATOR: This is iHub. It's in Nairobi, in Kenya. It opened in 2010. About 100 developers work here, making computer software.

NARRATOR: Developers at iHub make apps to help people. They also make mobile games.

NARRATOR: People who like technology are called techies. Techies come to iHub to talk about their ideas.

NARRATOR: Joe Njeru works at iHub. Joe thinks this is a good time for technology in Africa. He says it can solve some of Africa's problems.

JOE NJERU, SPEAKING (ENGLISH): There has never been a better time to be a developer in Africa, we have so many problems and they need solutions, which can use technology.

NARRATOR: For developers like Joe, this is an exciting time to make new apps for Kenya. And iHub is where they meet to do it.

Unit 9: Jobs

NARRATOR: Erik Groszyk was a banker, but now he is a farmer. Erik doesn't like spending each day behind a desk. He wants to do something else.

NARRATOR: His farm is not a normal farm. It is a farm in the centre of New York City.

It is in a 40-foot container in a Brooklyn parking lot.

NARRATOR: Nabeela Lakhani also works on the farm.

NABEELA LAKHANI, SPEAKING (ENGLISH): I've always been interested in food ever since I was in high school. I read Fast Food Nation and I was like, "This is insane. I have to do something about it."

NARRATOR: Nabeela learned about food at New York University. She thinks fast food is bad for the health of American people.

NABEELA LAKHANI, SPEAKING (ENGLISH): I want to figure out the problem before, you know, before the food ruins our society.

NARRATOR: Erik and Nabeela sell their products to local businesses who want food they can trust.

Unit 10: Skills

NARRATOR: These young people want to be Olympic champions. They are at the Schichahai sports school in Beijing. Children first come here when they are eight years old. They do many sports.

NARRATOR: But they also have normal lessons. Zhang Jing is a teacher at the school.

ZHANG JING, SPEAKING (CHINESE): Some people like doing sports a lot. They can work hard and be champions. But everybody needs to learn. After all, there can only be one champion.

NARRATOR: Today, children at sports schools in China learn more than just sports. Students at Shichahai go to school five days a week.

NARRATOR: They have lessons in the morning and do sports in the afternoon.

ANSWER KEY

UNIT 1 SELF

Discussion point

1

1 Japan 2 Four 3 China

2

Students' own answers

Video

Before you watch

1 d 2 a 3 c 4 b

While you watch

1 two
2 four (including the narrator)
3 happy
4 weather

After you watch

Students' own answers

Reading 1

A Vocabulary preview

1

1 March 5
2 19
3 Saudi Arabia
4 Cairo
5 555-7711
6 family
7 France
8 2018

2

1 language
2 birthday
3 hobby
4 name
5 email address
6 city
7 age
8 country

B Before you read

A title, pictures, captions

C Global reading

1 new
2 four
3 different countries

D Close reading

1

1 F (Bianca is from Brazil.)
2 T
3 T
4 F (Nilay's birthday is on April 10.)
5 F (Bianca studies sports science.)
6 T

2

1 Kenichi
2 Nilay
3 Kenichi, Bianca
4 Ahmed, Nilay
5 Ahmed, Kenichi
6 Bianca, Kenichi

E Over to you

1 and 2

Students' own answers

Study Skills

1 and 2

Students' own answers

Reading 2

A Vocabulary preview

1

1 c 2 d 3 a 4 b 5 h 6 g 7 f 8 e

2

1 favorite
2 class
3 first
4 movie
5 club
6 easy
7 second, third

B Before you read

1 three
2 students
3 student magazine

C Global reading

1 They speak English.

D Close Reading

1

	Leila Abboud	Diego Garcia	Ji-won Kim
Age	20	18	21
Year	second	first	third
City	Sharjah	Tijuana	Busan
Country	United Arab Emirates	Mexico	South Korea
Studies	biology	music	east Asian history
Languages	Arabic, English, French	Spanish, English	Korean, English, Japanese, Chinese

2

1 old
2 movie
3 soccer
4 music
5 Chinese
6 teachers

E Over to you

1

Students' own answers

2

Students' own answers

3

Students' own answers

Topic vocabulary

1

1 France
2 Russia
3 Thai
4 Japanese
5 Thailand

2

1 France
2 Russia
3 Italy
4 China
5 Japan

3

1 Spanish
2 Korean
3 German
4 Portuguese
5 Thai

4

Students' own answers

Vocabulary builder

1

1 c 2 f 3 a 4 e 5 d 6 b 7 h 8 g

2

1 Marta studies business.
2 David studies music.
3 Kwame studies art.
4 Ana studies history.
5 Kurt studies sports science.
6 Yumiko studies geography
7 Lucy studies film studies.
8 Omar studies science.

Writing model

A Analyze

1 c 2 e 3 a 4 b 5 d 6 h 7 i 8 j 9 g 10 f

B Model

2

1 e 2 a 3 f 4 b 5 c 6 g 7 h 8 d

Grammar

1

1 is	3 am	5 is	7 is
2 am	4 is	6 are	

2

1 is	4 is	7 is	10 are
2 is	5 is	8 is	11 is
3 am	6 is	9 is	

3

1 Cassie is 23 years old.
2 Max is not in a club this year.
3 I am not a second-year student.
4 Tomas is a film student from Panama.
5 The teachers at this college are great. / The teachers are great at this college.
6 Korean and Chinese are not easy. / Chinese and Korean are not easy.

4

1 Are you 20 years old? Yes, I am.
2 What is your last name?
3 Where are you from?
4 Is your area of study English?
5 Are you a new student here?
6 How are your classes?

5 and 6

Students' own answers

Writing skill

1

1 Derek speaks Greek and Italian.
2 Karachi is a large city in Pakistan.
3 My friend Roberto is from Bogota, Colombia.
4 Berlin, Munich, and Cologne are cities in Germany.
5 People speak French and English in Canada.
6 Our teacher is from Los Angeles, California.

2

1 Isobel and Paul are first-year students.
2 Justine speaks English and Spanish.
3 Achara reads and writes Chinese.
4 Mark and Hassan are business students.

3

Students' own answers

Review

Vocabulary builder review

1 art   2 geography   3 history   4 film studies

UNIT 2 FAMILY

Discussion point

1

1 5%   3 a friend
2 8:00 and 9:00

2

Students' own answers

VIDEO

Before you watch

1 d   2 a   3 c   4 b   5 e

While you watch

1 China   3 buy
2 visit   4 cook

After you watch

Students' own answers

Reading 1

A Vocabulary preview

1

1 d   2 c   3 a   4 b   5 h   6 f   7 e   8 g

2

1 spend	3 apartment	5 pet	7 exercise
2 clean	4 Both	6 normal	8 cash

B Before you read

1

b families in the U.K.

2

Students' own answers

C Global reading

children, food, money, exercise

D Close reading

1

1 b   2 b   3 a   4 a   5 b   6 a

2

1 outside   2 cash   3 exercises   4 normal

E Over to you

1

Students' own answers

2

Students' own answers

Study skills

Students' own answers

Reading 2

A Vocabulary preview

1

1 c   2 a   3 d   4 b   5 h   6 f   7 e   8 g

2

1 once	3 meal	5 twice	7 special
2 keep	4 busy	6 Everyone	8 game

B Before you read

1

Students' own answers

2

Six students

C Global reading

Photo 1: Jared   Photo 2: Suzie

D Close reading

1

1 c   2 f   3 d   4 e   5 b   6 a

2

1 old	3 twice	5 once	7 pizza
2 fish	4 first	6 has	

E Over to you

1

Students' own answers

2

Students' own answers

Topic vocabulary

1

Male: brother, father, husband, grandfather, nephew, son, uncle
Female: aunt, daughter, grandmother, mother, niece, sister, wife

2

1 grandmother
2 niece
3 aunt
4 nephew
5 grandfather
6 uncle
7 brother
8 father

3

Students' own answers

Vocabulary builder

1

1 My mother cooks pizza once a week. / Once a week my mother cooks pizza.
2 I chat with my brother every night. / Every night I chat with my brother.
3 I talk with my parents twice a month. / Twice a month I talk with my parents.
4 I cook for my family every week. / Every week I cook for my family.
5 My aunt and uncle visit us twice a year. / Twice a year my aunt and uncle visit us.
6 My family goes to a restaurant three times a month. / Three times a month my family goes to a restaurant.

2

1 I text my sister every day.
2 My family calls once a week.
3 My grandparents visit me three times a year.
4 My mother has breakfast with my father every day.
5 I watch an old movie with my mother twice a month.
6 My father takes my picture once a year.

3

Students' own answers

Writing model

A Analyze

2

✓ her parents' names
✓ her brothers' ages
✓ what her mother always does
✓ how often they go to school
✗ what her father sometimes does
✗ how often Talia goes to school
✓ her brothers' names
✓ how often Talia studies

B Model

1 e 2 h 3 a 4 d 5 g 6 b 7 f 8 c

Grammar

1

1 They
2 She
3 his
4 We
5 your
6 My
7 His
8 My, Its

2

1 her
2 Their
3 Its
4 Their
5 His
6 Her
7 Their
8 Our

3

1 They
2 We
3 Our
4 His
5 You
6 It
7 My
8 She
9 We
10 Their

4

1 My uncle has a new car. It is / It's very nice.
2 I don't live with my family. I live alone.
3 Do you and your brother live with your family?
4 Our parents live in Los Angeles. They visit me once a month.
5 My sister lives in Germany, but her daughter lives in France.
6 My father likes sports. His favorites are baseball and soccer.
7 I want to write to your niece. Do you have her email address?
8 Mr. Hariri and his new wife live in Oman. Their children live there, too.
9 I really like your new home. It is / It's a special place for your family.
10 My nephew and I like to play games. They are fun on a Sunday afternoon.

Writing skill

My family is very special to me. I live with my parents and my grandmother. We live in an apartment in Shanghai.
My father is a taxi driver. He works all day. My mother works in a restaurant. Her restaurant is open all day. They both work very hard.
I go to college. It is very good, and I get good grades. I like my teachers. They help me a lot. I study business. It is not easy.
I have a sister. Her husband is a college professor. They live in Wuhan. They have a new baby boy. His name is Jinhai.

Review

Vocabulary builder review

1 business 2 once a year 3 music 4 every week

UNIT 3 STUDY

Discussion point

Students' own answers

VIDEO

Before you watch

1 b 2 a 3 d 4 c

While you watch

1 T
2 F (The weather is cold and it snows.)
3 F (The hotel is in big metal boxes.)
4 T

After you watch

Students' own answers

Reading 1

A Vocabulary preview

1

1 a 2 c 3 d 4 b 5 g 6 e 7 h 8 f

2

1 shelves
2 bed
3 closet
4 dresser
5 roommate, sofa
6 poster, dorm

B Before you read

1

Students' own answers

2

Picture 1: window, bed(s), desk(s), chair(s), lamp(s), TV, dresser(s), shelf / shelves
Picture 2: window, bed(s), desk(s), chair(s), lamp(s), TV, dresser(s), closet(s), poster(s)
Picture 3: window(s), bed, desk, chair, lamp, sofa, dresser, shelves, closet

C Global reading

Picture 1: Megan
Picture 2: Kyle
Picture 3: Rachel

D Close reading

1

1 Megan, Kyle
2 Kyle, Rachel
3 Megan, Kyle
4 Megan, Kyle
5 Megan, Kyle
6 Megan, Kyle
7 Kyle
8 Rachel

2

1 T
2 F (Megan doesn't have a picture of her closet.)
3 T
4 F (He keeps his books on the floor.)
5 T
6 F (Her room has a desk lamp.)
7 T
8 F (She lives alone.)

E Over to you

Students' own answers

Study skills

1

1 parents
2 kitchen
3 printer
4 teachers
5 library
6 photocopier

2 and 3

Students' own answers

Reading 2

A Vocabulary preview

1

1 c 2 d 3 b 4 a 5 f 6 h 7 e 8 g

2

1 plant
2 electricity
3 light
4 neat
5 office
6 best
7 messy
8 open

B Before you read

b where people work

C Global reading

Messy is best 4
Keeping it green 3
Family and friends 1
Lots of light 2

D Close reading

1

1 b 2 c 3 c 4 c 5 a

2

1 work
2 neat
3 open
4 spaces
5 pictures
6 make

E Over to you

Students' own answers

Topic vocabulary

1

1 The book is on the table.
2 The phone is under the bed.
3 The lamp is in the closet.
4 The man is by the shelves.
5 The book is in front of the TV.
6 The plant is behind the sofa.
7 The TV is on the dresser.
8 The poster is on the wall.
9 The box is under the chair.

2

Students' own answers

Vocabulary builder

1

1 map
2 folder
3 tablet
4 notebook
5 highlighter pen
6 calendar
7 printer
8 flash drive

2

1 map
2 tablet
3 notebook
4 highlighter pen
5 calendar
6 printer
7 flash drive
8 folder

3

Students' own answers

Writing model

A Analyze

1 d 2 e 3 f 4 b 5 a 6 c

B Model

b

Grammar

1

1 has
2 has
3 have
4 Does, have
5 has
6 have
7 Do, have
8 has

2

1 don't have
2 has
3 doesn't have
4 doesn't have
5 don't have
6 don't have
7 doesn't have
8 don't have

3

1 Do Ken's walls have posters on them?
2 Does your office have a big window?
3 Does their room have blue walls?
4 Does Maria have a small dorm room?
5 Does your teacher have office hours from 1:00–2:00?
6 Do they have a class at 10:00?
7 Does Paul have a room on the third floor?
8 Do your parents have four bedrooms in their house?

4

1 Joe and his roommate have a dorm with a big closet.
2 Do you have chairs in your room?
3 We don't have class on Friday.
4 Does Mr. Wilson have many students in this class?
5 Does your university have a lot of green space?
6 Sarah doesn't have a roommate this year.
7 Do you and your friends have fun in class?
8 Jake doesn't have a computer now.

5

Students' own answers

Writing skill

1

1 I have a poster and a calendar on my wall.
2 Dan's room has two dressers and one closet.
3 My study space is in the corner and on the second floor.
4 Jim and his roommate have a large red chair.
5 Emiko's dorm is very big and sunny.

2

1 She also has a small desk lamp.
2 He has a table in front of the sofa, too.
3 Patricia's dorm is also on the third floor.
4 He has a big closet, too.
5 Paula's room also has three windows.

Writing task

Brainstorm

Possible answers

desk, wall, shelves, laptop, flash drive, soccer poster, digital clock, calendar, printer, paper, highlighter pens

Review

Vocabulary builder review

1 science
2 notebooks
3 every morning
4 highlighter pen

UNIT 4 MONEY

Discussion point

Students' own answers

VIDEO

Before you watch

1 d 2 c 3 b 4 a

While you watch

1 c 2 d 3 a 4 b

After you watch

Students' own answers

Reading 1

A Vocabulary preview

1

1 d 2 c 3 a 4 b 5 g 6 e 7 h 8 f

2

1 gift, type
2 save, grow
3 careful, credit card
4 dream, worry

B Before you read

Students' own answers

C Global reading

1

b

2

1 The Saver
2 The Giver
3 The Builder
4 The Spender

D Close reading

1

1 Givers
2 Builders
3 Spenders
4 Givers
5 Savers
6 Builders
7 Savers
8 Spenders

2

1 d 2 b 3 a 4 c

E Over to you

Students' own answers

Study skills

1

A 35% Brazil
B 30% Mexico
C 20% Japan
D 10% China
E 5% Oman

2

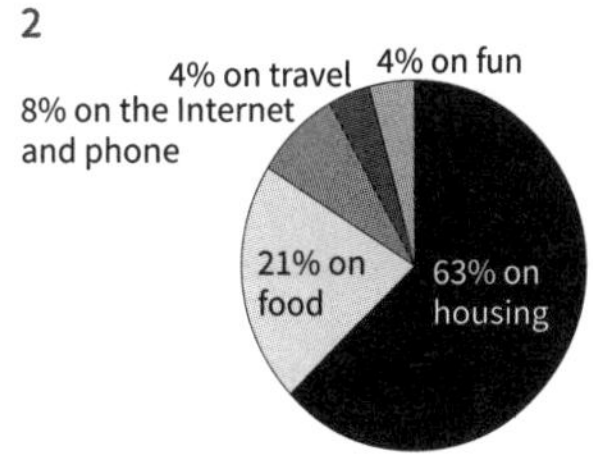

3

1 James
2 Paul

Reading 2

A Vocabulary preview

1

1 d 2 c 3 b 4 a 5 f 6 h 7 g 8 e

2

1 cost
2 add
3 daily
4 snack
5 gas
6 bill
7 rent
8 fast food

B Before you read

a class website

C Global reading

1

1 three
2 day
3 cell phone

2

1 c 2 b 3 c

D Close reading

1

Marissa Carlson

2

1 T
2 T
3 T
4 F (He usually has his meals at home.)
5 F (She lives in a dorm.)
6 T

3

1 rent
2 food
3 coffee
4 bus
5 dorm
6 car

E Over to you

Students' own answers

Topic vocabulary

1

1 800
2 12
3 6,202
4 77
5 14
6 105
7 3,200
8 563
9 18
10 25,000

2

Students' own answers

Vocabulary builder

1

1 b 2 a 3 d 4 c 5 h 6 g 7 f 8 e

2

1 about
2 between
3 one-fourth
4 over
5 exactly
6 around

3

1 e 2 b 3 f 4 c 5 h 6 d 7 a 8 g

Writing model

A Analyze

2

1 month
2 one-half
3 10%
4 exactly
5 over

B Model

1 month
2 one-half / half / 50%
3 $540
4 exactly
5 over

Grammar

1

1 costs
2 doesn't save / does not save
3 buys
4 grows
5 don't spend / do not spend
6 don't worry / do not worry
7 doesn't have / does not have
8 use

2

1 like
2 has
3 costs
4 worry
5 live
6 grows
7 give
8 spends

3

1 I don't like / do not like to spend money.
2 Sally doesn't have / does not have $400 in the bank.
3 Gas doesn't cost / does not cost a lot right now.
4 They don't worry / do not worry about money.
5 I don't live / do not live with my parents.
6 My money doesn't grow / does not grow in that bank.
7 My parents don't give / do not give me $25 a week.
8 David doesn't spend / does not spend a lot on rent.

4

Students' own answers

Writing skill

1

1 Tom spends $6 on food.
2 This car costs $30,000.
3 Danni pays for gas.
4 She makes $1,200 a month.
5 The price of this computer is $699.
6 There are several dollars on the floor.

2

1 I save $80 a month.
2 There are three people in the classroom.
3 These two bus tickets cost $14.
4 We need to pay our rent today.
5 Jennifer spends $25 a week on fast food.
6 Kendra makes $1,100 a week.

3

Students' own answers

Writing task

Brainstorm

1 are
2 makes
3 one-third
4 15%
5 over

Review

Academic words review

1 three times a day
2 map
3 One-half
4 exactly

UNIT 5 TASTE

Discussion point

Students' own answers

VIDEO

Before you watch

1 d 2 b 3 e 4 a 5 c

While you watch

1 b 2 a 3 b 4 a

After you watch

Students' own answers

Reading 1

A Vocabulary preview

1

1 d 2 a 3 b 4 c 5 g 6 e 7 h 8 f

2

1 photographer
2 serve
3 menu
4 chef
5 magazine, price
6 assistant, company

B Before you read

1 c 2 d 3 e 4 b 5 a

C Global reading

1

1 jobs 2 do 3 do 4 like

2

1 food taster
2 food photographer
3 chef's assistant
4 food writer
5 food-truck owner / food-truck chef / food-truck driver

D Close reading

1

1 Bert eats ice cream.
2 Jennifer makes dishes look nice.
3 Dan writes emails.
4 Tina writes about desserts.
5 Paul serves food.

2

1 T
2 T
3 F (She takes pictures for books, websites, and menus.)
4 F (She puts oil on meat.)
5 F (He doesn't help in the kitchen.)
6 T
7 T
8 F (She describes how the desserts taste and how much they cost.)
9 T
10 F (He serves Korean food on Tuesday. He serves Turkish food on Wednesday.)

E Over to you

Students' own answers

Study skills

1

a Students' own answers b Teddy's Kitchen restaurants
c Students' own answers

Reading 2

A Vocabulary preview

1

1 c 2 d 3 b 4 a 5 h 6 f 7 e 8 g

2

1 fresh
2 dish
3 staff
4 quick
5 high
6 order
7 mean
8 customer

B Before you read

1 and 2

Students' own answers

C Global reading

1

b

D Close reading

1

1 b 2 b 3 a 4 a 5 b

2
1 drinks
2 check
3 22
4 American
5 fish

E Over to you
Students' own answers

Topic vocabulary

1
1 menu
2 a dish
3 a menu
4 a chef
5 the price
6 a restaurant
7 the check
8 a customer

2
1 Let's try Turkish food.
2 Glen eats breakfast with his family.
3 That café serves great ice cream.
4 Jaime has a snack at 10:00 p.m. / At 10:00 p.m., Jaime has a snack.
5 I don't want to order a big meal.
6 I cook dinner every night. / Every night, I cook dinner.
7 Ken doesn't drink tea or coffee. / Ken doesn't drink coffee or tea.
8 I want to taste your dessert.

3
Students' own answers

Vocabulary builder

1
1 e 2 c 3 b 4 a 5 f 6 d

2
1 low
2 slow
3 expensive
4 large
5 great
6 boring

3
1 c 2 d 3 e 4 a 5 f 6 b

4
1 terrible
2 cheap
3 small
4 boring
5 fast
6 high

Writing model

A Analyze

1
1 name of restaurant
2 what it serves
3 the meal size
4 the prices
5 the staff
6 what's good to order
7 what is not good about it
8 where it is

2
Positive things: large dishes, low prices, friendly staff, great desserts, fresh food, cheap food
Negative things: slow staff, where the restaurant is

3
1 American food
2 the cheeseburger
3 in a shopping mall (far from the / our college)

Grammar

1 an [use ***an*** before a vowel sound; use ***an*** before a singular countable noun that is not specific]
2 The [use ***the*** before something specific—not just any price, but the price (specifically) of fish]
3 The [use ***the*** before something specific—not just any staff, but the staff here]
4 the, the [use ***the*** before something specific; note that you can't use ***a*** because ***food*** is non-countable]
5 Ø, The [no article for things in general; ***the*** for something specific]
6 Ø [no article for things in general]
7 the [use ***the*** for something specific]
8 Ø [no article for things in general]

2
1 The [use ***the*** before something specific; context is important here—if you are in a restaurant, then you mean menus for that restaurant, not menus in general]
2 a [use ***a*** before a singular countable noun that is not specific; we haven't said what kind of snack, it's just a general snack]
3 a [use ***a*** before a singular countable noun that is not specific]
4 the [use ***the*** before something specific]
5 an [use ***an*** before a vowel sound; use ***an*** before a singular count noun that is not specific]
6 the [use ***the*** before something specific; it's the check for our meal, not just any check]
7 Ø [no article for things in general]
8 Ø [no article before non-countable nouns; in this case, dessert is non-countable]

3
1 hard
2 soft
3 weak
4 strong
5 thin
6 thick
7 hot
8 cold

4
Possible answers
1 Please have some hot soup.
2 She takes great pictures of food. / She takes pictures of fresh food.
3 Let's go to the new café.
4 I want to order some fresh bread.
5 The cold juice is on the table.
6 The small restaurant is popular with students. / The restaurant is popular with Chinese students.

5
1 I try not to have a snack at night.
2 The food at the Italian restaurant is expensive.
3 The chicken at the new chicken place is great.
4 The menu here is in five different languages.
5 There is a problem with the check.
6 Tom works as an assistant to a food photographer.
7 The thick noodles at the Chinese café are great.
8 I want to have dinner at a cheap place.

Writing skill

1
1 quick
2 terrible
3 busy
4 large
5 high
6 third

2
1 I don't like strong coffee. I need to add water.
2 We need a large table. There are 15 of us.
3 One-Dollar sushi is a cheap restaurant.
4 Pizza Pit is a small place. It has four tables.
5 Jill is a great chef. Everyone loves her food.
6 Daniel is a terrible chef. No one eats his food.

3
1 famous
2 large
3 happy
4 Indian
5 interesting
6 expensive

4
Students' own answers

Review

Vocabulary builder review
1 tablet
2 slow
3 once a month
4 around

UNIT 6 HEALTH

Discussion point
Students' own answers

VIDEO

Before you watch
1 e 2 d 3 c 4 a 5 b

While you watch
1 b 2 c 3 a 4 d

After you watch
Students' own answers

Reading 1

A Vocabulary preview
1
1 c 2 d 3 b 4 a 5 e 6 f 7 g 8 h

2

1 pretty	3 Several	5 sport	7 without
2 belong to	4 gym	6 point	8 find out

B Before you read
in magazines

C Global reading
sleep, Q9; sports, Q5; water, Q4; fast food, Q7

D Close reading
1
Students' own answers

2

1 week	3 30	5 often	7 day
2 6	4 2	6 10	8 6

E Over to you
Students' own answers

Study skills
Students' own answers

Reading 2

A Vocabulary preview
1
1 a 2 d 3 b 4 c 5 f 6 h 7 g 8 e

2

1 cold	3 hungry	5 strong	7 app
2 spend	4 at least	6 sick	8 actually

B Before you read
1 magazine 2 students 3 four 4 habits

C Global reading
1 f 2 d 3 b 4 a

D Close reading
1
1 T
2 F (He goes on Thursdays.)
3 F (She takes several thousand steps a day.)
4 T
5 F (She sometimes eats ice cream.)
6 T
7 F (He usually has a snack at night.)
8 T

2
1 Sean plays soccer every day.
2 Sean plays basketball once a week.
3 Caitlyn thinks walking is the best way to stay healthy.
4 Jill watches sports on TV. / Caitlyn's roommate watches sports on TV.
5 Natalie rarely eats fast food.
6 Natalie tries not to eat desserts.
7 Antonio doesn't exercise.
8 Antonio doesn't get a lot of sleep.

E Over to you
Students' own answers

Topic vocabulary
1

1 have	2 catch	3 have	4 play

2

1 feel	2 get	3 be	4 be

3

1 cold	3 hungry	5 stressed	7 snack
2 sick	4 sport	6 tired	8 habits

Vocabulary builder
1
1 Gina studies more than Erica.
2 Brian sleeps less than Yousef.
3 Jennifer works much more than me.
4 William sleeps a little less than Randy.
5 Ava exercises a lot more than her sister.

2
Possible answers
1 Peter sleeps (a little) more than David. / David sleeps (a little) less than Peter.
2 Tina's meal costs (a little) more than Layla's. / Layla's meal costs (a little) less than Tina's.
3 Kerry exercises (much / a lot) more than Diana. / Diana exercises (much / a lot) less than Kerry.
4 Oliver spends (much / a lot) less on gym classes than Adam. / Adam spends (much / a lot) more on gym classes than Oliver.
5 Trevor walks (much / a lot) less than Zac. / Zac walks (much / a lot) more than Trevor.

Writing model

A Analyze
1 K 2 S 3 K 4 S 5 K 6 S 7 S 8 S

B Model
1 three times a week
2 eats fast food
3 some fruit

Grammar
1
Students' own answers

2
1 How often do you go to the gym?
2 How often do you eat red meat?
3 Do you ever sleep in the library?
4 Do you ever drink coffee in class?
5 How often do you eat ice cream?
6 Do you and your friends ever play soccer?

3
Students' own answers

4

Possible answers

1 Maria studies every day. / Maria always studies.
2 Maria runs with Jesse twice a week. / Maria sometimes runs with Jesse.
3 Maria plays tennis once a week. / Maria plays tennis on Sundays.
4 Maria often goes to the gym. / Maria goes to the gym three times a week.
5 Maria never plays basketball. / Maria doesn't play basketball at all.

5

1 Paul usually plays tennis with his brother. (Frequency adverbs go before the verb.)
2 Megan runs twice a week. (*Twice a week* is a fixed expression.)
3 Rachel doesn't exercise at all / doesn't exercise very much. (fixed expression)
4 I sometimes catch a cold in the summer. / Sometimes I catch a cold in the summer./ I catch a cold in the summer sometimes. (Frequency adverbs go before the verb. *Sometimes* is an exception to this rule and can go at the beginning of the sentence or at the end.)
5 I always feel tired on Saturday morning. (Frequency adverbs go before the verb.)
6 How often do you get sick? / Do you ever get sick? (Choose one question or the other.)
7 Fouad hardly ever goes to the gym. (fixed expression)
8 Do you ever get hungry in the afternoon? (In a question, ***ever*** comes after the pronoun and before the verb.)

Writing skill

1

1 Zoe plays tennis and volleyball. / Zoe plays volleyball and tennis.
2 Kenichi loves to watch and play sports. / Kenichi loves to play and watch sports.
3 They run in the morning and go to the gym in the evening.
4 This app shows where I walk and tells me my steps.
5 I drink a lot of water, and I don't eat a lot of meat.
6 She does 30 pull-ups and 50 push-ups every morning.

2

1 Beth never exercises, but she stays pretty healthy.
2 I love to watch sports on TV, but I hardly ever play sports.
3 I sometimes eat meat, but I don't eat red meat.
4 Khadija has four meals a day, but she never snacks between meals.
5 I usually run on weekends, but I rarely run during the week.
6 Rory sleeps eight hours a night, but he's often sleepy in the morning.

3

Students' own answers

Writing task

Brainstorm

Positive habits

Emma: likes sports a lot, plays tennis twice a week, favorite dessert is fruit

Kath: runs several times a week, walks to and from college, sometimes eats fish

Negative habits

Emma: doesn't go to the gym, doesn't run at all, takes the bus to and from college, sleeps six hours a night

Kath: doesn't like sports very much, doesn't go to the gym, favorite dessert is ice cream, sleeps nine hours a night

Review

Vocabulary builder review

1 boring 3 folder
2 more 4 over

UNIT 7 PLACES

Discussion point

Students' own answers

VIDEO

Before you watch

1 b 2 a 3 d 4 e 5 c

While you watch

1 park 2 sun 3 phone 4 good

After you watch

Students' own answers

Reading 1

A Vocabulary preview

1

1 c 2 a 3 d 4 b 5 g 6 h 7 e 8 f

2

1 market 5 wide
2 traffic 6 crowded
3 park 7 popular
4 neighborhood 8 museum

B Before you read

Students' own answers

C Global reading

1 Ueno, Tokyo 3 Bellas Artes, Santiago
2 Gràcia, Barcelona

D Close reading

1

1 Gràcia, Bellas Artes 5 Ueno, Gràcia, Bellas Artes
2 Ueno, Bellas Artes 6 Ueno
3 Bellas Artes 7 Bellas Artes
4 Gràcia

2

1 overseas visitors 4 pretty cheap
2 crowded 5 two
3 is no traffic

3

1 the night market 3 the fish market
2 Park Güell

E Over to you

Students' own answers

Study skills

Students' own answers

Reading 2

A Vocabulary preview

1

1 c 2 a 3 d 4 b 5 h 6 f 7 g 8 e

2

1 air 4 tourist, drive
2 temperature 5 capital, once
3 cool 6 beautiful

B Before you read

Students' own answers

C Global reading

c

D Close reading

1

1 a 2 b 3 c 4 b

2

1 ten / 10	3 730	5 0 / no	7 Three / 3
2 11	4 22	6 1.4%	

E Over to you

Students' own answers

Topic vocabulary

1

1 b	3 d	5 g/c	7 f
2 c/g	4 a	6 h	8 e

2

1 The gas station is behind the bus station.
2 The post office is inside the shopping mall.
3 The movie theater is next to the fitness center.
4 The art museum is across from the department store.

3

Students' own answers

Vocabulary builder

1

1 four	4 a lot of
2 several	5 thousands of
3 many	6 millions of

2

1 Many older people live in Gràcia.
2 Gràcia has some great restaurants.
3 Several stores in Umeno sell Japanese clothes.
4 Millions of people live in Tokyo.
5 There are a lot of universities in Bellas Artes.

3

1 My city has two bus stations.
2 Thousands of people live in my neighborhood.
3 A lot of people visit the park every day.
4 There are several colleges in my town.
5 Many tourists come to the capital every year.
6 The fitness center costs hundreds of dollars a month.
7 I need to buy some clothes today.

Writing model

A Analyze

my street, lots of houses, my house, a school, small park, movie theater, restaurants, fitness center

B Model

1

Sunnyville is a good place to live.
One problem the author mentions is that the fitness center is too crowded.

2

Students check the following items: 1, 2, and 4

Grammar

1

1 The people in this neighborhood are very friendly.
2 The night market gets really busy around 10:00 p.m.
3 That restaurant has pretty good desserts.
4 My college isn't very expensive.
5 The cafés in this neighborhood are not nice at all.
6 The art museum is too crowded on weekends.
7 The streets around here aren't wide enough.
8 This neighborhood is really famous for its Italian cafés.

2

1 This café is not quiet enough.
2 That table is too small for us.
3 You're not old enough to see that movie.
4 The river is too cold to swim in.

3

1 There are three really old fountains in the park.
2 The fish in the market is too expensive.
3 The park next to the college is not very big / is very small.
4 You can get pretty good ice cream at that store.
5 The people in the neighborhood are not friendly at all.

4

Students' own answers

5

Students' own answers

Writing skill

1

Possible answers

1 There are two nice stores on my street.
2 My neighborhood has a big park.
3 The subway is next to a fountain.
4 The fitness center is behind the bus station.
5 My street has a great Japanese restaurant.
6 The shopping mall is too crowded.
7 There is an interesting sculpture near my house.
8 The highway is not wide enough.

2

Students' own answers

3

Students' own answers

4

Students' own answers

Review

Vocabulary builder review

1 every day 2 between 3 hundreds of 4 less

UNIT 8 PLANS

Discussion point

Students' own answers

VIDEO

Before you watch

1 b 2 d 3 a 4 e 5 c

While you watch

1 F (iHub opened in 2010.)	3 T
2 T	4 T

After you watch

Students' own answers

Reading 1

A Vocabulary preview

1

1 d 2 a 3 c 4 b 5 f 6 g 7 e 8 h

2

1 join, online	3 social media, interested
2 invitation, date	4 pleased, information

B Before you read

1

d an invitation

2

Students should check: a title, several headings, several pictures, several web links

C Global reading

1 a web page	3 invites
2 Tech Talk	4 learning

D Close reading

1

1 c 2 a 3 b 4 c

2

1 May 5
2 Dubai World Trade Centre
3 three
4 Friday, May 6

E Over to you

Students' own answers

Study skills

Students' own answers

Reading 2

A Vocabulary preview

1

1 b 2 d 3 a 4 c 5 f 6 h 7 g 8 e

2

1 free
2 probably
3 book
4 world
5 professor
6 company
7 document
8 describe

B Before you read

a

C Global reading

1 25
2 speak
3 asks questions
4 5

D Close reading

1

1 Khalid asks Claire to speak at the conference.
2 Khalid gives the dates for the conference.
3 Claire says she is interested in speaking at the conference.
4 Claire asks Khalid when he wants her to speak.
5 Khalid asks Claire to send him the title of her talk.
6 Claire attaches a document to her email.

2

1 an invitation
2 Dubai
3 travel
4 ABC Games
5 speakers
6 4:00
7 Khalid
8 airport

E Over to you

Students' own answers

Topic vocabulary

1

1 Sunday
2 Monday
3 Tuesday
4 Wednesday
5 Thursday
6 Friday
7 Saturday

2

1 January
2 February
3 March
4 April
5 May
6 June
7 July
8 August
9 September
10 October
11 November
12 December

3

1 at
2 on
3 on
4 in
5 on
6 on
7 on
8 on
9 in
10 at

Vocabulary builder

1

1 I will probably go to the cafeteria today.
2 The library is definitely closed tomorrow.
3 I am certain I can watch TV tonight.
4 I will possibly see my grandparents this weekend.

2

Students' own answers

Writing model

A Analyze

1 Mr. Sloane
2 before June 11
3 the Grand Hotel

B Model

1 Puebla University
2 September 14
3 conference
4 airport

Grammar

1

1 begins
2 gets
3 starts
4 doesn't end
5 goes
6 arrives
7 doesn't start
8 arrive

2

1 The conference starts on April 18.
2 Talk 1 begins at 9:00.
3 Lunch ends at 1:00.
4 People ask questions at 4:00.

3

Students' own answers

4

1 will call / 'll call
2 will book / 'll book
3 won't go / will not go / 'll not go
4 will go / 'll go
5 will stop / 'll stop
6 will invite / 'll invite
7 won't pay / will not pay / 'll not pay
8 will answer / 'll answer

5

Students' own answers

Writing skill

1

1 f 2 b 3 j 4 g 5 i 6 c 7 d 8 e 9 h 10 a

2

1 Please see attachment.
2 All the best,
3 Thanks for your email.
4 It's on Friday at 3:00.

3

1 b 2 a 3 d 4 c

Review

Vocabulary builder review

1 probably 2 printer 3 large 4 several

UNIT 9 JOBS

Discussion point

Students' own answers

VIDEO

Before you watch

1 c 2 d 3 e 4 b 5 a

While you watch

1 F (He used to be a banker but now he is a farmer.)
2 T
3 T
4 F (The plants grow in a shipping container under artificial light.)

After you watch

Students' own answers

Reading 1

A Vocabulary preview

1

1 c 2 d 3 b 4 a 5 h 6 g 7 f 8 e

2

1 part-time
2 skill
3 experience
4 education
5 full-time
6 manager
7 goal
8 program

B Before you read

Students' own answers

C Global reading

1

three, résumé

2

travel writer

D Close reading

1

Students' own answers

2

Students' own answers

3

1 full-time
2 company
3 Colorado
4 six
5 has
6 two
7 two languages
8 can

E Over to you

Students' own answers

Study skills

Students' own answers

Reading 2

A Vocabulary preview

1

1 b 2 d 3 a 4 c 5 g 6 f 7 e 8 h

2

1 forest
2 choose
3 pass
4 fire
5 alone
6 safe
7 outside
8 team

B Before you read

1 + 2

Students' own answers

C Global reading

Possible answers

1 Likes: working outside, working with people and animals Dislikes: working alone
2 Likes: to travel and go to some interesting places Dislikes: working on weekends, crowded planes
3 Likes: working with other people Dislikes: working long hours, low pay.

D Close Reading

1

Possible answers

Marcy: I look for any fires in the forest. I teach people. I sometimes work with groups of people.

Alex: I answer questions, help people with their bags, and serve food and drinks on planes. I also help keep people safe.

Lily: I look at the film one second at a time. I choose what to use and what not to use. I put the film together in an office.

2

1 Alex (and Marcy)
2 Marcy (and Alex)
3 Lily (and Alex)
4 Alex (and Marcy)
5 Lily
6 Marcy
7 Alex
8 Marcy

3

1 They need to pass a test.
2 Because he often works on weekends.
3 Most people are nice, but sometimes they aren't friendly.
4 They usually need a degree.

4

Students' own answers

E Over to you

Students' own answers

Topic vocabulary

1

1 musician
2 tour guide
3 police officer
4 artist
5 nurse
6 farmer
7 doctor
8 receptionist

2

1 c 2 a 3 b 4 d 5 g 6 h 7 f 8 e 9 j 10 l 11 i 12 k

3

Possible answers

a restaurant: a chef
a hospital: a nurse, a doctor (a dentist)
an office: a receptionist (a police officer)

Vocabulary builder

1

1 c 2 d 3 a 4 b 5 g 6 h 7 f 8 e

2

1 dean
2 lecturer
3 researcher
4 lab technician
5 career counselor
6 teaching assistant
7 tutor
8 librarian

3

Students' own answers

Writing model

A Analyze

1

Possible answers

Two things the student is interested in: art and computers
The job the student would like to have: a graphic designer
Three reasons why the student would like the job: they like to paint and draw; they love to make designs; a graphic designer can work with a lot of other people.

2

Possible answers

skills: computer skills, use several computer programs
degree: I would like to get my BA degree in graphic design ...
where to study: ... at the University of Art & Design in Helsinki, Finland.
where to work: I would like to work for a large design company in Europe.

3

Students' own answers

Grammar

1

1 Do you like
2 like
3 would you like
4 like
5 Would you like
6 don't like
7 like
8 like
9 would like

2

1 b 2 c 3 f 4 d 5 e 6 a

3

1 Do you like to use a computer?
2 What is the pay like at your job?
3 I don't like to work with numbers.
4 What company would you like to work for?
5 I wouldn't / would like to be a professor.
6 What is your new job like?
7 Where would you like to work someday?
8 Our office manager doesn't like to work on weekends.

4
Students' own answers

Writing skill

1
1 d 2 e 3 f 4 a 5 c 6 b

2

1 because	3 so	5 so	7 so
2 so	4 because	6 because	8 because

3
Students' own answers

Review

Vocabulary builder review

1 librarian 2 calendar 3 definitely 4 lecturer

UNIT 10 SKILLS

Discussion point

Students' own answers

VIDEO

Before you watch

1 e 2 d 3 c 4 a 5 b

While you watch

1 sports 2 teacher 3 afternoon 4 work

After you watch

Students' own answers

Reading 1

A Vocabulary preview

1
1 c 2 b 3 d 4 a 5 e 6 h 7 g 8 f

2

1 improve	3 remember	5 real	7 throw
2 during	4 try out	6 idea	8 future

B Before you read

(See ***Global reading***.)

C Global reading

a

D Close reading

1
Students' own answers

2
Possible answers
Stage 1 0 to 2: understand what they can see, feel, throw, or put things in mouth; understand things not in front of them (8 months); begin to understand language (2 years)
Stage 2 2 to 7: their use of language improves; they begin to understand words, numbers, and pictures; can remember information and talk about things not in front of them; tell stories that are not real; start to ask questions (age 4)
Stage 3 7 to 11: think about other people more; understand why things happen; begin to think like a scientist; can solve problems by trying out new ideas
Stage 4 11 to 15: think in an abstract way; use symbols; think about different ways to do things; think about what is possible in the future

3
1 c 2 a 3 e 4 b 5 d
Correct order for summary: 2, 3, 5, 1, 4

E Over to you

Students' own answers

Study skills

1
Topic: my nephew Jason
Topic sentence: My nephew Jason is seven years old.

2
Cross out sentence: He doesn't have a part-time job.

3
After: He also is good at music.

4 + 5
Students' own answers

Reading 2

A Vocabulary preview

1
1 d 2 a 3 c 4 b 5 f 6 h 7 g 8 e

2

1 hurt	3 leader	5 share	7 calm
2 wrong	4 accountant	6 fact	8 care

B Before you read

(See ***Global reading***.)

C Global reading

1
1 b 2 d 3 c 4 a

2
Students' own answers

D Close reading

1
Possible answers
see below

2
Possible answers

1 Positive: have clear goals and work hard to meet them, good with details Negative: don't always work well with different people / ideas Possible jobs: accountants, web designers
2 Positive: good people skills, work well on a team Negative: sometimes not good at solving problems Possible jobs: nurses, salespeople
3 Positive: they are good listeners, they are good at understanding other people Negative: they can forget about their own work Possible jobs: teachers, librarians
4 Positive: they are always fair, they are born leaders Negative: they can sometimes hurt others Possible jobs: managers and business people

3
1 Inspectors, Protectors
2 Inspectors, Givers (Protectors can remember details about other people.)
3 Givers, Protectors
4 Inspectors, Supervisors

E Over to you

Students' own answers

Topic vocabulary

1

1 drive a car	5 manage money
2 use a computer	6 lead a team
3 cook a meal	7 follow instructions
4 give a presentation	8 solve a problem

2

1 lead a team
2 follow instructions
3 use a computer
4 solve a problem
5 drive a car
6 cook a meal
7 manage money
8 give a presentation

3

Possible answers

Work skills: give a presentation, lead a team
Both: use a computer, manage money, follow instructions, solve problems, drive a car
Life skills: cook a meal

Vocabulary builder

1

1 c 2 b 3 d 4 a 5 g 6 h 7 f 8 e

2

1 creative
2 funny
3 friendly
4 sociable
5 fair
6 polite
7 easygoing
8 quiet

3

Students' own answers

Writing model

A Analyze

1

(See answers below in Exercise 2.)

2

Number the notes as follows:
1 people find her friendly, sociable
2 violin (in college band)
3 soccer, basketball, volleyball (leader)
4 yes, both
5 add very large numbers in her head

B Model

1

My classmate Suchin is a very friendly and sociable person and has some interesting skills.

2

Possible answers

I think Suchin can be a very good accountant or banker someday. It's clear that she has many useful skills and abilities.

Grammar

1

1 Mike can go to the library at 6:00.
2 What time can you come to your study group?
3 Kevin can't play soccer today.
4 Can Jessica speak another language?
5 Adam can be very unfriendly sometimes.
6 Where can we put our book bags?
7 These notes can't be right?
8 I think you can do anything you want in life.

2

1 I can't speak French.
2 I can help you study.
3 Rachel can't use a computer.
4 Ben can join your club.
5 Pete and his wife can't meet us.
6 We can't follow these instructions.

3

1 What can you cook?
2 Can you solve problems easily?
3 Can you manage money well?
4 Where can students study at your college?
5 Can your best friend drive a car?
6 What can you use a computer to do?

4

Students' own answers

5

Students' own answers

Writing skill

1

1 T
2 T
3 F (It is usually near the beginning of a paragraph.)
4 T
5 F (The concluding sentence usually ends the paragraph.)

2

Mainly about and topic sentence's main idea: Children ... when they are 11 to 15 ... think in an abstract way.
Concluding sentence: They have a deeper understanding now of what is right and what is not.

3

Possible answers

1 My aunt has several skills and can do many interesting things.
2 She can speak or understand several languages, such as Spanish and Portuguese.
3 She is very funny, and can make people laugh easily.
4 She can also do many things at the same time, and is always calm.
5 All of these things help her in her job as a nurse.

Extra sentence: She is sometimes tired and quiet.

4

Students' own answers

Review

Vocabulary builder review

1 reseachers 2 sociable 3 creative 4 expensive

Vocabulary builder

Vocabulary builder revision

Units 1-5

1 flash drive
2 five times a week
3 great
4 low
5 sports science
6 every night
7 one-quarter

Units 6-10

1 polite
2 fair
3 much more
4 Thousands of
5 certainly
6 dean
7 less than
8 quiet
9 a lot of

UNIT ASSIGNMENT MARKING SHEETS

MARKING KEY FOR ASSESSMENT CRITERIA

25 points: Excellent achievement. Student successfully fulfills the expectation for this part of the assignment with little or no room for improvement.

20 points: Good achievement. Student fulfills the expectation for this part of the assignment, but may have a few errors or need some improvement.

15 points: Satisfactory achievement. Student needs some work to fulfill the expectation for this part of the assignment, but shows some effort.

5 points: Poor achievement. Student does not fulfill the expectation for this part of the assignment.

UNIT 1 SELF

Student name: ______________________________

Date: ____________________

Unit assignment: Write sentences about your classmate

	25 points	20 points	15 points	5 points
The student completed the task successfully.				
The student correctly used the verb *be* in their sentences.				
The student used appropriate vocabulary to refer to countries, languages, and subjects of study.				

Total: ______ **/ 75**

Comments:

UNIT 2 FAMILY

Student name: ______________________________

Date: ____________________

Unit assignment: Write sentences about your family

	25 points	20 points	15 points	5 points
The student completed the task successfully.				
The student correctly used subject pronouns and possessive adjectives.				
The student used appropriate vocabulary to refer to family members, and to describe how often things happen.				

Total: ______ **/ 75**

Comments:

UNIT 3 STUDY

Student name: ______________________________

Date: ______________________________

Unit assignment: Describe your study space

	25 points	20 points	15 points	5 points
The student completed the task successfully.				
The student used the verb *have* in correct structures to complete the description.				
The student appropriately used prepositions of place and vocabulary related to classroom and college objects.				

Total: ______ **/ 75**

Comments:

UNIT 4 MONEY

Student name: ______________________________

Date: ______________________________

Unit assignment: Describe how much money a family spends

	25 points	20 points	15 points	5 points
The student completed the task successfully.				
The student used correct verb structures in the simple present tense.				
The student used appropriate vocabulary to refer to numbers and to describe numbers in more detail.				

Total: ______ **/ 75**

Comments:

UNIT 5 TASTE

Student name: ______________________________

Date: ______________

Unit assignment: Describe a restaurant

	25 points	20 points	15 points	5 points
The student completed the task successfully.				
The student correctly used articles and adjectives with nouns.				
The student used appropriate collocations and adjectives in their descriptions.				

Total: _____ / 75

Comments:

UNIT 6 HEALTH

Student name: ______________________________

Date: ______________

Unit assignment: Compare two people's health habits

	25 points	20 points	15 points	5 points
The student completed the task successfully.				
The student used adverbs of frequency to correctly describe how often things happen.				
The student used appropriate vocabulary to talk about health, and to describe or compare actions.				

Total: _____ / 75

Comments:

UNIT 7 PLACES

Student name: ______________________________

Date: ____________________

Unit assignment: Describe your neighborhood

	25 points	20 points	15 points	5 points
The student completed the task successfully.				
The student used appropriate structures to modify the adjectives in their writing.				
The student used correct vocabulary to refer to places, buildings, and quantity of things.				

Total: ______ **/ 75**

Comments:

UNIT 8 PLANS

Student name: ______________________________

Date: ____________________

Unit assignment: Write an email invitation

	25 points	20 points	15 points	5 points
The student completed the task successfully.				
The student used appropriate present and future structures to describe plans and schedules.				
The student used correct vocabulary to refer to days, months, time, and likelihood of things happening.				

Total: ______ **/ 75**

Comments:

UNIT 9 JOBS

Student name: ______________________________

Date: ______________

Unit assignment: Describe a job you would like to have

	25 points	20 points	15 points	5 points
The student completed the task successfully.				
The student used *like*, *would like* and *be like* correctly.				
The student correctly used vocabulary relating to popular jobs or college jobs.				

Total: ______ / 75

Comments:

UNIT 10 SKILLS

Student name: ______________________________

Date: ______________

Unit assignment: Describe your classmate's skills and abilities

	25 points	20 points	15 points	5 points
The student completed the task successfully.				
The student described ability and possibility using *can*.				
The student correctly used collocations and adjectives to describe people and their skills.				

Total: ______ / 75

Comments: